INFORMATION LAW IN PRACTICE

Information Law in Practice

Second Edition

Paul Marett

Ashgate

Published by
Ashgate Publishing Limited
Gower House
Croft Road
Aldershot
Hants GU11 3HR
England

Ashgate Publishing Company
131 Main Street
Burlington VT 05401-5600 USA

British Library Cataloguing in Publication Data
Marett, Paul
Information law in practice. – 2nd ed.
1. Intellectual property – Great Britain
I. Title
346.4'1'048

Library of Congress Cataloging-in-Publication Data
Marett, Paul.
Information law in practice / Paul Marett. – 2nd ed.
p. cm.
Rev. ed. of: Information law and practice / Paul Marett. 1991.
Includes bibliographical references.
ISBN 0-566-08390-6
1. Intellectual property – Great Britain. 2. Copyright – Great Britain. I. Marett, Paul.
Information law and practice. II. Title.

KD1269 .M37 2002
346.4104'8–dc21
2001053605

ISBN 0 566 08390 6

Typeset in 10pt Century Old Style by Bournemouth Colour Press, Parkstone.
Printed in Great Britain by MPG Books Ltd., Bodmin, Cornwall.

Contents

Preface

Ten years is a venerable age for a law book. Law is a fast-moving field and since the first edition of this book was published in 1991 there have been tremendous changes in the subject matter dealt with here. There has been a spate of European Union legislation on copyright. The UK has a new Defamation Act, a new Data Protection Act, a new Trade Marks Act, to mention only some of the new developments. The Internet has raised new questions, although we cannot yet provide the answers. The financial returns from intellectual property continue to grow and the attraction to pirates grows correspondingly. Litigation goes on and new judgments provide new interpretations of existing law. A new edition of this book is called for. I have had to rewrite and rearrange a very substantial part, and this is almost a new book. The publishers suggested a small change in the title, from *Information Law and Practice* to *Information Law in Practice*.

The first edition grew out of a series of lectures which I gave each year to postgraduate students in what is now the Department of Information Science in Loughborough University. I have attempted to paint a broad picture of the legal environment of information, aimed more particularly (but not exclusively) at professionals in the information field, librarians, information scientists, and others who exercise a management function in the information and media fields. This is not really a textbook, though I hope that it will prove a useful basis for courses on intellectual property law and related professional issues in university departments of information science, as well as for students of media studies and other subjects in the same broad area. Nor is it just a work of reference. Rather it is an introduction and guide to a very interesting and important area of law. I anticipate that readers will range from those with a knowledge of law to those for whom the law is a complete mystery. So I have included, particularly in Chapter 1, some basic information about law in general and how it works, and I apologize to more knowledgeable readers who will skip these details.

Intellectual property is of fundamental importance to the information and media professions. The Copyright, Designs and Patents Act 1988 states right at the beginning that copyright is a property right, reflecting the fact that copyright has been recognized as a piece of personal property for well over two centuries. As information is seen more and more as a marketable commodity, so the tangible expression of marketable information is one of the main subjects of copyright, and its legal protection is particularly important to the information owner and provider. The law of copyright is concerned with a great deal more than information in its narrow sense, indeed it is a truism that information pure and simple, like ideas, cannot be the subject of copyright. It is only the information (or idea) as expressed in words or figures or musical, graphic or electronic form which can be protected. The work of the novelist or poet, the artist or musical composer, the computer programmer, are among the subjects of copyright protection.

Although copyright is the most important area of intellectual property for the information professional, there are other areas of considerable importance. Patents are very important as the legal means of protecting that intellectual property which can be brought within the definition of inventions. Patent records also form a most valuable source of information on scientific and technological developmments: companies within these fields watch the patenting activities of their competitors carefully, scientists and inventors scan patent applications for new ideas. Industrial designs have their own protective regimes. Trade marks can be worth a lot of money to their owners: though somewhat outside our remit, they are the third major area of intellectual property. Confidential information and trade secrets are protected by law.

Intellectual property, particularly copyright, is of prime importance to the information or media professional and it receives a lot of attention in this book. However, other fields of the law will touch the professional's work. Data protection and privacy are important. Defamation is generally newsworthy and always interesting. Freedom of information contrasts with official secrets and censorship. Everyone has views on pornography or obscenity, and so has the law. Incitement to racial hatred is a criminal offence, so is blasphemy (though many people do not know this). Law has the reputation of being a dull and arcane study. This is not at all true, certainly not for the subjects dealt with here, and I have tried to write something which can be read with interest by the non-lawyer. I have also taken the utmost care to be accurate and up to date but changes in legal matter can take place fast, and therefore I disclaim legal responsibility for any loss resulting from reliance on my book.

In the first edition I thanked the Controller of Her Majesty's Stationery Office for permission to reproduce statutory material. Since October 1999 Crown copyright is waived for reproduction of statutes and statutory instruments, subject to limited conditions and the following acknowledgment: 'Material from the Copyright, Designs and Patents Act 1988 is reproduced under the terms of Crown

Copyright Policy Guidance issued by HMSO.' This brings the UK into line with many other countries. Finally, I should like to thank my publishers for their help and forbearance in the long drawn-out process of writing this book.

Paul Marett
MA *Cantab* BA *Bristol* BA *CNAA*
MPhil *De Montfort* BSc(Econ) BCom PhD
London FCIArb FRHistS of Gray's Inn Barrister

Glossary and abbreviations

Note: (1) Abbreviated titles of law reports are given at the beginning of the Table of Cases.

(2) With the recent civil justice reforms a number of familiar terms have been superseded by new, supposedly simpler, expressions. The older terms will, of course, have been used in law reports and other writings up to the date of the reforms, so it will be a very long time before they cease to be needed. These, and other obsolete expressions, are marked below with an asterisk.

account	reckoning of amount gained by defendant by a wrongful act, to be paid to claimant
A-G	Attorney-General: senior government legal officer
anor	another
Anton Piller order*	court order authorizing claimant to search defendant's premises to uncover additional evidence for a civil lawsuit, now called 'search order'; not to be confused with 'search warrant' granted to police to search for evidence in criminal matter
appellant	person (or body) making an appeal
author	includes the creator of a literary, dramatic, musical or artistic work, or a computer program
bis, ter, quater, quinquies	literally two, three, four, or five times, used to number new articles interpolated in a treaty, convention etc
CDPA	Copyright, Designs and Patents Act 1988
Circuit judge	judge ranking below High Court judge, trying civil matters in County Court and all save the most serious criminal matters in the Crown Court: addressed as 'Your Honour'

civil law	law regulating relations between parties, cf criminal law
Civil Law	law derived from Roman law, current today in Europe (except England and Ireland) and Latin America
claim form	*see* writ
claimant	*see* plaintiff
common law	(1) traditional and judge-made law, as opposed to statute law; (2) legal system of England and most former possessions (including USA)
costs	a party's legal expenses in an action, usually paid by the loser to the winning party
County Court	court hearing civil cases: there are over 200 County Courts
criminal law	law of acts condemned and punished by the state
Crown Court	court where criminal cases (except minor ones heard by magistrates) are heard
damages	recompense paid by losing party to winner
de minimis non curat lex	the law does not concern itself with trifles
District Judge	judge with a wide range of responsibility for preliminary matters in the courts, and jurisdiction in relatively smaller cases
Divisional Court	two or three High Court judges hearing certain special appeals
DPP	Director of Public Prosecutions
droit d'auteur	author's right, loosely translated as 'copyright' but emphasizes individual creativity rather than pure economic rights
droit de suite	artist's right to a percentage of later sale proceeds after disposing of a work
ECJ	European Court of Justice (European Union)
ECHR	European Court of Human Rights
EEA	European Economic Area: EU plus Norway, Iceland and Liechtenstein
EPO	European Patent Office
EU	European Union
ex parte	(a) on behalf of; (b) refers to an application made to the court without notifying the other party (when speed and secrecy are necessary)
freezing injunction	*see* Mareva injunction
High Court	hears the most important civil cases: the Chancery Division hears intellectual property among other

	matters, the Queen's Bench Division hears particularly tort and contract cases
industrial property	patents, trade marks, designs
injunction	order from court to carry out, or desist from, some activity
intellectual property	includes copyright, patents, trade marks, designs, confidential information
interim	before the full trial
interlocutory*	interim
J	High Court judge, addressed as 'My Lord' or 'My Lady'
JP	Justice of the Peace, unpaid lay magistrate hearing a wide range of fairly minor matters in the Magistrates' Court
Law Lords	senior judges granted life peerage to exercise judicial function of the House of Lords and Privy Council
LC	Lord Chancellor, head of the legal hierarchy (but a political appointment) and a very senior judge; sits (sometimes) as a Law Lord
LCJ	Lord Chief Justice, second highest in the legal hierarchy and head of the Queen's Bench Division of the High Court
LJ	Lord, or Lady, Justice, in Court of Appeal
Mareva injunction*	court order to freeze a party's assets to prevent their being spirited away; now called 'freezing injunction'
moral rights	rights of authors to be identified as such, to object to derogatory treatment of their work and not to have a work falsely attributed to them
MR	Master of the Rolls, head of the Court of Appeal
ors	others
PA	Patents Act 1977
plaintiff*	person making a claim in a civil action, now called 'claimant'
pma	*post mortem auctoris*, after [the end of the year of] the death of the author
Privy Council	a large body of cabinet ministers and others: the Judicial Committee, of Law Lords, hears certain appeals
R	Rex or Regina, The King or Queen
Recorder	barrister or solicitor sitting as a part-time judge
respondent	defendant in an appeal
search order	see Anton Piller order

SI	Statutory Instrument: extra-statutory regulations
Stipendiary Magistrate	paid, legally-qualified magistrate
taxation*	assessment of costs by a court official
TMA	Trade Marks Act 1994
tort	a civil wrong, eg defamation, personal injury
V-C	Vice-Chancellor, senior judge, head, under the Lord Chancellor, of the Chancery Division of the High Court
WIPO	World Intellectual Property Organization
writ*	document initiating a civil lawsuit, now 'claim form'

Table of cases

ABBREVIATED TITLES OF LAW REPORTS

Note: The convention is that when the year is an essential part of the reference it is placed in square brackets. If the volume number is a sufficient reference, the year (if given) is placed in round brackets.

AC	The Law Reports, Appeal Cases [House of Lords and Privy Council]
All ER	All England Law Reports
App Cas	Appeal Cases [1875–90]
Ch	The Law Reports, Chancery Division
CLR	Commonwealth Law Reports [Australia]
Cr App R	Criminal Appeal Reports
Cr App R(S)	Criminal Appeal Reports (Sentencing)
Crim LR	Criminal Law Review
EHRR	European Human Rights Reports
EMLR	Entertainment and Media Law Review
ER	English Reports Reprint [1210–1865]
FSR	Fleet Street Reports
FSupp	Federal Supplement [USA]
ILR	Indian Law Reports
Ir CL	Irish Common Law Reports [1850–78]
IRLR	Industrial Relations Law Reports
KB	The Law Reports, King's Bench Division
LJCh	Law Journal, Chancery
LJKB	Law Journal, King's Bench
LR Ch	Law Reports, Chancery [1865–75]
LR CP	Law Reports, Common Pleas [1865–75]

UNITED KINGDOM AND COMMONWEALTH (INCLUDING FORMER COMMONWEALTH)

UNITED STATES OF AMERICA

FRANCE

JAPAN

EUROPEAN PATENT OFFICE

Statutes, statutory instruments and European Union measures

STATUTORY INSTRUMENTS

EUROPEAN UNION MEASURES

1 Introduction

The supply of information has been revolutionized over the past two or three decades. Even before the Internet took off new technology had added a fresh dimension to storing and accessing information. Data which had previously been kept on shelves full of books or in paper-filled filing cabinets and laboriously extracted by turning over the pages or handling the files could now be stored for instant retrieval in the memory of computers. Paper has not disappeared: it probably never will. In fact the advent of new electronic technology has made possible a vast expansion of paper-based information. Newspapers, journals, magazines have grown in number and bulk. Book publishing has expanded. In every organization, business, professional, educational or leisure-oriented, the photocopier has generated reams and reams more paper. The invention of paper many centuries ago in China and its introduction to Europe around the fourteenth century, was probably the most significant factor in the expansion of human communication, far more significant than the invention of printing, which could never have been utilized without a cheap medium on which to print. There is no sign that we can begin to ignore paper yet, if ever. The information revolution is not simply a phenomenon of the computer age but, of course, it is the computer which has added a vast new dimension and the Internet is the latest manifestation of this.

This book is about Information Law so the first priority is to set bounds on the meaning of the term. The bounds will be set widely, to look at the law covering anything which is communicated, or is capable of communication, between human beings, or to or from or between computers or other information-holding devices, or between such devices and humans. Thus it can cover the material held in an encyclopaedia or dictionary or other reference book or paper. It can relate to such various fields as scientific information, legal information, business information and a host more. To avoid setting arbitrary boundaries included also are other products of the human intellect or spirit such as literature, music and art, even though those do not, perhaps, come within any ordinary definition of information. In other words, our concern is with the material handled by the modern information professional, librarian, archivist or information scientist. We are interested in ownership, purchase, sale and theft, use and misuse. We shall also stray a bit beyond the proper bounds of the subject in order to present a rounded picture of the law as it affects particularly the information professional, as well as the creator, collector and user of our subject matter in the wide definition set here.

The dissemination of information takes in, then, a greatly expanded field of conventional paper-based publishing, transformed by new technological methods, the publishing of information and other material on new physical carrier media, tape, disk and others, and online services which can give access, via the Internet or otherwise, to stores of data in every field of human activity. It overlaps with telecommunications and satellite communication, and merges into the field of broadcasting. The collection and utilization of this involves every possible means of handling it, from pen on paper to the most advanced electronic tools known, or likely to be known in the foreseeable future.

The commitment to this in terms of labour, expertise and capital can be large and very costly, from the work of the originator, through the various stages of dissemination, to the librarian or information broker, or by other means finally to the end user. The protection of that investment is the principal function of information law. The fact that information needs legal protection is rather upsetting to some people. Information is free, they say, there to be picked up by anybody, like pebbles on a seashore. Moreover, they consider it right that it should be free: freedom of information is a basic human right, like freedom to breathe the air around us. Librarians often feel a professional commitment to the freest possible information regime. However, although information in its raw state may be freely available (and this is indeed open to question), it is of no use until it has been sorted and packaged and transported to the end user. The analogy of pebbles on the seashore is less apt than, shall we say, the analogy of North Sea oil. It is there under the sea for anybody who can burrow deep enough, but to extract it, refine it, prepare it for use, and transport it, involves a major investment in skill and training, labour and capital.

Strictly speaking, as will be made clear later, the law does not generally recognize any ownership rights in information as such, or at least that is what the copyright experts say. The Roman lawyers recognized a property right in naturally occurring things once they came into the ownership of an individual, and that is a close analogy to the situation with regard to the ownership of information. Once information has been captured, packaged and recorded in some way, an ownership right, defensible in law, comes into existence. This is the basis of the most important area of information law, copyright, as we shall see later.

In the Middle Ages there was no protection for the products of human intellectual endeavour. The great medieval writers laboured for the glory of God, for the enlightenment of their fellow human beings and, doubtless, for their own reputation, in the sure and certain knowledge that their works would be copied and re-copied, plagiarized and anthologized, with no material recompense to themselves. Indeed it was not until the sixteenth, seventeenth, even the eighteenth century, that owners' rights in their intellectual property, whether technological or literary, gained acceptance. As society grew more complex, particularly in the nineteenth century, there came an increasing need for the law to protect the products of human inventiveness and intellectual endeavour. There was a general expansion of human knowledge, with great rewards available to those who could satisfy the requirements of an increasingly literate and prosperous populace desirous of things, both material and intangible, which their forebears had lacked. So the idea of intellectual property law to protect those rewards was born, and rationalized by the invention of the concept of intellectual property.

INTELLECTUAL PROPERTY

The terms 'ownership' and 'property' have been used in the previous paragraphs. The greatest part of this book is concerned with 'intellectual property'. This is a fairly new term but a useful one, covering the non-tangible products of human inventiveness and intellectual endeavour. It includes information that has been captured or recorded, to the extent that it has been given a definite shape and some more or less permanent form by an author or editor or compiler, in writing, for example, or on a computer or on a sound recording. Intellectual property goes beyond pure information as conventionally understood, for it covers works of imagination and inventiveness as well. The property rights in intellectual property are the subject of intellectual property law.

The area of the law of intellectual property which is probably of most importance to information work is copyright. This covers the right of authors (including editors, compilers, composers, programmers, artists) to defend their compositions (including written works, musical compositions, artistic works, computer programs, sound recordings, films) against infringement by others. Next in importance, but of considerable economic importance, comes the law of patents, which protects inventions that can be produced by, or applied in, industrial processes. Quite apart from their legal aspect, patents are important sources of scientific and technological information. The third major area of intellectual property concerns trade marks and passing-off. These fit in rather uneasily with the general definition of intellectual property and they are of less relevance to the aims of this book so, although it is a fascinating field, we shall look at it only in outline. Confidential information, whether personal or commercial, including trade secrets, is certainly relevant to our theme. Patents and trade marks, with perhaps trade

3

secrets, are sometimes subsumed under the term 'industrial property'. A good deal of this book is devoted to copyright in its various manifestations, relating as it does not only to the provision of information as such, but also to the whole field of publishing, to broadcasting and also to the entertainment industries.

However, the legal issues involved in the production and communication of what we have loosely defined as information are not confined within the conventionally drawn bounds of intellectual property law. The particular problems relating to data held and accessed electronically have given rise to a specialism in informatics law: such problems include data protection issues and privacy. Every facet of our field is likely to be touched by the legislation on human rights but here we are on uncertain ground until a body of case law has had time to build up. More certain are the legal pitfalls discussed in Chapter 9 in the law of defamation, obscenity, racial hatred and official secrets. Intellectual property cannot be confined within national frontiers, particularly now that it is possible to transfer data to the other side of the world at the touch of a few computer keys. Certain international agreements protect intellectual property transnationally. Nearly every country has its own laws in this field and may, or may not, grant the same level of protection as the foreign owner of intellectual property expects in their home country. These questions have to be discussed.

The remainder of this chapter will be devoted to outlining essential legal background: the framework and divisions of the law, legal sources and processes, legal relations and crime, on the assumption that most readers will not be lawyers.

PROPERTY AND THEFT

Suppose someone is a skilled craftsman and makes, say, a chair. Somebody else takes the chair from his house without permission and keeps it. This is theft:

> A person is guilty of theft if he dishonestly appropriates property belonging to another with the intention of permanently depriving the other of it. (Theft Act 1968, s. 1, (1).)

The thief can be prosecuted in the criminal courts and can be punished with up to 10 years imprisonment (Theft Act 1968, s. 7) though in a comparatively trivial case like this the punishment will, of course, be much less. Usually the law will be set in motion by the police and subsequent proceedings will be in the hands of the Crown Prosecution Service, not the victim of the theft. (Private prosecutions are not so common.) The victim will get the property back if it has been recovered or, in certain cases, the court has powers to order the thief to pay compensation. However the victim will often have to be content with seeing the thief punished.

Take the case of an author who has written a book. A person takes the manuscript, makes a copy without permission and returns the manuscript. You might say that this person has 'stolen' the author's ideas and words and work, but in the eyes of the law this is not theft: there was no intention of 'permanently depriving' the author of the manuscript. Here are two actual examples of this. In the case of *Oxford* v. *Moss*, 1978, a student at Newcastle University (not Oxford: that was the name of the person prosecuting) had obtained a proof copy of an examination paper, read it and returned it. He had not stolen anything (except perhaps the confidential information in the examination paper, and the Theft Act does not regard that as property) so he was not guilty of theft. The men who borrowed films to make pirate copies, *R.* v. *Lloyd and ors*, 1986, were equally not guilty. (The abbreviations 'ors' and 'anor' for 'others' and 'another' are frequently met in case names.) Although the defendants were not guilty of the criminal offence of theft, the owner of copyright in the films could have brought a civil action for infringement of copyright. (Also, depending on the actual circumstances, commercial dealings in pirated copyright material can be a different criminal offence, as we shall see later.) So, unless it is tangible property (or, for example, money in a bank account), the criminal law of theft is not applicable. In any case, the first concern of the owner of intellectual property is not to see the infringer locked up. What the owner wants is:

1.   that the other should stop exploiting the owner's intellectual property, and
2.   that the owner should get compensation for any loss suffered.

That is just what the law provides. The main remedies for infringement of a person's intellectual property are:

1.   an order (called an 'injunction') to stop the infringer, and
2.   damages to compensate for the loss suffered (including, of course, any gain that the victim should have made were it not for the infringement).

In the UK the law always used to take a rather materialistic view of intellectual property rights; compensation was usually for the quantifiable pecuniary loss suffered. In many other countries (most notably France) the law has long protected an author's 'moral rights', for example the right to be recognized as author and the right to prevent the work being reproduced in a manner derogatory of the author's reputation. The protection of moral rights was an innovation in the UK in the Copyright, Designs and Patents Act 1988.

TERMINOLOGY

Some people are a little confused about the terminology relating to the civil and criminal law. Contrary to the popular view the legal system is not primarily concerned with the 'criminal' law, that is the punishment of malefactors. The main function of the law is to regulate the relations, commercial and personal, between individual persons (a legal person can include a company or other corporation as well as an individual) and to settle the disputes between them. This is known as the 'civil' law. (Rather confusingly, 'Civil Law', usually with capitals, is also used to describe the continental legal systems rooted in Roman law, the law protecting the citizen, *civis*, contrasted with the English 'Common Law' system.) For example, practically the whole of the legislation on copyright or patents is concerned with civil law and not criminal law. If somebody's copyright is infringed the victim will sue the infringer in the civil courts. The judge will decide the rights and wrongs and award an appropriate remedy to the victim if the decision is in his or her favour.

However, the criminal law will step in on occasion when commercial exploitation of material infringing intellectual property rights takes place. There are penal provisions in the Copyright, Designs and Patents Act and severe punishment can be meted out in the worst cases of piracy. Sometimes action is initiated by local Trading Standards Officers under trade descriptions legislation against manufacturers and traders with counterfeit clothing, videos, sound recordings or computer software. The offender will be prosecuted in the Magistrates' Court or Crown Court and punished by a fine or imprisonment. This will probably put a stop to the offender's nefarious activities (at least for a while) but since it does not give the copyright or trade mark owner any compensation the owner may well bring an action in the civil courts as well. It is worth stressing, though, that 90 per cent of the law in general, including nearly all the areas dealt with in this book, is concerned with the civil law, with settling disputes between two parties.

Words such as 'prosecute', 'offence', 'punish', 'fine', and 'crime' refer to the criminal law. In civil cases we are likely to see the terms 'sue', 'bring an action', 'damages', 'injunction', 'dispute', 'lawsuit', or 'civil wrong'. We can talk of 'criminal liability' or alternatively 'civil liability'. The word 'guilty' ought really to be confined to criminal guilt but in fact is often used in relation to somebody whose acts constitute only a civil wrong. Cases are referred to by the names of the parties. Civil cases usually have such titles as *Jones* v. *Robinson* (read aloud as Jones and Robinson), the first-named being the 'claimant' (formerly 'plaintiff'), the party bringing the action, and the other the 'defendant' (in Scotland the 'pursuer' and 'defender'). When one party appeals to a higher court against the decision of the court below the party appealing becomes the 'appellant' and the other party is the 'respondent'. (In appeals to the House of Lords the name of the appellant is placed first, thus *Jones* v. *Hulton* (a famous libel case) became *Hulton* v. *Jones* in the House of Lords.) Most criminal cases are brought in the name of the Crown and take the form *R.* v. *Jones* (R. standing for Rex or Regina) read aloud as The Crown against Jones. Where there is a private prosecutor R. is replaced by the prosecutor's name. In certain criminal appeals you may see the Director of Public Prosecutions, DPP, standing in place of the Crown.

SOURCES OF LAW

The framework of the law of copyright in the UK is to be found in the Copyright, Designs and Patents Act 1988 (which we shall refer to as the CDPA). As its name suggests, the Act also includes the updated (to 1988) law on industrial designs and the rights of performers in their performances are included, but the Act has only a few, largely administrative, provisions regarding patents. As regards copyright it is the most important single source of information and anyone working in the information field, whether as a librarian or in any other area, should get to know it thoroughly. The other main fields of intellectual property are covered in the Patents Act 1977, the Trade Marks Act 1994 and the Registered Designs Act 1949 (which is conveniently available, amended up to 1988, as a schedule at the end of the CDPA).

It would be helpful if the whole law of intellectual property could be found within the compass of these statutes. Unfortunately that is not so. A written enactment cannot possibly answer every question. Most Acts of Parliament make provision for the appropriate Minister to make Regulations filling in the detail which would have made the Act unreasonably wordy. A Regulation will be published as a Statutory Instrument (SI), one of thousands made each year covering every field of government. Many Regulations are in force in the field of intellectual property. Even then situations can arise for which there is no solution in the written text. For example, what exactly did the drafters of earlier copyright statutes mean when they used the term 'literary work'? The definitions in the Acts help but still leave a lot of questions unanswered. Does it include a railway timetable or an examination paper or a transient image produced on a computer screen? Suppose some newsworthy person recounts his or her life story to a journalist who then writes it down and publishes it: who is the 'author'? These are actual examples of questions which judges have been called upon to settle in the law courts.

Most people know that there is, alongside the statute law, what is often called 'judge-made law'. In theory judges only interpret the law. However, in practice, a decision by a judge on a tricky point will form a precedent which will be followed in later cases unless another judge can ingeniously distinguish the facts of the later case from the earlier, or unless it is overruled by a higher court. This strong reliance on precedent is one of the main marks of the Common Law tradition of England and Wales (also of most countries of the Commonwealth, and the USA). The situation is different in the Civil Law countries on the continent and elsewhere (including to some extent in Scotland) where the courts can look to earlier decisions (and to textbook writers) but are not obliged to follow them. In this book, therefore, much attention is given to real-life cases, which is much more interesting than learning the principles out of context.

LAW REPORTS

Reliance on precedent presupposes accurate reports of previous cases. Law reports of some kind (the *Year Books*) go back to the thirteenth century (long before there was any copyright law). (Although this book concentrates on more recent cases, eighteenth-century cases are not infrequently cited in the law courts, and occasionally even earlier ones.) Reporting of law cases has been very largely a matter of private enterprise, though the standard of reporting has generally been high and the major series of reports are accepted in the courts as authoritative.

Older series of reports are generally known by the name of the compiler and are most conveniently consulted in the 176 volumes of reprints known as the *English Reports* (ER) which go up to 1865 and will be found in law libraries. The most important series for modern cases is known simply as the *Law Reports*, published in periodical parts, brought together annually in one or more separate volumes for each of the separate courts: House of Lords Appeal Cases (AC), Chancery Division (Ch), Queen's Bench Division (QB) and Family Division (Fam). The *Weekly Law Reports* (WLR) include cases which will subsequently appear in the various parts of the Law Reports, as well as some others. The other major current general series is the *All England Law Reports* (All ER) which started in 1936: a selection of earlier cases (back to the sixteenth century) can be found in the *All England Law Reports Reprint* (All ER Rep).

There are two specialized series of reports in the intellectual property field, the *Reports of Patent, Design and Trade Mark Cases* (RPC), published by the Patent Office, and the *Fleet Street Reports* (FSR). Both report cases across the whole field of intellectual property and sometimes include cases from other countries if they are of particular importance. Related areas of law will be covered in various specialized and general series of reports, and a large law library will probably subscribe to some of the law reports of Commonwealth countries and perhaps of the USA. (Cases from Common Law jurisdictions outside England and Wales may be regarded as 'persuasive', even though not authority in the English courts.)

The Times and other major newspapers publish short but reliable reports which appear within days (not months, as is common with the larger series) and often include cases which are not subsequently reported elsewhere. Legal journals, specialized or general, have proliferated in recent years and many include short reports of recent cases within their fields of interest. One thing must be remembered: despite the considerable bulk of law reports available, they represent only a small fraction of cases which the higher courts have decided, selected usually because they decide some legal issue of importance. The vast majority of law cases are born to blush unseen, unnoticed by anyone save the immediate participants. However, with the growth of electronic sources of legal information more reports of varying value have become available to the ardent searcher and the courts have had to clamp down on the growing tendency of counsel to cite numbers of obscure precedents of often marginal relevance.

The law of the European Union (EU), covered in more detail in Chapter 8, has grown to importance, in intellectual property no less than in other areas relevant to our present interest. European legislation usually appears as Directives or Regulations. A Regulation is immediately applicable in each EU State without further action by government. A Directive, on the other hand, must be incorporated by each State into its own law: only then is it effective in that State. Matters relating to EU law are adjudicated in the European Court of Justice (ECJ) and Court of First Instance: cases are reported in the *Common Market Law Reports* (CMLR) and the *European Court Reports* (ECR) (and generally make rather turgid reading).

A standardized system of citing law reports is in use in legal writings and is a useful piece of general knowledge for any librarian or other information specialist. The year is given in brackets, followed by the volume number, if any, abbreviated title of the series and the page number on which the report commences. For example the famous *Anton Piller* case is at [1976] 1 All ER 779 (the volume number in this case refers to the first volume of the year 1976). In the Law Reports there was only one volume of Chancery cases for that year so the reference to the report of the same case in that series is [1976] Ch 55. The square brackets indicate that the date is an essential part of the reference. Some other series of reports number the volumes consecutively and the year is not really necessary. This was so with the *Reports of Patent Cases* until 1960. The convention is that the year, if not necessary, is given in round brackets. For example, *Haig* v. *Haig* (a trade mark case picked at random) is at (1957) 74 RPC 381. For those who do not have easy access to the actual law reports there are various case books which give useful extracts from leading cases. An example is *Cases and Materials on Intellectual Property* Professor by W.R. Cornish. These books usually give a summary of the bare facts with an extract from the judgment explaining the legal point settled. However, where possible it is best to look at the fuller reports to appreciate the real-life situations behind them.

BOOKS AND JOURNALS

Over the past few years many new works have appeared on the topics dealt with in this book, intellectual property, media law, defamation, data protection and all sorts of related areas. A selection is given in the Bibliography. Updated editions of standard texts come out regularly and some old friends reappear in a new edition every few years. It is doubtful if W.A. Copinger would have recognized his book, first published in 1870, by the time it had reached its eleventh edition just over a hundred years later, and it is still the standard text in its latest edition, now as *Copinger and Skone James on Copyright*. *Terrell on the Law of Patents* first appeared in 1884, and *Kerly's Law of Trade Marks* goes back to 1894. For most of their long lives these three have been the bibles of practitioners in their fields. One stern warning is necessary: always check that you are using the latest editions. Law books become out of date probably more quickly than texts in any other field. Updating supplements are issued regularly for some works, sometimes even with the original volume at the time of publication, so quickly can the law change. Loose-leaf works can be updated without scrapping the whole book but the subscription for the updates can be very expensive (and the task of removing dead pages and inserting new pages is indescribably boring).

Lawyers and law students have a large number of aids to keep them up-to-date and there are various guides to legal research and using legal materials. It is worth mentioning *Current Law*, a monthly publication with a cumulative index, noticing new cases, legislation, Statutory Instruments and much more, cumulated in annual volumes. New law journals and magazines keep appearing, ranging from practical newsletters to scholarly publications. Highly recommended (though expensive) for the worldwide intellectual property situation is the *European Intellectual Property Review* (EIPR). A newcomer is the *Intellectual Property Quarterly* with substantial refereed articles.

INITIATING A CIVIL LAWSUIT

What happens when the machinery of the law is put in motion in a civil case, for example a case of infringement of intellectual property? If the owner of intellectual property, whether a patent, copyright or other, finds out that somebody is infringing the rights in that property the first recourse may well be a stiff letter to the infringer, perhaps written by a solicitor. It is necessary to be careful about such a letter: if it is not clear, accurate and complete it may be held against the writer at a later stage of the proceedings. This may stop the infringement, particularly if it was committed in all innocence. However, the other party may believe, for one reason or another, that this is not infringement. The product in question may appear to be outside the scope of the complainant's patent, or the alleged infringer's written work is not in fact a copy. Of course, the infringer may just decide to go ahead with the infringement, particularly if there is not a great deal of evidence to prove the complainant's case. If an initial letter had no effect there may well be lengthy negotiations, probably conducted through the two parties' solicitors. In well over 90 per cent of cases a settlement will be reached without its coming to court. (This is so with all kinds of civil actions: only a very small proportion of those commenced are pursued to the stage of an actual trial. A court case is expensive and time-consuming and it generally makes sense to avoid it if at all possible.) Perhaps the infringer will desist, or a licence fee or compensation may be negotiated, or perhaps the first party may realize that there is not a very strong case after all and will decide to drop the matter.

However, even while negotiations are proceeding the claimant may play safe by taking the first procedural steps to bringing the case to court. This may be particularly desirable if the prospective defendant looks like being obdurate because there is a time limit within which the case must be started. (This is normally six years from the date when the cause of action arose but in defamation actions it is only one year and in negligence actions (other than personal injuries) it can be three years after the claimant knew that he had a claim or six years after the negligent action had its effect.) The claimant may do everything without professional legal advice, but it is always wise to use a solicitor who will know the ins and outs of legal procedure. Even after the civil justice reforms of 1999 legal procedure is very complicated: one of the standard guides for lawyers, the *Civil Court Service* published by Jordans, runs to around 2000 pages and is updated three times a year. Bigger firms of solicitors will often have one or more experts in the field of intellectual property: there are some firms of solicitors, particularly in the City of London, which have large departments specializing in this area and there are also barristers' chambers which bring together a number of intellectual property specialists.

Civil lawsuits are, with rare exceptions, heard by a judge sitting alone without a jury. The main exception to this is a claim of defamation when either party may call for a jury. The judge rules on the law and indicates to the jury the facts which must be proved to constitute defamation. The jury not only decides whether defamation has been proved but also the level of damages. Juries, doubtless influenced by newspaper stories of high libel damages, frequently used to make quite ridiculously high awards of damages: modest reforms to procedure a few years ago improved the situation.

CIVIL COURTS

One point of possible confusion may perhaps be cleared up at this stage. When a textbook or other source refers to 'the court' as making some decision or taking a particular step this normally refers to the judge handling the case. The hierarchy of courts in civil matters runs as follows. 'Small claims' (where the amount at issue is not more than £5000 (£1000 for personal injuries and a few other things)) get a hearing, which may be relatively informal, before a District Judge. Depending on the financial value of the claim and the complexity of the case, where the financial value is over £5000 it will go to a County Court to be heard by a Circuit Judge who wears a black robe with lilac facings, or the High Court before a High Court Judge in scarlet. Appeals go to the Court of Appeal, Civil Division, before two or three Lords Justices of Appeal (who are not, in fact, lords though when first appointed to the High Court they will have received a knighthood or, if women, a DBE with the title 'Dame', and are thenceforth addressed as 'My Lord' or 'My Lady' in court (a Circuit Judge is 'Your Honour')). The work of the Court of Appeal is very demanding: plain black robes and grinding hard work as one Lord Justice described it. Appeals can sometimes go beyond the Court of Appeal to the House of Lords where particularly weighty cases, or those with a crucial point of law at issue, are finally determined by five Law Lords (who are lords, very senior judges specially granted life peerages to exercise the judicial function of the House of Lords: they wear plain clothes, though counsel appearing before them are robed). (The Law Lords also sit as the Judicial Committee of the Privy Council to hear now dwindling final appeals from a few Commonwealth countries, from Crown dependencies such as the Channel Islands and the Isle of Man, as well as some miscellaneous appeals from bodies such as some professional disciplinary councils, including the General Medical Council.) Incidentally, a judge in court wears a short wig, not the long wig beloved of cartoonists which is reserved for ceremonial occasions. In England (and Scotland, which has its own legal system) judges are appointed by rigorous selection from senior practising barristers, and now solicitors, who have many years of legal experience behind them. In many Continental countries, for example France, Germany and Italy, there is a career judiciary, a young law graduate opting to join the judiciary rather than legal practice and gradually progressing from junior positions. Whilst both systems have their supporters, the high level of probity, impartiality and ability of English judges, with very rare (and usually highly publicized) exceptions, is a matter of pride.

Intellectual property matters are heard in the Chancery Division of the High Court, or as Chancery business in the County Court. There is a specialist Patents Court within the Chancery Division where a judge expert in the intellectual property field deals with 'Patents Court business', primarily claims under the Patents Acts and Registered Designs Acts. Two judges, who sit singly, are assigned specially to the Patents Court and there is a Patents County Court for rather less weighty cases. Copyright cases are also heard in the Chancery Division and in fact the Patents Court judges frequently take these on. Most other civil actions on matters dealt with in this book go to the Queen's Bench Division of the High Court, or to a County Court.

A CIVIL ACTION

To bring a civil action the claimant, or usually his or her solicitor, fills in a 'claim form'. (Remember when reading any case before the civil justice reforms came into effect on 26 April 1999 that the 'claimant' would be referred to as the 'plaintiff'.) The procedure has been streamlined in the new reforms and the claim form is now a simple two page document requiring the claimant's and defendant's names, brief details of the claim and its value, and a signed statement of truth. The second page provides space for more detailed particulars of the claim, or these may be attached or sent separately. There are detailed notes and further information is available from the court. The claim form succeeds a more ponderous document, the writ, which came ostensibly from the Sovereign (though really from the plaintiff). (A writ, *breve* in Latin, was once used to convey royal administrative, not only legal, orders and dates back to Anglo-Saxon times.) Once completed the claim form must be taken or posted to the court where it is 'issued', that is sealed and recorded, on payment of a fee. It is then 'served' on the defendant, usually by first class post, by the court or the claimant. There are many examples in older law reports of the means by which wily defendants tried to evade service, and the ingenuity used to overcome them. In one old case the court accepted that a writ had been properly served by placing it in a basket and hanging it over the defendant's garden wall. On receipt of the claim form the defendant must return to the court the Acknowledgment of Service and a form stating whether the claim is admitted, or alternatively a statement of his or her defence, within 14 days. Time limits are tight: one aim of the civil justice reforms is to prevent dilatory parties from prolonging the case.

Under the new procedure the court (that generally means the District Judge) now allocates the case to one of three 'tracks', normally on the basis of a questionnaire to the parties. The Small Claims Track is for cases of no complexity which are for no more than £5000 (£1000 in personal injury and certain other cases) to be heard by a District Judge. Cases worth over £5000 and up to £15 000 go on the Fast Track if the trial will last no more than one day. They will be heard in a County Court, if possible the nearest to the defendant's address, within 30 weeks. Other claims, including all Patents Court and Patents County Court business, go on the Multi-Track: a number of criteria will decide whether the trial will be in the County Court (usually up to £50 000 in value) or the High Court.

The court will give directions to the parties of the various steps which must be taken before trial. One feature of English civil procedure which can seem strange to foreign lawyers is the duty of Disclosure of documents (formerly known as Discovery). As part of the preparations for trial each party is required to provide a list of documents relevant to the case which they hold or have held and to allow the other party to inspect them. This normally means all documents which the party will rely on and any which are adverse to their case. There are some very limited exemptions; one which frequently attracts criticism is when a party (often an organ of government) asks the court's permission to withhold disclosure of a document on public interest grounds. Communications between a party and lawyers are also privileged from disclosure.

It is a general rule that a fact relied upon by either party at a trial which needs to be proved by the evidence of witnesses must be proved by their oral evidence given in public. However, the court will now, during the preparations for trial, order each party to take signed witness statements of their evidence from their witnesses and pass them to the other party. The witness will still have to attend the trial but will not usually have to repeat the evidence in the statement, though the witness can be cross-examined on the contents, on oath, by the other party's counsel.

One other matter which has to be settled before the trial and which can be particularly important in highly technical patent cases is the use of expert witnesses. An expert witness is exactly what it sounds like, an expert in a particular field, perhaps computer programming or pharmaceutical chemistry (though expert witnesses may be used in many types of case, automobile engineers in road accident claims, medical practitioners in medical claims, accountants in cases involving the examination of accounts for example). The expert is there to give impartial guidance to the court: this is the expert's duty and it overrides any obligation to the party who has instructed or is paying him or her. To keep costs down and to avoid confusion the court can restrict the number of experts, ideally to one witness agreed by both parties. Expert evidence is given in a written report unless the court orders otherwise and, particularly in Fast Track cases, the expert may not be required to attend the trial.

Meanwhile, negotiations for an out-of-court settlement will be continuing between the parties or their lawyers right up to the last minute: even after the issue of a claim most cases will be settled without reaching an actual trial. If the case does finally come up for trial it will certainly be many months, and probably much longer, after the claim was issued. To some extent delay is inevitable: witnesses must be approached, tricky legal points considered, documents prepared. The civil justice reforms have tightened up the time limits for the different procedural stages but even so a dilatory party still has some chance of dragging out the legal procedure however expeditiously the other party may proceed. In addition there will probably be a queue of litigants waiting for time in the court's busy schedule.

COSTS

All this time costs are mounting up. Litigation is very expensive: lawyers are highly skilled, take a lot of responsibility and have to charge accordingly. Numerous other matters will have to be paid for. Costs for a simple case soon mount into thousands of pounds: in a hard-fought patent action between two big companies the bills will be in hundreds of thousands. Generally speaking the loser will have to pay the winner's costs as well as the loser's own, though this is not always so. Sometimes there is little merit in the case of a litigant who may be technically successful and the judge may leave the winner to bear his or her own costs. Either party who has introduced unnecessary complications before or during the trial, or did not try to resolve the dispute, may be penalized in costs. The 'standard basis' allows costs which are reasonable and proportionate to the matters in issue: any doubts will be resolved in favour of the paying party. The 'indemnity basis' is more favourable to the receiving party. In any case there may well be a detailed assessment of the costs by a court officer, a procedure which used to be known rather confusingly as 'taxation of costs', and the winning party is unlikely to recover everything which has been disbursed. Any private individual, or indeed any small company or organization, would be very ill-advised to contemplate litigation without discussing the likely cost with a solicitor.

INJUNCTIONS AND ORDERS

Very often in an infringement action the claimant wants immediate action to stop the infringement and will apply for an 'interim injunction' (formerly known as an 'interlocutory' injunction). This is a temporary order from the court, requiring the other party to cease the behaviour complained of, for example allegedly infringing the applicant's copyright, until the matter comes to trial (prohibitory injunction), or more rarely ordering that party to do something (mandatory injunction). The judge will hear briefly what the parties want to say and will weigh up various factors before deciding whether to grant the injunction. Although this is only a preliminary decision, intended really to stabilize the situation until trial, the defendant will often take it as an indication of the way the court is likely to decide in the end and may decide that it is not worth the trouble and expense of carrying on. Very often an interim injunction marks the effective end of an infringement action. If the case does go on to trial and the claimant wins the court may well issue a permanent injunction ordering the defendant to stop the behaviour complained of, infringement of an intellectual property right, for example, or perhaps defamation, for all time. Although an injunction is a civil remedy the court can show its teeth if the person against whom it has been made fails to comply. The party seeking to enforce the injunction may apply to the County Court or High Court, whichever made the original injunction, to commit the defaulter to prison for contempt of court. A court hearing will normally be in public and the defaulter may in the last resort be sentenced to a term of up to two years in prison, or to a fine (the latter being the normal penalty if it is a company in default). A defaulter who decides then to comply may apply to 'purge his contempt', or hers as the case may be. One interesting reported case is *Phonographic Performance Ltd* v. *Amusement Caterers (Peckham) Ltd*, 1963. Amusement Caterers played sound recordings in which PPL had copyright, in their juke boxes and, despite an injunction, it took the threat of proceedings for contempt of court before they caved in and cut the wires to their juke boxes.

If the claimant has suffered loss the court will award a compensatory sum of money, damages. Damages are intended to compensate for actual loss suffered, which may include, of course, profits or other gains which would have been made if it were not for the defendant's actions. Sometimes additional damages may be awarded to compensate the claimant for particularly objectionable behaviour by the defendant; these are known as 'aggravated damages'. An especially vicious libel may call for additional damages above those which would normally be considered sufficient to compensate for the claimant's loss of reputation. Alternatively, the court may disapprove of the behaviour of the defendant, which went far beyond normal acceptable standards, and award 'exemplary damages'. There is a fine line between aggravated and exemplary damages. One very readable case is *Lady Anne Tennant* v. *Associated Newspapers*, 1979. Lady Anne, a lady-in-waiting to the Queen's sister Princess Margaret, took photographs of the princess and a friend in fancy dress at a party. By a somewhat suspicious route these came into the possession of the *Daily Mail* and were published. The editor should have been on his guard in these circumstances: Lady Anne won her case for infringement of copyright in her photographs and the judge felt that this was the sort of case where additional damages could be called for. (English law, unlike French, did not give a remedy for invasion of privacy – the position will have changed under recent human rights legislation – so the princess herself would have had no cause of action.)

SEARCH ORDERS

It is not always easy for someone who knows that his or her intellectual property rights are being infringed to get proof that will satisfy a law court. Since 1974 the courts have been willing to grant what came to be known as an 'Anton Piller order' after the leading case, and is now renamed a 'search order'. This draconian instrument is not a final remedy but simply an interim order allowing the claimant to search the defendant's premises to uncover further evidence. EMI, the record company, brought an action against a Leicester dealer, Kishorilal Pandit, in respect of copyright infringement in certain recordings of Indian music. EMI obtained an interlocutory (interim) injunction to stop Mr Pandit from parting with or selling the allegedly infringing material, and an order for him to hand over the names and addresses of his suppliers and customers and copies of any relevant documents in his possession. He thereupon produced the name of one supplier, with a post office box address in Dubai, two customers only (who were already known to EMI) and a single letter purporting to be from EMI. The plaintiffs (claimants) were convinced that Mr Pandit's operations were much more extensive than he admitted. Their counsel, Mr Hugh Laddie (now Mr Justice Laddie) went back to the court without notice to the respondent (the parties to an application for an injunction are the 'applicant' and the 'respondent') producing convincing evidence to back up the suspicions, and obtained an order to enable the applicants to enter Mr Pandit's premises, to inspect and photograph tapes, packaging and documents, as well as typewriters and photocopiers, and to remove into EMI's solicitors' custody any infringing tapes. The order also forbade Mr Pandit to destroy, remove or alter any relevant material (*EMI* v. *Pandit*, 1975). This was actually the fourth such order to be made but the first to be reported: three others had been made earlier in the same year, 1974. Of course, only a very tiny proportion of cases heard find their way into the law reports.

The order took its familiar name, however, from *Anton Piller KG* v. *Manufacturing Processes Ltd*, 1976, which went before the Court of Appeal and so had the authority of three of the most senior judges behind it. The claimants were German manufacturers and the defendants their agents in the UK. Fearing, with enough evidence to back this, that the defendants were passing on confidential and copyright material to rival firms, Anton Piller sought an order to enter Manufacturing Processes' premises, inspect documents and remove or copy them, in order to collect additional evidence sufficient to support their case at trial. The High Court judge refused the order but the Court of Appeal, where the application went as a matter of urgency, granted it.

A search order must not be confused with a search warrant granted to the police in criminal matters. It can happen that criminal proceedings in respect of, for example, counterfeit goods, may be proceeding at the same time as a civil lawsuit, but the directions for a search order forbid its being carried out at the same time as a police search warrant. It was previously common practice for the solicitors to arrange for a policeman to be on hand in case of trouble, but the police will not interfere unless there is a breach of the peace.

The search order has proved an important weapon in the fight against piracy in the intellectual property field, which is where its main use has been found. Together with the Mareva injunction, now known as a 'freezing injunction', which freezes a respondent's assets if there is a danger that they will be spirited away, it has been described as one of the 'two nuclear weapons of the law'. It must be remembered, however, that a search order can be very expensive. The attendance of the applicant's solicitors and others, often for a lengthy search, perhaps at two or three premises to be searched simultaneously, can soon run up a substantial bill. The cost of the supervising solicitor (see below) alone for a typical search is likely to be in the region of £3000.

Whilst it was originally envisaged that this invasion would be allowed only rarely, in fact the orders came to be granted in large numbers: one firm of solicitors obtained 300 Anton Piller orders between 1974 and 1986. Slackness crept in and in *Columbia Picture Industries* v. *Robinson*, 1986, the defendant struck back with a counterclaim, and although the plaintiffs won their case on infringement, he was awarded £10 000 damages in view of serious irregularities in the obtaining and execution of the order. Important and relevant matters had not been disclosed in the original application, material not covered by the order had been seized and the solicitors had lost some of the material while it was in their custody. Other cases came under criticism and it was after *Universal Thermosensors* v. *Hibben*, 1992, that the Lord Chief Justice issued a Practice Direction in 1994 reforming the process.

Perhaps the most important reform was that instead of the claimant's solicitor being wholly in charge an independent 'supervising solicitor' with relevant experience and not a member of the applicant's firm of solicitors (recommended – and paid – by the applicant's solicitor, and paid ultimately of course by the claimant, but approved by the court) must be appointed to serve the order and ensure that the search is properly conducted. The independence of the supervising solicitor is stressed. In France a rather similar procedure exists, *saisie contrefaçon*, which is carried out by an officer of the court. There is a rather curious provision in the current Practice Direction that if the supervising solicitor is a man and the person in charge of the premises is likely to be an unaccompanied woman (as was the case in *Universal Thermosensors*) then at least one of those taking part must also be a woman. (The courts still retain on occasion Victorian ideas of feminine frailty.) The whole procedure is now regulated to prevent abuses: unless the court orders otherwise the order must be served in the daytime on a weekday and the persons undertaking the search are limited to those mentioned in the order. The respondent will probably never have heard of a search order and it is the supervising solicitor's duty to explain it and make it clear that the respondent may call a solicitor. In theory the respondent can refuse entry but must then make an immediate application to the court to set the order aside or risk action for contempt of court.

Surprise is the essence of a search order, and indeed of its cousin the freezing order, and the application to the court will probably be made without notice to the respondent, *ex parte* in the concise term used until the civil justice reforms of 1999 banned the use of Latin. (In another context *ex parte* can also mean 'on behalf of'.) Whilst most judges have the power to grant other injunctions, a search order may be made only by a High Court judge or rarely by another judge specially authorized. Usually counsel for the applicant drafts the order using the model in the Practice Direction and seeks the judge's approval or emendation. In really urgent cases out of working hours application may be made to the duty High Court judge by telephone. The Anton Piller order faced a challenge in the European Court of Human Rights, *Chappell* v. *United Kingdom*, 1989, but its use was held not to breach the human rights convention: this seems a sensible decision (something not always apparent in the decisions of the human rights court).

THE CRIMINAL COURTS

Criminal proceedings are likely to concern the information professional at work only to a very small extent, if at all. However, a few matters dealt with in this book may entail criminal penalties so this topic needs some brief discussion. Most criminal cases in the UK are relatively minor and are dealt with in the Magistrates' Courts where they are heard by two or more lay Justices of the Peace, or in some cities by a legally qualified stipendiary (paid) magistrate. Lay magistrates have sentencing powers up to six months imprisonment. Some matters dealt with in this book, relating to obscene publications or false trade descriptions for example, may, if they are not too serious, be heard by magistrates. More serious matters are dealt with in the Crown Court where, depending generally on the seriousness of the offence, they will be dealt with by a Circuit judge or, for the most serious, a High Court judge (known sometimes as a 'scarlet judge'). (Circuit judges wear black with red facings for criminal cases, magistrates have no special dress.) A judge in the Crown Court is responsible for all questions of law, including the admissibility of evidence and the sentence, whilst the jury determines whether the evidence shows the defendant to be guilty or not. Criminal appeals go (generally on points of law only, or on sentence) to the Court of Appeal, Criminal Division, where they are heard by two or three judges without a jury, and, rarely, to settle a particularly important point of law, to the House of Lords. Certain 'either way' offences may be tried either by magistrates or in the Crown Court: the defendant may have the choice of submitting to trial by the magistrates or going to the Crown Court where there is a risk of a longer sentence but, it is popularly believed, a greater likelihood of acquittal by the jury. (Restrictions on the right of a defendant to elect trial by jury are being introduced.)

The decision whether to prosecute or not, and the general conduct of the prosecution, used to be taken by the police: this is now the responsibility of the Crown Prosecution Service which is staffed largely by lawyers. In fact, however, anybody can bring a criminal prosecution and a few private individuals do (usually when the authorities refuse to act). Quite a number of prosecutions are brought by local authorities (for example, regarding trade descriptions) or by other public or semi-public bodies.

CRIMINAL OFFENCES

The few criminal offences which are specially relevant to information work are discussed elsewhere in this book. Libel is normally a civil matter but very rarely a prosecution may be brought for exceptionally vicious or persistent conduct.

Obscene publications, racial hatred and breach of official secrets can all trigger criminal prosecution. What can broadly be described as commercial dealings in infringing copyright material, in other words piracy, can now attract fairly stiff maximum penalties. False use of a trade mark is a serious offence. Since the Video Recordings Act 1984 came into force there is provision for classification of video recordings as suitable for general viewing, viewing by or supply to persons over a certain age, or for supply only in a licensed sex shop: it is an offence to supply videos otherwise than as provided for. This is the only pre-publication censorship in this country and it is backed by penal sanctions. The Trade Descriptions Act 1968 has proved a useful weapon against the production and sale of counterfeit recordings and computer software: suppliers are prosecuted, often on the initiative of local trading standards officers, for applying a false trade description to counterfeit goods, that is describing them as genuine.

LEGAL RELATIONS

It is outside the scope of this book to go into the law of contract in any detail (there are plenty of textbooks on the subject) but this branch of the law becomes more and more important in relation to the supply of information as information is recognized as a valuable form of property. A contract can be a very simple legal relationship (for example, the exchange involved in purchasing a tin of beans in a supermarket) or it can be extremely involved. To form a contract under English law all that is needed is an offer, acceptance of the offer, and some sort of payment or recompense (the law calls this 'consideration'). Except for a few special categories (the best known example is the sale of land) a contract does not have to be in writing, though except for the very simplest contracts it normally will be written down to avoid future dispute as to its terms. Thus if A says to B 'Get me this information and I will pay you £50' and B says 'OK', they have a contract. There is an offer, acceptance, and the consideration is £50. (We assume, naturally that they intend to create a legal relationship, even if they do not think of it in those words: it would be otherwise if the exchange took place over a game of Monopoly.) In modern commerce, of course, the owner of intellectual property rights very frequently has no contractual relation with the ultimate purchaser. This has caused problems over computer software, games and so on, bought off the shelf in the high street: the purchaser's contract is with the retailer, not with the owner of the copyright. One attempted solution has been the so-called 'shrink-wrap agreement'. The wrapping of the product bears a message stating that opening the wrapping will constitute acceptance of the contractual terms set out.

The provider and user of, for example, an online information service will agree to a fairly detailed contract which will set out the rights and duties of both parties.

This will probably be on the service provider's standard terms: most suppliers of more expensive goods and services present the purchaser with a take it or leave it agreement. Standard form contracts are also common in many major business areas, commodities trades, carriage of goods, insurance or chartering ships. These will often be drawn up by a trade association and the parties will agree to the standard terms without having to negotiate all the details in every transaction. Breach of the terms of the contract could have various legal results depending on the facts and the seriousness of the breach. The aggrieved party might be able to say that the contract is now void and he or she is not bound to perform his or her side of the bargain. The party might go to the court and get damages for breach of contract, or an order for the defaulting party to do what that party had contracted to do, or the court might order the cancellation (rescission) of the contract. Contracts for the supply of computer hardware and software, for online or Internet services, or contracts between publishers and authors, are examples of contracts which have particular relevant to information work. All these pose their particular problems and there are books and online sources giving advice and specimen forms. Publishing of textbooks and other reference works on CD-ROM has been with us for some time, often as an alternative to the printed form, and is particularly useful for material in fast-moving fields such as law which needs frequent updating. Use of the CD-ROM will probably be controlled by a detailed contractual licence which may be set out in the accompanying documentation. Entry will be denied without a password which will be supplied, perhaps by telephone, when the user agrees the terms, thus concluding the contract.

In a good many areas relevant to information, licensing agreements or contracts are important. The supplier of computer software does not normally sell it outright but licenses the other party to use it within the limits agreed. This will generally, for example, restrict copying of the software by the user, forbid others to be allowed to use it and restrict use to particular systems or sites. Publishing agreements are sometimes outright sales of all rights in a work, but they may simply license the publisher to produce, perhaps, a single edition of the work, or to publish it in a foreign country, or to produce it on television. Licences may be granted for one or more performances of a copyright musical work or play. The owner of the intellectual property rights does not lose these rights, but only permits the licensee to use the work within defined limits. A patent may be exploited by the original patentee but frequently he will grant a licence to a manufacturer to produce the patented product or use the patented process. Compulsory licensing can arise in certain circumstances. Under the Patents Act 1977 an application may sometimes be made if the patentee is not exploiting the patent and the applicant may be granted a compulsory licence to do so: the rationale is, at least in part, that the benefits of inventiveness should be made available for the public good. Under international conventions the government of a developing country may require the publisher of a copyright textbook published elsewhere to grant a licence for a local edition: again, the public good of a poor country's population is the justification. Sometimes a licensee may be granted exclusive rights in the subject matter, excluding, that is, any other person: under the Copyright, Designs and Patents Act 1988 an exclusive licensee has the same rights to take legal action as the owner in cases of infringement. A non-exclusive licensee, when there may be other licensees, will usually have to leave enforcement of the copyright to its owner.

TORT AND THE *HEDLEY BYRNE* CASE

'Tort' is the term applied to behaviour causing loss or harm to another person where no contract is involved. It can apply to personal injury, damage to property, defamation, and a host of other matters, most of which are not directly relevant to us here. Tort often involves the idea of negligence or carelessness in some form or other. What happens if A carelessly gives inaccurate information to B as a result of which the latter suffers loss? If the provider of information is providing a fee-based service he will have a contract with the client who will be able to claim under the terms of the contract. But suppose (as is often the case with libraries) information is supplied gratuitously. Has the recipient of the information any redress for loss suffered as a result of using inaccurate information? This question came up in *Hedley Byrne* v. *Heller and Partners*, 1963. Hedley Byrne, a firm of advertising agents, placed TV and press advertisements for a client on credit. They asked their own bank to check with the defendants, who were the client's merchant bankers. The defendants gave a guarded but basically favourable reference as to the client's standing. As a result of relying on this ill-considered reference the plaintiffs (claimants), Hedley Byrne, lost a lot of money when the client went into liquidation. The House of Lords held that there can be cases where a person undertaking to supply information has a duty to take reasonable care, the sort of care that a person in that position or profession ought to take, that the information is accurate. In such cases the supplier of information could be liable for any loss which the recipient suffers through relying on it. Obviously there are limits to this. It will exclude casual or social enquiries. If you ask me the time and I know my watch is unreliable but nevertheless tell you, so that you miss your train and lose an important contract, you can hardly be said to have a claim against me. It seems that the information provider must have assumed some responsibility to provide the information: it is probably within the scope of that person's business or profession. As it happened, Heller and Partners had cautiously headed their letter 'Without responsibility' and this saved them: they thus avoided the liability which their Lordships would otherwise have held them to have incurred.

Since the original decision, the Hedley Byrne principle has come up in a variety of situations involving the supply of information where there was no direct contractual link between supplier and recipient. One fairly recent House of Lords case was *Spring* v. *Guardian Assurance*, 1994, concerning a damning reference given by Guardian for an insurance agent. He had been employed by a company connected with Guardian and now found it impossible to get a similar job in the light of that reference. The case was complicated by various other issues but it was held that the Hedley Byrne principle could apply in this case.

Although Hedley Byrne has been treated cautiously by the courts, the implications for an information service are clear. Obviously the first essential is to ensure that the information is accurate: if there is the least doubt about it the position should be clearly explained to the recipient and a disclaimer added. In particular, giving legal advice could have nasty repercussions and the information professional will need to cover him or herself very carefully if asked about a client's legal rights.

ALTERNATIVE DISPUTE RESOLUTION

Although over ninety per cent of legal disputes are settled by the parties before they actually get into the courts, there remains a hard core for which a trial seems inevitable. But litigation can be expensive and long drawn out so there is growing interest in alternative methods of dispute resolution. Indeed the courts will now frequently ask, in the early stages before trial, whether the parties have tried to settle the dispute by Alternative Dispute Resolution (ADR) and will encourage them to do so. Although there are various ways to produce a settlement instead of negotiation or trial, they really boil down to two, arbitration and mediation. Arbitration has been with us for centuries, particularly in the commercial field. The parties make a binding agreement in advance to accept the award of an independent arbitrator, commonly a person (or sometimes a panel of more than one) with particular knowledge of the subject area of the dispute. Often a contract, particularly in the construction industry, will include a clause binding the parties to submit any disagreement over the contract to arbitration. Methods of selecting the arbitrator vary: the parties may agree on a name or they may leave the appointment to the president of their trade association or professional body. The procedure in an arbitration is much more flexible than in the courts and to a large extent is determined by the parties themselves. A simple consumer matter, for example between a tour operator and a disappointed customer where the scheme operated by the travel agents' association comes into play, may be determined on documents only with the arbitrator deciding on the basis of written submissions by the parties. More complicated cases may involve more complicated procedures, with an oral hearing before the arbitrator. The hearing may be quite informal or it may be not dissimilar to a trial, with the parties represented by lawyers and witnesses examined on oath. Arbitration has advantages: at its best it can be quick and inexpensive (though it is not always so); the arbitrator, unlike a judge, is often an expert in the field; it is not exposed to the public like an open trial; and the award (equivalent to the judgment in a trial) is binding because the parties have agreed that it should be so. Although the courts have some residual functions in relation to arbitrations they are deliberately kept minimal. Rather surprisingly, there is a substantial body of law on the conduct of arbitrations with several weighty textbooks and an important statute, the Arbitration Act 1996. Whilst any suitable person can be chosen as an arbitrator, the Chartered Institute of Arbitrators, among many other functions, provides training courses and examinations. It is in the construction industry that arbitration is most widely used, with the interpretation of multi-million pound building contracts submitted to experienced civil engineers or surveyors. Arbitration is internationally recognized and international trading contracts often contain an arbitration clause. Although less used in intellectual property matters, there is a feeling that its use will expand: the World Intellectual Property Organization (WIPO) in Geneva has an arbitration centre which facilitates arbitration.

Arbitration is sometimes included in the blanket term Alternative Dispute Resolution, and sometimes treated separately. ADR, more narrowly defined, centres on mediation (virtually interchangeable with 'conciliation') where a trained mediator uses techniques to bring the two parties into agreement. CEDR, the Centre for Dispute Resolution, has pioneered mediation and related methods. A high level of success is claimed and one of the great advantages of mediation is that there is no winner–loser result inhibiting future business relations.

THE LAW IN SCOTLAND

There are six separate legal jurisdictions in Great Britain, each with its own court system and, to some extent, its own separate laws. England (with Wales) is the largest: the others are Scotland, Northern Ireland (these three constitute the UK), Jersey, Guernsey and the Isle of Man. Laws passed by the UK parliament at Westminster prima facie extend to Scotland (and Northern Ireland) unless stated otherwise. (An Order in Council is generally necessary to extend a statute to the other three jurisdictions.) Statutes which apply only to Scotland normally have 'Scotland' in the title. Although Scots law has been heavily influenced by English law, particularly since 1800, Roman law struck deeper roots in Scotland in such fields as moveable property, contract and delict (tort): Scotland may be regarded as a Civil Law jurisdiction.

The court structure is quite different from that in England, although at the lowest level lay Justices of the Peace hear the minor criminal cases, and at the top of the system civil appeals (not criminal) go to the (UK) House of Lords. (It is the custom for at least two Law Lords to be Scots.) There is a Sheriff court in most towns, with legally qualified salaried Sheriffs, hearing a range of civil cases, also criminal cases (but not the most serious). The Court of Session approximates to the English High Court and Court of Appeal. The Outer House hears civil cases at first instance (including intellectual property, for which judges are specially selected): civil appeals go to the Inner House (whose judges have the courtesy title 'Lord' but are not peers). The same judges form the High Court of Justiciary for criminal cases and appeals. Sheriffs wear black robes. In the Court of Session judges wear dark blue robes with maroon facings and scarlet crosses on the facings: for criminal cases the robes are red with white facings and scarlet crosses. Sheriffs and judges are addressed as My Lord or My Lady in court. The legal profession is divided (as in England) into advocates and solicitors.

Scots law has its own terminology, for example the claimant is called 'pursuer' and defendant is 'defender'. There is no Scots equivalent of the English Patents County Court, all patents actions being heard in the Court of Session. Arbitration is totally different: the Arbitration Act 1996 does not extend to Scotland where the law is much closer to the European model. The law of real property (land) retains elements of the old Norman feudal law which have disappeared in England. Until 1995 archaic and obscure law governed the execution of documents: this was swept away and for most purposes a contract can be created without writing, or if writing is required or used a simple signature suffices. The law of defamation in Scotland differs from that of England. There is no distinction between libel and slander, and an insulting defamatory statement made to the pursuer alone may be grounds for action. A defence of *rixa* exists where a defamatory statement was made in the heat of a quarrel. Whilst the search order, or Anton Piller order, was an English invention, the Sheriff Court and Court of Session have extensive powers, put in statutory form in 1972, to order inspection and custody of documents or other property likely to be relevant in a court case.

In the Civil Law tradition the Scottish courts formerly did not accept previous judicial decisions as binding. English influence, which has been pervasive in modern times, has broken that down and the courts' attitude to precedent has come to equate more closely to the English. The principal series of law reports is the Session Cases (S.C.) which are cited by the year and page of the annual volume, for example 1975 S.C. 123. (Square brackets are not used but round brackets are used when the date is not essential, i.e. in earlier volumes which were numbered serially.) House of Lords decisions in Scottish appeals are bound in with the Session Cases, as are Justiciary (criminal) cases. These are abbreviated S.C. (H.L.) and J.C. respectively. Scottish Criminal Case Reports, S.C.C.R., and Scottish Civil Law

Reports, S.C.L.R., are other series containing reports with critical notes. There is a number of specialized series of reports, as well as old private reports (cited by the reporter's name).

2 **Protection of written works**

WHAT WORKS ATTRACT COPYRIGHT?

This chapter concentrates on UK law. Chapter 7 describes the features of copyright law in other countries.

Section 1 of the Copyright, Designs and Patents Act 1988 explains that copyright is a property right which subsists in accordance with the first Part of the Act in nine different categories of work in three groups. These are:

(a) original literary, dramatic, musical or artistic works,
(b) sound recordings, films, broadcasts and cable programmes, and
(c) the typographical arrangement of published editions.

Leaving aside (c) for the time being, it will be seen that the essential difference between the two groups (a) and (b) is that literary, dramatic, musical and artistic works are really 'primary' works, whilst recordings, films, broadcasts and cable programmes are 'secondary' in the sense that they nearly always have a primary work behind them. Thus, a recording will usually be of a musical work, a film will have a script behind it, a broadcast may be of a play, or a piece of music or a scripted talk, and so on. (Though, of course, our definition is not quite watertight: a sound recording may be of a steam locomotive, a broadcast may be of an unscripted discussion.)

The problems relating to dramatic works do not differ very much from those of literary works so we shall include them here, but musical works will be considered separately in Chapter 3 and artistic works in Chapter 4. The expression 'literary work' is a little misleading. It is defined in s. 3(1) to mean 'any work, other than a dramatic or musical work, which is written, spoken or sung'. It accordingly includes:

(a) a table or compilation, (other than a database),
(b) a computer program, and

(c) preparatory design material for a computer program,

(d) a database.

Thus, a 'literary work' may be far from literary in the accepted sense of the word: the term 'written work' seems rather closer and has been used for the title of this chapter. A database is in a special position: it is made clear that it is not to be regarded as a table or compilation, but is listed separately. A database used to be treated like any other literary work. Then the European Union stepped in with the Database Directive of 1996. In the UK the main criterion for copyright protection has always been the hard work put in by the author, rather inelegantly described as 'sweat of the brow', irrespective of intellectual creativity. On the Continent *droit d'auteur* depended on whether the product was the author's own intellectual creation: obviously any database which is simply a routine assemblage of data is not, however much labour it may have involved. The UK fought a rearguard action but in the end we had to capitulate and s.3A was added to the CDPA taking away copyright from a database created after 27 March 1996 unless by reason of the selection or arrangement of the contents it constitutes the author's own intellectual creation. In other words, there must be something definitely creative in the way the author has handled the material if it is to attract copyright. As a consolation prize, a new *sui generis* database right was introduced, described below.

A film script, but not the actual film or its sound track, will normally count as a dramatic work. Rather less obviously, a dramatic work includes a work of dance or mime, s.3(1). As a musical work excludes any accompanying words or action it follows that these must come within the definition of a literary, or dramatic, work. In this chapter we shall deal with the question of how copyright is acquired, what rights are covered by copyright, who gets the copyright and what rights copyright gives the owner. We shall see how the bounds delimiting copyright have been set in previous cases.

HOW IS COPYRIGHT ACQUIRED?

In the UK copyright in a written work is automatic. There is no need to apply for it, register it or anything like that. As soon as it has been recorded, in writing or otherwise (including electronically), the work is protected by copyright. It does not have to be a major piece of writing: a short poem or a letter is equally protected. The copyright line, the word 'copyright' – often abbreviated to © – with the owner's name and date of publication, commonly appears on books and other material published in the UK to give notice in certain other countries, but it is not essential in the UK (though it can be useful if anyone wants to know who owns the copyright in order, perhaps, to seek permission to copy from the work).

DURATION OF COPYRIGHT

Copyright in an unpublished written work formerly endured indefinitely but under the CDPA the position is the same for published and unpublished works. The general rule is that copyright lasts until 70 years after the end of the year in which the author died, *post mortem auctoris* (*pma*) in the concise Latin phrase. (In the case of a work of joint authorship it is 70 years after the last surviving co-author, or co-author whose identity is known if others are still unknown, died.) The period used to be 50 years but a Directive in 1993 harmonized the copyright term throughout the EU, choosing the longer term which was already in force in Germany. (One of the reasons for the longer term was the appalling slaughter of two world wars which had cut short many authors' lives prematurely.) The change was introduced by amendments to the CDPA in 1995 inserted by the Duration of Copyright and Rights in Performances Regulations 1995, and came into force on 1 January 1996. This has created some complication where copyright had expired under the old rule but now revived (see Part III of the Regulations). For convenience of calculation the duration of copyright, and other rights, always runs from the end of the calendar year: thus Rudyard Kipling died on 18 January 1936 so his works came out of copyright after 31 December 1986 and various publishers took advantage of this to produce new editions early in 1987. Then, on 1 January 1996 the 70-year term came into force, the copyright was revived in favour of whoever had been entitled before the 50-year term had ended and Kipling's heirs enjoy copyright until 31 December 2006 (70 years after his death).

Section 12 of the CDPA deals with the duration of copyright in literary, dramatic, musical and artistic works. There are slightly complicated provisions in the Regulations relating to anything done, or for which arrangements were made, in the interregnum before the copyright was revived: these things do not infringe Reg. 23. In addition, someone who wants do anything restricted by the revived copyright may do so subject to giving notice to the copyright owner and paying reasonable remuneration, Reg. 24.

If the work is of unknown authorship copyright expires 70 years after it is made, or if made available to the public (that includes performance in public or broadcast), 70 years after being made available, unless the author's identity becomes known during one of those periods when the 70-year *pma* period applies. Time runs, as usual, from the end of the year. Copyright in a computer-generated work that has no human author lasts for 50 years from the end of the year in which it is made.

SPECIAL CASES

PERPETUAL COPYRIGHT

Under the Copyright Act 1775 the six old universities of England and Scotland, as well as three public schools, enjoyed perpetual copyright in certain works. This provision was at last repealed by the CDPA though the rights will not be extinguished until 50 years after the 1988 Act came into force. Rather curiously, after abolishing one set of perpetual rights Parliament created a perpetual right (a little short of full copyright) to receive royalties on any public performance, commercial publication or broadcast (or cable programme) of Sir James Barrie's play *Peter Pan* in favour of the Great Ormond Street Hospital for Sick Children, s. 301. The Hospital had enjoyed the benefit of the copyright which expired at the end of 1987 and the passage of the CDPA through Parliament coincided with a rather emotive appeal for funds by the Hospital. When the general duration of copyright was extended to 70 years *pma* the full copyright has, of course, now revived and will expire in 2007 but the right to receive royalties will continue after that.

CROWN AND PARLIAMENTARY COPYRIGHT

Crown copyright (in any work made by Her Majesty or by any officer or servant of the Crown in the course of his or her duties) lasts for 125 years, but if the work is published commercially in the first 75 years the period is 50 years from publication, s. 163. The Queen also owns copyright in Acts of Parliament (and, as Supreme Head of the Church of England, in Measures of the General Synod) for 50 years from the royal assent, s. 164. Parliamentary copyright applies to works produced under the direction or control of the House of Lords or the House of Commons and lasts for 50 years: it may be owned by either House, or by both jointly, as appropriate, s. 165. This includes Parliamentary Bills but in this case copyright ceases after the Bill is passed, rejected or withdrawn, s. 166. As usual, time runs from the end of the year for Crown or Parliamentary copyright.

NATIONAL LIMITS TO COPYRIGHT

There are three possible situations in which a written work gets copyright protection in the UK. These are, first, if it is first published in the UK (or if the author has a direct connection with the UK), secondly, if provisions of the Act 'extend' to the country where it was published (or where the author comes from), and, thirdly, if the Act has been 'applied' to the country in question. The Act extends to England and Wales, Scotland and Northern Ireland and may be extended to any colony as well as the Channel Islands and the Isle of Man, s. 157. It may be applied to signatory states of the international copyright conventions and member states of the European Union, also to other states which give adequate protection to British works, s. 159.

The first situation is fairly simple. A work qualifies for copyright if it is first published in the UK, or if the author was a 'qualifying person'. This means a British citizen or someone who comes within the various other (generally overseas) national categories within the meaning of the British Nationality Act 1981, or someone resident or domiciled in the UK, s. 154. ('Domicile' is a concept of private international law distinct from residence or nationality: it refers to the country where a person is deemed to have his or her permanent home. Everybody has one domicile, and only one at a time. The 'domicile of origin' is normally that of one's father, but may be superseded by a 'domicile of choice' acquired by residence and a firm intention to settle in the new country.)

Secondly, the Act may be extended by Order in Council to any of the Channel Islands, the Isle of Man and any colony, and this puts works first published there, and authors resident or domiciled, in the same position as those in the UK. The Channel Islands of Jersey and Guernsey (with Alderney and Sark), are the last vestiges of the old Duchy of Normandy and have their own legal systems. They are not in the UK (nor in the European Union) but are self-governing dependencies of the British crown. The Isle of Man, which came under Scottish rule in the thirteenth century, has a similar status.

Thirdly, the UK copyright law protects works first published in a country to which the Act has been applied by Order in Council, or the authors of which are citizens or subjects of that country, or resident or domiciled there. This relates mainly to other signatory states of the international copyright conventions which the UK has joined, but may include non-members with which bilateral copyright protection has been agreed.

To put it in the simplest possible terms, it is safe to say that the UK Copyright Act protects in the UK practically any written work from any country in the world (except the very few which have not signed either of the two major conventions and have not concluded a bilateral agreement). The provisions are set out in detail in sections 153 to 160 of the Act. It must, of course, be remembered that it is the British law of copyright which is enforced and this may give greater or less protection than the law of the state from which the work or author originates. However, if this state is outside the European Economic Area (EEA) then the duration of copyright is that of the state in question (unless it is longer than the UK duration, s. 12(6)). The EEA consists of the (currently 15) European Union states plus Norway, Iceland and Liechtenstein.

OWNERSHIP OF COPYRIGHT

Copyright can be a valuable piece of property and it is important to know who owns it at any particular time. Normally the author of the work is the first owner of copyright, s. 11. However, when an employee produces a work in the course of his or her employment the employer owns the copyright (subject to any agreement which they may have made to the contrary). Some tricky questions can arise as to whether a person is an employee or self-employed. These are really questions of employment law which need not be answered here. It is possible for an employee to make an arrangement with the employer but there is no provision in the CDPA like s. 40 of the Patents Act 1977 which gives an employee a statutory right to compensation if the employee's invention is of outstanding benefit to the employer.

If an employee works at home in the employee's own time and on his or her own account then the employer has no claim to copyright. A couple of examples relate to artistic, rather than literary, works but the principle is the same. A map publisher claimed (unsuccessfully) that copyright in a map produced by a cartographer formerly in the firm's employment belonged to them. Although he had started work on his own map at home before leaving the plaintiffs' employment, this fact gave the employers no claim to the copyright, *Geographia* v. *Penguin Books*, 1985. On the other hand, a designer who did a lot of work designing a racing car in his own drawing office at home, this being the particular project on which the employer required him to work, did not own copyright in the designs, *Nichols Advanced Vehicle Systems* v. *Rees*, 1979.

Like other pieces of property, copyright can be sold, given away, bequeathed or, if there is no will, inherited by the author's heirs. It is quite possible for an author to assign only part of the rights, perhaps rights of translation, or film rights, or rights in a specified country, or for part only of the duration of copyright. When a publisher agrees to publish an author's work the two parties may agree that the copyright is assigned, in effect sold, to the publisher: the copyright becomes the publisher's property, whether totally or partially depending on the agreement. Alternatively, the author may retain the copyright but license the publisher to produce an edition of the work. If a licence is exclusive nobody may do anything covered by the licence during the time it subsists, and the exclusive licensee, just like the owner, can bring an action against an infringer. An assignment must be in writing, signed by, or for, the copyright owner. Section 90 deals with these provisions and they also cover database right.

Some tricky questions of ownership can arise. A spiritualist medium writing under the guidance of a long-dead spirit guide owned the copyright in the writings, the judge holding that his jurisdiction did not extend to the realms in which the spirit moved, *Cummins* v. *Bond*, 1927. On a rather more down to earth note, copyright in a computer-generated work belongs to the person who makes the necessary arrangements for its creation, s. 9(3).

NO COPYRIGHT IN IDEAS

For practical reasons a literary work has to be recorded, in writing or otherwise, (with or without the author's permission) before it can be protected by copyright, s.3. Obviously ideas floating around in the author's head are not capable of protection by the courts. Recording will, of course, include means of fixing the work other than simply writing it down on paper, like dictating it into a tape recorder or keying it into a computer's memory. Copyright exists in the actual words (or figures, or whatever) written down or otherwise recorded, not in the ideas or information behind them. In *Wilmer* v. *Hutchinson*, 1936, an ingenious plot for a film was reproduced in a short story by another writer. There was no copyright in the idea. (The idea was that a man, wrongly convicted of murder, serves out his sentence and then seeks out the 'victim', who is actually alive, with the intention of killing him, knowing that he cannot be tried again for the same crime.)

Two interesting cases from some years ago illustrate the situation when one person supplies information which is then written up by another. Hadji Lello Zeitun had an adventurous career as a freelance detective. In a series of interviews he recounted his adventures to a writer named Evans who then wrote up the information. A dispute arose when Zeitun subsequently had it published. The judge accepted that Evans was the sole author, as the person alone responsible for the literary form of the matter. It was fallacious to talk of Zeitun's being a joint author although he supplied the ideas, *Evans* v. *Hulton*, 1924. This case was followed in *Donoghue* v. *Allied Newspapers*, 1938. Steve Donoghue was probably the most famous jockey of his day. Allied Newspapers paid him £2000 to give information about his career to their reporter and to no other newspaper. The reporter wrote up the material and it was published in a series of articles in the *News of the World*. When the reporter (with Allied Newspapers' consent) started to republish the articles in amended form in another paper, Steve Donoghue tried to stop him. He was unsuccessful. The judge was clear that copyright exists in the particular form of language in which ideas are conveyed: there is no copyright in the ideas themselves.

WHAT RIGHTS DOES COPYRIGHT GIVE THE AUTHOR?

Once it has been established who actually owns copyright in a written work, the next question is what rights this ownership provides. Only the copyright owner has the right to take certain actions in relation to the work in question, and only the copyright owner has the authority to authorize these to anyone else. These actions are listed in s.16 to 21 of the CDPA. They consist of copying the work, issuing copies to the public (in effect, publishing it), renting or lending the work to the public, performing it in public (appropriate to a dramatic work), broadcasting it or including it in a cable programme, or making an adaptation of it (or doing any of the above to an adaptation). The provisions on renting or lending were not in the original Act but were added in 1996 by Regulations implementing the EU Directive on rental and lending right of 1992. Section 18A was added to comply with the Directive. It is infringement of copyright in a literary, dramatic, musical or (with exceptions) artistic work, a film or a sound recording, to rent it out, or to lend it through an establishment which is accessible to the public. The difference between rental and lending is that the former provides direct or indirect economic or commercial advantage, while the latter does not. There are exceptions, which are spread over ss. 18A, 36A and 40A. They include on-the-spot reference use, inter-library loans, lending by educational establishments, lending by public libraries of books which are within the public lending right scheme, and lending by certain non-profit libraries.

COPYING AND PUBLICATION

Making copies and issuing them to the public are sufficiently closely related to justify dealing with both these aspects of infringement of the author's copyright together. Section 17 of the CDPA defines copying and s. 175 gives the meaning of publication (and commercial publication). (Incidentally, it is worth remembering that there is a convenient index of expressions relating to copyright which are defined in the Act, to be found in s. 179, and about a couple of dozen minor definitions in s. 178.)

The ban on copying means that anyone who makes a copy of a substantial part of a copyright work is prima facie infringing the copyright owner's rights. It need not be more than a single copy, it can be handwritten, or indeed engraved in stone on a monument, it will still constitute infringement (unless it is exempted by one of the special provisions discussed below). Defining a 'substantial part' is tricky. Various guidelines have been issued at different times for different types of material: 10 per cent of the text, or a single chapter, have been regarded as a rough cut-off but pretty obviously this could hardly apply to a 3000-page legal textbook. The photocopier, of course, has provided the easiest and commonest method of illicit reproduction so far and is still a serious worry to the publishing industries, but the Internet may well have caught up by now. Not very long ago it was possible for a student in Singapore to borrow a library book, take it to a copy shop and collect a complete copy in a neat paper wrapper an hour or two later for 3 cents (roughly 1¹/₄p) a page. Reputable publishers could not compete and local textbook writers suffered accordingly. 'Copying' a work means reproducing it in a material form and that includes storing by electronic means as well as making copies which are transient.

As we have already seen, ideas or information in themselves are not protected by copyright. So it is not infringement of copyright to reproduce the information contained in a written work provided the actual form or expression of the author is not taken. For example, it would be infringement to make a photocopy of a table of statistics (unless it came within one of the statutory exceptions). It would equally be infringement to take a ruler and pen and make a handwritten copy. Now, would it be infringement to use the statistics in writing an article on the subject to which they refer? In *Graves* v. *Pocket Publications*, 1938, the publishers of *Lilliput* magazine extracted figures of earnings in 26 occupations from various chapters of the plaintiff's book *Other People's Money* and published them in the form of a table. Mr Graves had compiled the information at considerable cost and trouble to himself and the judge held that, although the actual literary form had not been copied, the compilation was entitled to protection. But this is a rather blatant case where the defendants' article was no more than a reproduction, somewhat rearranged, of material from the plaintiff's book and it does not derogate from the principle that there is no copyright in information as such. Any writer of a serious work of non-fiction stands on the shoulders of earlier writers and will incorporate information from earlier works. It is impossible to lay down exact rules as to how far the author may go in taking the incidents, characters or other material. In *Harman Pictures* v. *Osborne*, 1967, the plaintiffs owned the film rights in Cecil Woodham-Smith's book *The Reason Why*. The court had to compare incidents and situations and words in detail to decide whether the defendant's film script on Balaclava infringed copyright in the book.

ORIGINALITY

Copyright subsists in an 'original' literary work. This means that the work must be the product of the author's own creative labour: it must not be copied from somebody else. However, unlike a patent, copyright does not confer a monopoly right if somebody else produces a similar work quite independently. In an old case, *Bailey* v. *Taylor*, 1830, the author of tables of the value of leases and annuities was entitled to protection even though some of the tables had been published previously. When he made his own calculation of these the results were, of course, the same as the earlier versions but that did not debar him from protection provided that he had not copied anything. It would strain the court's credulity if a defendant claimed to have written an identical novel without copying, but two identical, or very closely similar, versions of, say, a mathematical table, a business form or a computer program, might easily arise quite independently. In that case each author would have copyright in his or her own version and could stop somebody else from copying it. It would be a good defence to show that an allegedly infringing version had been made without reference to the claimant's work.

The question of originality can be a bit tricky. The requirement that to attract copyright a work must be original does not mean that it must have come entirely from the brain of the author. In various cases the courts have allowed copyright in new versions of pre-existing works, or new selections of pre-existing material. The parameters were set quite a long time ago. Some of these cases were decided before the word 'original' was introduced by the 1911 Act but it is, to say the least, probable that they provide good guidance today. A decision of the highest Australian court persuades us that the word 'original' adds nothing to the pre-1911 use of the word 'author', *Sands and McDougall* v. *Robinson*, 1917.

Somebody who transcribes and edits ancient Welsh manuscripts would seem to most people to be deserving of copyright in that skilled and laborious production, and so the court held in *Evans* v. *Tout*, 1909. In an Indian case a similar decision had been reached in relation to an edition of a well-known Sanskrit religious work: a great deal of skill and labour had been put into rearranging and annotating the old text, *Gangavishnu Shrikisondas* v. *Moreshva Bapuji Hegishte*, 1889. An account of the famous trials of Oscar Wilde, heavily abridged and edited from an original transcript of the court proceedings, was a literary work in its own right, and one in which copyright subsisted, *Warwick Film Productions* v. *Eisinger*, 1969. In all these cases someone had used a lot of labour, a lot of skill and a lot of judgement in putting the existing text into a form which would be of value to the readership for which it was intended, whether Welsh scholars, Indian pandits or readers interested in the scandalous case of a well-known society figure. Obviously the authors (it might be better to say editors in these cases) could not claim copyright in the texts themselves but what they had done, in effect, was produce something new, worthy of being regarded as an original literary work in its own right.

In *Macmillan* v. *Cooper*, 1923 (an appeal to the Privy Council from Bombay) it was held that a selection of passages from an earlier translation (not copyright) of a classical Greek text did not involve enough 'knowledge, labour, judgement or literary skill or taste' to give copyright in the selection (though it was otherwise with the explanatory notes added to the text). On the other hand, some 30 years earlier the same plaintiffs had been successful in upholding the copyright in Professor Palgrave's *Golden Treasury* against another pirate in India. Compiling this famous anthology of poems had required 'extensive reading, careful study and comparison, and the exercise of taste and judgement in selection', *Macmillan* v. *Suresh Chandra Deb*, 1890. The defendant had copied a selection of poems from the fourth book of the *Golden Treasury* (a set book in Bombay and Calcutta universities), rearranged them and added his own notes. Although the defendant had taken a few notes and some titles from the original, the case turned on whether the actual selection of poems was copyright: the judge held that it was. The defendant's case was weakened by the fact that he had obviously copied from Palgrave's book rather than going back to the original books of the poets. He certainly did not make a very good impression on the court and the decision might have been different if he could have persuaded it that he really had taken no more than the list of poems from Palgrave. In a later case a selection of 13 essays, taken from 127 written by Hazlitt, did not impress the court as worthy of copyright, *Cambridge University Press* v. *University Tutorial Press*, 1928.

The test for originality is not really whether the work is completely new, but whether the author has put a substantial amount of creative skill, labour and judgement into its production. If he has, then anyone copying it is in peril.

ADAPTATIONS

Whilst straight copying is perhaps the commonest form of infringement of a written work, it is also infringement to make an adaptation of it or, even if the adaptation has not been recorded, to do any of the acts constituting infringement in relation to that adaptation. Section 21 deals with adaptations in detail. An adaptation specifically includes turning a literary work into a play, or vice versa, or a literary or dramatic work into a strip cartoon. Strictly speaking anyone doing any of these things is infringing, but legal action is unlikely to follow unless it is deliberate piracy. An adaptation made with the copyright owner's permission enjoys copyright in its own right so it would be infringment to re-translate a translated work into a third language (or, indeed, back into its original language).

AUTHORIZING INFRINGEMENT

The infringer does not have to act in person: it is equally infringement to authorize another to infringe. The Australian case *Moorhouse* v. *University of New South Wales*, 1976, sent shivers through librarians who provided photocopying facilities. The university library provided coin- or token-operated photocopiers, still something of an innovation at that time, and a certain Mr Brennan, a graduate of the university, made two copies of one story (about 10 pages long) from a book by the plaintiff. This was in fact prearranged, to allow the plaintiff, with the support apparently of the Australian Copyright Council, to bring a test case. The Australian copyright law closely followed the UK Copyright Act 1956, current at that time, so the case was highly persuasive in the British courts. The High Court, the highest Australian court, decided that the university was authorizing the infringement, in the sense of sanctioning, approving, countenancing or permitting it. Much play was made of the inadequate supervision and warning notices over the photocopiers.

Most academic institutions have now covered themselves, with warning notices and licences from the relevant bodies: students (and, some people suggest, particularly law students) are among the worst offenders. However, it is open to question how far the innumerable little copy shops and other facilities are really aware of the law.

COPYING

It is not unknown for somebody to try to disguise the fact of copying by altering the words or arrangement of the original. Sometimes this may be done quite honestly (but innocent copying is still infringement). This can give rise to difficulties. First, is the second work sufficiently close to the original to be regarded as a copy? Secondly, did the author of the second actually copy the original, or was it a case of a work produced independently, notwithstanding the similarities? *Bailey* v. *Taylor*, 1830, discussed above, is an interesting old case where these questions arose. Where two works were produced from common sources it may be very difficult to get at the true situation, and the author of the allegedly infringing version may well be questioned closely about his or her method of working. The selection of the same items or incidents, the use of the same language, the existence of the same mistakes, may all be pointers to copying. In James Herbert's thriller *The Spear* a neo-Nazi group has obtained possession of a supernatural spear giving immense power. The history of the Hofburg Spear had been recounted in a semi-historical, semi-mystical work, *The Spear of Destiny*, by the plaintiff, and this history was interwoven in the defendant's book. The judge found similarities of language and selection which could only be explained by copying, even though Herbert had not reproduced any part of the plaintiff's work exactly (*Ravenscroft* v. *Herbert*, 1980).

INNOCENT COPYING

Innocent or unconscious copying is no exception to the law. The copier may believe wrongly that there is no copyright in the work copied, or perhaps that the right owner has given permission. This is still infringement (but if the defendant did not know and had no reason to believe that the work was subject to copyright then the claimant is not entitled to damages, but may pursue any other remedy, s. 97(1)). Unconscious copying is more likely to come up in relation to music (see Chapter 3) but it would be quite possible for somebody to reproduce, say, a poem dredged up from the depths of the unconscious memory without realizing that it was not original.

PARODIES

Parodies of copyright material are usually taken in good part by the author of the work parodied so there is not much authority in the form of decided cases. Provided the parodist has produced something original, and has not taken a substantial part of the original work, then it is likely to be safe. So, a poem about Prince Philip, loosely based on a pop song, escaped, *Joy Music* v. *Sunday Pictorial*, 1960, but a 'Schlurppes' bottle label did not, *Schweppes* v. *Wellingtons*, 1984. Another case, *Clark (Alan)* v. *Associated Newspapers*, 1998, concerned a spoof diary supposed to be by the plaintiff which appeared in the *Evening Standard*. Mr Clark, a government minister, had published his (genuine) political diaries. The *Evening Standard* parody bore a note that it was no more than a parody but the general effect was that it was genuine. There was no copyright issue, it did not copy, but imitated, Mr Clark's work. However, Lightman J held that there was passing off of the spoof as genuine, also infringement of the plaintiff's moral right not to have a false attribution of authorship to him.

THE INTERNET

Issues relating to the Internet fit most conveniently in Chapter 5. At this point it is enough to say that the law applies to the Internet just as it does elsewhere. If a work would have copyright in print it would equally have copyright on the net. Downloading copyright material is infringement, so is copying such material onto the net. The trouble is how to enforce it. The present author published a small book on an Indian religion a few years ago. One day somebody told him, your book is on the Internet, expecting him to be pleased! Somebody in the USA had scanned it in without seeking permission, actually with the best intentions to give it a wider circulation. In this case the book has no great commercial value but the same could happen to a work representing a considerable investment in labour and money by the author and original publisher which they expected to recoup. Perhaps even more worrying is the use that could be made of the pirated work: for example, republication in inaccurate or distorted form.

SPEECHES AND LECTURES

If there is no copyright until a work is recorded, what is the position with regard to a lecture or speech taken down and published by one of the speaker's audience?

The Earl of Rosebery was a prominent political figure in the 1890s. Speeches which he made were taken down by reporters for *The Times* and were published in that newspaper, verbatim save for a little tidying up, punctuation and so on. The defendant subsequently copied the speeches from *The Times* and published them in a book. The question which had to be decided was whether the reporters (or in fact their employers, the newspaper proprietors) owned the copyright in their written reports of the speeches. The House of Lords said that they did (*Walter* v. *Lane*, 1900). Lord Davey said 'There is no copyright in a speech ...' and Lord Rosebery made no claim to copyright. (Doubtless he was pleased to have his speeches reported.) *Walter* v. *Lane* has been questioned, *Sands and McDougall* v. *Robinson*, 1917, an Australian case, on the ground that the word 'original' (literary work) did not appear in the statute then in force, the Literary Copyright Act 1842, but was added in the Copyright Act 1911 (and is now in s. 1 of the CDPA). In other words, the reporters' reports were not original works and would not have earned copyright after the law was changed in 1911 (though reports of public political speeches would not infringe). The question re-emerged in *Express Newspapers* v. *News (UK)*, 1990, when it was held that *Walter* v. *Lane* is still good law. So, effectively there can be two copyrights in an extempore speech or lecture, that of the original author, the lecturer, and that of the reporter (provided, probably, that some skill or labour was involved in recording it). If the speaker had written out the speech in advance, or otherwise recorded it, the situation might be different. In any case, once the work has been recorded by someone the author has copyright and it would be infringement to make a further copy or to issue copies to the public without the author's permission (CDPA, ss. 17 and 18).

We do have an old case of a student's publishing his professor's lectures, *Caird* v. *Sime*, 1887. A student made shorthand notes of the lectures of the Professor of Moral Philosophy in Glasgow University, and a Glasgow bookseller published these. The House of Lords recognized a common law right of property in a lecturer's composition, but this was abolished in 1911 leaving statutory copyright as the sole form of copyright. The case is now of historical interest only. If a work is dictated to a secretary there is no problem: the secretary is simply acting as the agent of the author and will not have any rights in it.

BIBLIOGRAPHIES

One area which closely affects anyone working in the information field is that of bibliographies. Compiling a bibliography can involve a great deal of very hard work, as well as a great deal of skill and judgement in locating and selecting the material. Section 3(1)(a) of the CDPA in its original form said that the expression 'literary work' includes a table or compilation, and this would clearly cover a bibliography. However, the adoption into UK law of the EU Directive on the legal protection of databases, 1996, has made important changes. The effects of these are considered in Chapter 5 but here we can just note that a database where the data are arranged in a systematic or methodical way and are individually accessible by electronic or other means, s.3A, does not now attract copyright unless by the selection or arrangement it constitutes the author's own intellectual creation. (Note that a paper-based database is included, not just one held on computer.) In *Whitaker* v. *Publishers' Circular*, 1946, the judge held that the skill and labour involved in collecting commonplace material into a convenient list was sufficient to confer copyright on the compilation. That would no longer be the case, the compiler would have database right only: the right, limited to 15 years, to prevent extraction or re-utilization of material. In *Whitaker* the plaintiffs owned the periodical *The Bookseller* in which they included weekly lists of recently published books compiled from various sources. Suspecting that the defendants were copying these lists in their own publications, they introduced 400 deliberate errors over an eight-month period and the same errors appeared in the defendants' lists!

LETTERS

When one person writes a letter to another the actual physical ownership of the letter may belong to the recipient but the writer retains the copyright and can prevent its being published. This made headlines in the popular press recently when there was a threat to publish letters from the late Princess Diana to one of her lovers. An earlier more commercial case was *British Oxygen* v. *Liquid Air*, 1925. A company got possession of a letter written by a trade rival to one of the latter's customers and made photographic copies with a view to circulating them. The court forbade that company from infringing its rival's copyright in the letter. The rule applies both to personal and business letters. The marriage of the Earl and Countess of Lytton had been characterized by sordid disputes. After the death of both parties the executrix of Lady Lytton proposed to publish letters which Lord Lytton had written to his wife. This was in order to counter aspersions on Lady Lytton's character in his son's biography of the late Lord Lytton. The son, now earl, as executor of his father's estate, was successful in preventing publication, *Earl of Lytton* v. *Devey*, 1884. The court did recognize a possible very limited exception to the general rule where publication was to vindicate the recipient's character but did not apply it in this case: the exception would almost certainly not be recognized today.

In practice, as we all know, letters received by business and other organizations, and indeed by individuals, are regularly photocopied, perhaps to circulate to staff or to pass on to somebody else concerned. It is highly unlikely that a court case would result from an ordinary routine situation. In the cases above the letters were particularly sensitive for business or personal reasons. Of course the author of a letter has the right to publish or reproduce it, as well as to stop publication or reproduction, though if the recipient had destroyed it (as he or she is entitled to do) or refused to part with it there might be some difficulty unless the author had kept a copy. There are some circumstances when a licence to publish may be inferred, particularly when a letter is addressed to the editor of a newspaper.

TITLES AND SLOGANS

The law does not concern itself with trivialities: *de minimis non curat lex*, in the neat Latin phrase. Various attempts to claim copyright in titles or slogans have met with no success. The Standard Oil Company, which already used the trade mark Esso, undertook lengthy research to find a new short distinctive name which would be devoid of any other meaning in almost 100 countries. They came up with the word 'Exxon' and in 1972 changed the company's name to Exxon Corporation. Aggrieved by Exxon Insurance Consultants' use of this same invented word, they tried to assert copyright: they had already registered 'Exxon' as a trade mark but under trade mark law then current this covered use only on their goods. Neither the judge in the Chancery Division nor the Court of Appeal was prepared to regard this single word as a literary work attracting copyright (though the plaintiffs did secure an order, on grounds unrelated to copyright, that the defendants should change their name), *Exxon Corporation* v. *Exxon Insurance Consultants International*, 1982. If Exxon Corporation had won their claim to copyright this would have given them a virtual monopoly in any use of the word (and might even have stopped the Bishop of Exeter from signing his name 'Exon.', albeit with only one 'x'!)

A slogan (*sluaghgairm* in Gaelic) was originally a Scottish Highland war cry. The battles between companies over use of a few words are less bloody but still hard-fought. An advertising slogan 'Beauty is a social necessity, not a luxury' was regarded as so trifling that the court could not attach any proprietary right to it in a dispute between two beauty specialists, *Sinanide* v. *La Maison Kosmeo*, 1928. The defendants' version was 'A youthful appearance is a social necessity'. In another case, although the *Canadian Copyright Act 1921* did recognize that copyright in a work included the title (provided that it was original and distinctive), the Privy Council on an appeal from Canada, refused to treat the title as a separate work and in any case regarded it as too insubstantial to attract copyright. The defendants had used the title 'The Man who Broke the Bank at Monte Carlo' for a film, which bore no relation at all to the plaintiffs' song with the same title, *Francis Day and Hunter* v. *Twentieth Century Fox*, 1940. Anyone aggrieved by a trade rival's adopting their name or slogan is unlikely to succeed in establishing copyright. A passing off action stands more chance of success (see Chapter 6).

In *Noah* v. *Shuba*, 1991, the court spelled out the requirement to qualify as a literary work as sufficient information, instruction or literary enjoyment. In this case it was not a slogan at issue but a terse seventeen-word medical instruction: this was not a literary work.

DISHONEST WORKS

Does an author have copyright in an irreligious, obscene, libellous or fraudulent work? The answer seems to be that the author does, but the courts will not give any help in asserting that right. The justification for this course of action is that it would not be in the public interest to assist the publication of such material. There are some old cases but little if any modern authority. In *Lawrence* v. *Smith*, 1822, the plaintiff had published *Lectures on Physiology, Zoology and the Natural History of Man* which had been delivered at the College of Surgeons, a respectable enough provenance one might think. However, he questioned the immortality of the soul, and on the grounds that this impugned the doctrines of the Scriptures, the Lord Chancellor (who in those days presided in the Court of Chancery) refused him any relief in respect of a pirated edition. A month earlier the Lord Chancellor had made a similar decision in *Murray* v. *Benbow*, 1822, over a pirated edition of Byron's poem *Cain*: such a work would hardly be denied protection today. It might be otherwise with a work of hardcore pornography, if the author or publisher were bold enough to bring an action. The *Memoirs of Harriette Wilson* were both indecent and libellous. In spite of that (or perhaps because of it) a pirate found it worth his while to print 5000 copies. The court refused the plaintiff publisher any relief, *Stockdale* v. *Onwhyn*, 1826.

Elinor Glyn enjoyed a considerable reputation as a romantic novelist in the early years of the twentieth century, and her book *Three Weeks* was reprinted four times within four months of publication in 1907. The story seems innocuous enough today and is light and entertaining. A young man meets a mysterious lady travelling incognito… She goes home to the country where her husband is king and a child is born. The book was condemned by the critics and banned by libraries. It was also burlesqued in a film, and the authoress sued, *Glyn* v. *Weston Feature Film Co*, 1915. Mr Justice Younger's strictures should be read in full in the law report. It is enough to say that he emphatically refused it protection.

The same happened just after the outbreak of the Second World War over a spoof leaflet masquerading as the last will and testament of Herr Hitler, *Bloom & Sons* v. *Black*, 1939. It was not pornographic, just vulgar and indecent, and the judge refused an interlocutory (interim) injunction to restrain publication until a full trial. The work refused protection in *Slingsby* v. *Bradford Patent Truck Co*, 1905, was different but the principle is the same. The plaintiff's catalogue was deceptive in claiming patents which he never had and in other ways exaggerating the scale of his business.

TYPOGRAPHICAL ARRANGEMENT OF A PUBLISHED EDITION

Copyright also subsists in 'the typographical arrangement of published editions', CDPA, s. 1(1)(c). This means the image on the page, the actual printing and layout. So, if a newly-typeset edition of a work is published (even if the original is out of copyright) it is infringement to make a facsimile copy. This does not apply (s. 8) to the extent that the typographical arrangement reproduces that of a previous edition. Protection lasts for 25 years only.

PUBLICATION RIGHT

If someone publishes a previously unpublished work after the expiry of copyright then the publisher has a right equivalent to copyright called 'publication right' but lasting for 25 years only. This applies only if first publication is in the European Economic Area and the publisher is a national of an EEA state, and it is not done without the consent of the owner of the physical medium on which the work is recorded. This right was put into effect by the Copyright and Related Rights Regulation 1996, reg. 16, following an EU Directive of 1992.

DATABASE RIGHT

The EU Database Directive 1996 has been implemented in UK law by the Copyright and Rights in Databases Regulations 1997 which (a) make certain amendments to the CDPA, and (b) introduce the new database right into UK law.

A database is defined as a collection of independent works, data or other materials which are arranged in a systematic or methodical way and are individually accessible by electronic or other means, s. 3A. As mentioned above a database attracts copyright only if the author has used real creativity in the selection or arrangement of the material. It is then treated, as regards copyright, like any other written work but it does have, in addition, database right, described below. (An older copyright database, made before 28 March 1996, keeps its copyright for the full term, subject to certain conditions.)

However, if the selection and arrangement are just normal routine processes then the creator is limited to database right. Database right is something *sui generis*, different from copyright. It protects the contents of the database from being extracted or re-utilized without the owner's permission. This applies whether the extraction or re-utilization is of the whole or a substantial part (and may include repeated and systematic extraction or re-utilization of insubstantial parts). Database right lasts for 15 years (or, if made available to the public in that period, from the time it is first made available). (Time starts to run from the end of the year.) However, any substantial change or accumulation starts off a fresh term. (This looks a very tricky provision: at what point does a regularly updated database become eligible to start a new term?) Remember that a database can have copyright and database right at the same time if the selection or arrangement show real creativity.

REMEDIES FOR INFRINGEMENT

Sections 96 to 115 of the CDPA deal in some detail with the remedies available to the copyright owner whose copyright is infringed. Copyright is a property right (s. 1(1)) and s. 96(2) makes it clear that the claimant is entitled to the same remedies, damages, injunction, account or otherwise, as for the infringement of any other property right. ('Account' means that the claimant may recover from the defendant the latter's profit or other ill-gotten gains from the infringement.) In a case where the infringement has been particularly flagrant, or has resulted in excessive benefit, then additional damages may be awarded. Conversely, if infringement was innocent then the claimant is entitled to any remedy except damages. The copyright owner may apply to the court for infringing articles to be delivered up, s. 99. The owner also has the right to seize infringing articles which are on sale or for hire, but should read section 100 carefully before exercising this right as there are strict conditions (including notifying the police in advance).

CRIMINAL LIABILITY

Section 107 deals with what may be broadly described as business dealings in infringing material and imposes criminal sanctions with penalties up to two years imprisonment and a very substantial fine. These include manufacture for sale or hire, selling or letting (or offering to do so) for sale or hire, or distributing in the course of business. Importing into the UK other than for the defendant's private or domestic use is also covered, and so is distributing, not in the course of business, to such an extent as to affect prejudicially the copyright owner. This last provision would catch someone who, perhaps because of a grudge against the author, gives away quantities of pirated copies of the author's work. It is also an offence to make or possess an article which is specially made or adapted to make infringing copies of a particular copyright work for sale, hire or business use. In all these cases the defendant has a good defence if he or she did not know, or have reason to believe, that the article was infringing (or was to be used to make infringing copies).

In practice, the courts seem reluctant to impose more than a few months in prison, though fines can be be high. Prosecutions nearly always seem to refer to the fairly large-scale operations of counterfeiters of fashion clothing, music recordings or computer software (in all of which the city of Leicester has acquired an unenviable reputation), rather than of literary works.

EXEMPTIONS TO THE COPYRIGHT OWNER'S RIGHTS

A fairly substantial Chapter III of the CDPA covering ss. 28 to 76 deals in some detail with acts which are permitted notwithstanding the subsistence of copyright. These provisions are quite complicated and recourse to the full text of the Act is advisable if there is any doubt. The provisions particularly relevant to written works are dealt with here (others are considered elsewhere in this book): they relate to

s. 29 Research and study
s. 30 Review and reporting
ss. 32–36 Education
ss. 37–44 Libraries
ss. 45–50 Public administration

FAIR DEALING FOR RESEARCH AND PRIVATE STUDY

Section 29 introduces the nebulous concept of fair dealing. Fair dealing with a literary or dramatic work for research or private study does not infringe copyright. Note the position of the word 'private'. Research does not necessarily mean academic research. While the CDPA was still at its formative stage there was some feeling that the fair dealing exemption should not extend to profitable research by commercial firms and the White Paper proposed that commercial researchers should no longer be able to take advantage of this provision when the new legislation came into force. Where that would have left academic research backed by a commercial sponsor is not at all clear and in the end the concession was not limited to private researchers. However, the position with regard to databases is slightly different following changes to s. 29 introduced by the Copyright and Rights in Databases Regulations 1997. Fair dealing with a database for research or private study does not infringe copyright in the database (remember that a database has copyright to the extent that it is the author's creative work) but doing anything with a database for commercial research is not fair dealing. Apart from copyright, database right is not infringed by a lawful user dealing even with a substantial part of a database which has been made available to the public if it is for illustration for teaching or research and not for a commercial purpose, reg. 20 of those Regulations. In all cases with databases the source must be indicated.

What is fair dealing? In s. 16(3)(a) of the CDPA we see that infringement may relate to a work as a whole or to a substantial part of it. It is easy to confuse the test for fair dealing with a substantial part. Really a two-stage test should be applied: has a substantial part been infringed, and then has the defendant a defence on the ground of fair dealing? Whilst a 'substantial part' will usually refer to quantity it may well be defined by quality, *Ladbroke* v. *William Hill*, 1964 (a case referring to football pool coupons). In an old case, a single page explaining the offside rule was taken from a large book on football: this was sufficient to constitute a substantial part, *Trengrouse* v. *Sol Syndicate*, 1901. It was, of course, the advent of the photocopier in academic libraries which brought fair dealing into focus. A medieval student needing an essential text would go to the *stationarius* for his parchment and writing requisites, at the same time hiring a quire (usually 24 sheets) of the text for a small sum. He would return to his lodging and laboriously make a copy for his own use. There was no copyright to worry about in those days. Cynics may assert that modern students use photocopying as a substitute for reading: certainly they use it extensively as a substitute for book buying. To some extent licensing schemes operated by the Copyright Licensing Agency and other bodies, together with guidelines on the acceptable limits of fair dealing have done a lot to regularize copying for research and private study. One point was clarified as far back as 1916: the private study exemption did not leave the way open for a publisher to publish London University examination papers even though they were intended for private study by students, *University of London Press* v. *University Tutorial Press*. That is why law students (and others) who buy collections of model answers to past examinations have to obtain the actual examination papers from the examining body.

FAIR DEALING FOR CRITICISM, REVIEW OR NEWS REPORTING

The other fair dealing exemptions, in s.30, refer mainly to publishing. Book reviews or other published criticism may need extensive quotation from the work reviewed (or sometimes from another work). Provided that it is sufficiently acknowledged and can be regarded as fair dealing this does not infringe copyright. The position is similar for a report of current events which takes material from a copyright work. Both defences failed *The Sun* newspaper when it published one whole letter and part of another from the correspondence between the late Duke and Duchess of Windsor. The *Daily Mail* had exclusive rights in the letters. *The Sun* appended no criticism or review to the material they took and there was no reporting of a current event involved (*Associated Newspapers* v. *News Group Newspapers*, 1986). There is one other exemption relating to reporting current events in s.58. It is not infringement of copyright to use a first-hand record (written or otherwise) of spoken words for reporting current events, though there are slightly complicated restrictions in that section.

EXEMPTIONS FOR EDUCATION

If we take literally the ban on copying it means that a teacher who copies something on the blackboard, or a pupil who copies it in an exercise book, is infringing copyright. That would be ridiculous, so s.32 of the Act exempts copying by a teacher or lecturer, pupil or student, in the course of instruction (including preparation) at a school or elsewhere. However, this does not allow copies to be made by a reprographic process (except for examination purposes, and even then copying a musical work is not permitted). The definition of a reprographic process in s.178 is wide enough to include just about any known process, even carbon paper (though that is rarely seen nowadays), and specifically includes copying by electronic means a work held in electronic form. There is a further concession to educational establishments in s.36: up to one per cent of a published work may be copied by reprographic means in each quarter-year, but only if no licence for copying is available. Since the CDPA came into force the restrictions on copying have been softened by the availability of licensing schemes by or on behalf of publishers allowing, usually for a fee, restricted copying of published works.

A limited exception allows inclusion of a short extract, with acknowledgment, in an anthology for school use, s.33. Not purely educational but worth mentioning at this point is the provision that a public reading or recitation by one person of a reasonable extract with acknowledgment is permissible, s.59. A marathon reading of a copyright work to get into the *Guinness Book of Records* would require the copyright owner's permission.

LIBRARY EXEMPTIONS

Libraries and archives have some limited privileges as regards copying, laid down in ss. 37 to 43 and further explained in regulations made by the Secretary of State. The exemptions apply only to libraries of a description prescribed in the regulations (which includes nearly all libraries except those run for profit). There are five things which a librarian or archivist (including a person acting on their behalf) may do:

1. supply a copy of a periodical article for research or private study (s. 38);
2. supply a copy of part of a published work for research or private study (s. 39);
3. supply a copy of a periodical article or the whole of a published work to another prescribed library if the copyright owner cannot reasonably be traced (s. 41);
4. make a copy of an item in the permanent collection to replace or preserve that item, or for supply to another prescribed library, where that item has been lost, damaged or destroyed (s. 42);
5. supply a copy of the whole or part of a document for research or private study (s. 43).

These fairly generous provisions are hedged around by restrictions (see below) and the librarian or archivist would be well-advised to become thoroughly acquainted with the provisions of the Act and the regulations.

It must first be noted that the concessions apply to literary, dramatic and musical works, including the typographical arrangement of a published edition, but not to artistic works, except illustrations accompanying the text. The Act, of course, states the law: licensing arrangements may well be in place to permit additional exemptions and these should be carefully studied for their exact provisions.

Whilst a periodical article may be supplied under s. 38 to a person who satisfies the librarian with a signed declaration that it is needed for research or private study, the concession is limited to a single copy of a single article from any single issue of a periodical to any one person. A charge covering the cost plus overheads must be paid to the library, as also under s. 39. Only a reasonable proportion (undefined) of a work may be supplied under s. 39 and only one copy to any one person. Section 40 is largely aimed at a group of individuals all requesting the same material (for example, a class of students attempting to evade the ban on multiple copies). The regulations shall require the librarian to be satisfied that an individual's requirement is not related to that of another person before material may be supplied under ss. 38 or 39. The effect of this is, of course, to give legal force to any licensing agreement by or on behalf of publishers which extends the bounds of the exemptions.

The concession under s. 41, supply to another library, applies only if the person entitled to authorize a copy, normally the copyright owner, cannot reasonably be traced. Section 42 allows a librarian or archivist to make a copy of an item in the permanent collection (but not an item which is available for lending) to preserve that item, or to replace it in their own or another library, but regulations must provide that this is permissible only when purchase is not reasonably practicable. This would seem to cover cases, for example, when a book is rare and extremely expensive, or out of print and rarely obtainable secondhand. It would not apply if the librarian sought to save money by photocopying the library's badly-worn copy of *Copinger on Copyright*.

Section 43 permits the supply of a copy for research or private study of the whole or part of a document in a library or archive. The same conditions apply as in ss. 38 and 39: one copy only, payment of costs and a signed declaration. However, the concession is not available if the work had been published before deposit or the copyright owner has prohibited copying and the librarian or archivist ought reasonably to have known about this. Obviously, this concession is of importance to scholars studying relatively recent historical or literary documents which are still in copyright. It is also relevant to the troubled area of university theses. Under the old law universities had to obtain permission, either in each specific instance or under some sort of general licence (voluntary, or enforced by university regulations) from the author at the time of deposit in the university library. A university is unlikely to draw its postgraduate students' attention to the law but the risk to the author of the work's being plagiarized or even published in some country where copyright enforcement is unsatisfactory is not to be discounted.

EXCEPTIONS IN THE AREAS OF JUSTICE AND PUBLIC ADMINISTRATION

Sections 45 to 50 lay down (in fair detail) that copyright is not infringed by anything done for the purpose of the proceedings of Parliament, a Royal Commission or a statutory enquiry, or of judicial proceedings, or for the purpose of reporting them. So, for example, copyright material can be reproduced if it is needed as evidence in a lawsuit, and the material could appear in a law report. (The reporting exception does not apply to a Royal Commission or inquiry not held in public; s. 46.) The other major exceptions in this field cover copying of material open to public inspection pursuant to statutory requirement, s. 47, and public records as defined in s. 49.

CROWN AND PARLIAMENTARY COPYRIGHT MATERIAL: EXTRA-STATUTORY CONCESSIONS

Her Majesty's Stationery Office should be consulted with regard to the copying of this material: the following notes are to draw attention to policy, which could be changed, with regard to certain categories. After an embargo period from the date of publication of six months for statutes and three months for Statutory Instruments (SIs) during which time no more than 30 per cent may be published or photocopied, these may be published or photocopied. Extracts not forming a substantial part of of the reports of parliamentary proceedings (Hansard) may also be copied or published. None of this material may be used as camera-ready copy for publication. There are similar concessions with regard to other parliamentary papers.

LEGAL DEPOSIT AND PUBLIC LENDING RIGHT

Before leaving the subject of written works reference must be made to two matters which strictly speaking do not concern copyright but which are nevertheless relevant here. In some countries deposit of one or more copies of a book with the appropriate authority is a prerequisite to copyright protection. Signatory states of the Berne Convention (see Chapter 8 for details) are required to give protection without any such formalities. However, in the UK (as in other countries) a system of legal deposit obtains requiring a publisher to deposit a copy of every published book with certain specified libraries, automatically with the British Library and, if specifically demanded, with the Bodleian Library in Oxford, the Cambridge University Library, the National Libraries of Scotland and Wales, and Trinity College, Dublin. There are some minor exclusions. The reason has nothing to do with copyright, though it is contained in s. 15 of the Copyright Act 1911 as amended (the only part of that Act not subsequently repealed), it is to preserve the nation's literary output for posterity. With an ever-increasing amount of publishing now taking place in transient and mutable electronic form, legal deposit is losing its universality, though it will be a very long time, if ever, before paper-based publishing ceases to be important.

Following a vigorous campaign by authors the Public Lending Right Act was passed in 1979. This provides modest remuneration for authors whose books are loaned by public libraries. There is a Registrar of Public Lending Right to whom application is made to place a book and author (also illustrator) on the register. By sampling in a number of libraries an estimate is made of total loans of each registered book across the country and a sum of money provided by Parliament is divided pro rata. No payment is made if the number of loans is very small, and there is a top limit for payment to any individual author. The author must be a British or EU citizen and resident in the UK but there is provision for reciprocal arrangements with other countries.

3 Entertainment and related media

This chapter brings together a rather diverse collection of subjects which have, nevertheless, a certain unity in that they all form part of the large (and prosperous) sector of industry devoted to entertainment. Hence it is not only convenient but logical to include them in one chapter. Music is the first area to be covered, that is musical compositions and recordings. Recordings, of course, are not always musical, nor are live performances which form the next topic. Broadcasting and cable services are obviously an important area, but equally obviously they represent too vast an area to cover comprehensively in a single section of a single chapter. Next, the chapter looks at films and videos (one of the most profitable fields for the pirate). In the course of dealing with these topics it will be necessary to look at rental right, censorship of films and videos, and piracy and safeguarding of rights, insofar as these matters are not dealt with in other chapters. One important topic, the Internet, will be more appropriately dealt with in Chapter 5.

For those who think of industry only in traditional terms of metal-bashing and factories producing utilitarian goods, it may be a surprise that 'creative' industries contribute over £112 000 million a year to the UK economy, according to government figures (*The Times*, news item, 14 March 2001), around nine per cent of which is earnings from exports. The areas dealt with in this chapter alone account for around £21 000 million and employ well over 300 000 people.

OWNERSHIP AND DURATION

Copyright belongs to the 'author', that is to say, to the person who creates the work: in the case of a piece of music we would say the composer. The author of a sound recording is the producer, s. 9(2)(aa), of a film it is the producer and the principal director, s. 9(2)(ab), and with regard to a computer-generated musical work the author is the person who made the necessary arrangements for its creation, s. 9(3).

The author of a broadcast or cable programme is defined in the same section of the Copyright, Designs and Patents Act as the person who transmits the broadcast, s. 9(2)(b), provided that this person has responsibility for content, s. 6(3), or who provides the cable programme service, s. 9(2)(c).

The provisions for copyright in a piece of music are similar to those for written or artistic works. Moral rights apply and the qualifications for copyright are the same (see Chapter 2). Duration of copyright in a piece of music is also the same, 70 years from the end of the year in which the composer died, or if the identity of the composer is unknown, until 70 years after the end of the year in which it was made, or if it was first made available to the public during that period then 70 years from the end of the year in which it was first made available by public performance, broadcast or inclusion in a cable programme service. A computer-generated work gets only 50 years from the end of the year in which it was made. A sound recording gets 50 years copyright from the end of the year in which it was made, or if released in that period, 50 years from the end of the year of release. Fifty years from when a broadcast is made or a cable programme was included in the service (calculated from the end of the year as usual) is the duration of copyright in broadcasts and cable programmes. There is no extension for repeats.

Apart from the extension to 70 years from 50 to accord with the EU Directive on the duration of copyright, these provisions are basically the same as in the original version of the Act, though the relevant sections, ss. 12 to 14, were replaced by new versions under the Duration of Copyright and Rights in Performances Regulations 1995. Copyright in films, however, which was lumped together with sound recordings in the original version (s. 13) was completely changed by the 1995 regulations. The duration of copyright is now linked to the death of the leading figures in the creation of the film, the principal director, the author of the screenplay, the author of the dialogue, or the composer of music specially created for and used in the film: copyright lasts until 70 years after the last of these dies, s. 13B. This follows the EU Directive on duration of copyright, Art. 2, and demonstrates the *droit d'auteur* stemming from personal creativity in the Civil Law tradition, rather than the mainly economic approach of the Common Lawyers. Exact details relating to the duration of copyright can be found in the amended ss. 12 to 14 of the CDPA.

MUSIC

There are three aspects to legal protection of rights in music. First it is necessary to consider protection of the actual musical composition, or musical work as the Act calls it. That means the tune, pop song, symphony, pibroch or whatever. For sheer practical reasons this will not have copyright until it is fixed in some permanent form, on paper or in a recording or, nowadays, stored in a computer, s. 3(2). Secondly, there is protection for a particular recording, on tape or on disc or on whatever other medium technology can produce. Thirdly, a particular live performance gets protection. If, for example, Angela composes a piano concerto, Brian gets somebody to play it into his recording equipment, and Clarissa also plays it at a concert, Angela has composed a musical work, Brian has made a sound recording and Clarissa has given a live performance.

Musical works are included in s. 1(1)(a) of the CDPA and share the same copyright regime as literary, dramatic and artistic works. Sound recordings appear in s. 1(1)(b) with films, broadcasts and cable programmes, the difference being, of course, that these are secondary to the works in s. 1(1)(a). Before the CDPA came into force various Acts on performers' protection made dealings in illicit recordings of a live performance a criminal offence, but rather unfairly gave no recompense to the performer. This was remedied by the provisions of Part II of the Act.

Where there are words attached to a musical composition the words will enjoy copyright separately as a literary work. Often, of course, the words and music will have been composed by different people so each will have copyright in his or her own work. In can happen that new words are composed for an old tune: the words will be copyright even though copyright in the tune lapsed long ago. When the Roman Catholic church for some reason virtually abandoned the Latin mass some years ago the vernacular translation of an ancient Latin prayer set to a 1500-year-old plainsong chant would have copyright as an original literary work even though the music, and the Latin words, as the compositions of long-dead authors, escaped copyright by very many centuries.

As the actual musical composition, or musical work, is lumped together with literary and dramatic works in s. 1 of the Act, the acts constituting infringement are the same. Only the copyright owner, or someone to whom the owner has given permission, may reproduce the work in any material form, issue copies to the public, perform it in public, broadcast it or include it in a cable programme, adapt it, or do any of these things in relation to an adaptation of it. (An adaptation means an arrangement or transcription of a musical work.) These provisions apply also to sound recordings, so it is infringement if anyone copies a recording or plays it in public. The provisions regarding infringement are to be found in ss. 16 to 21: as these are the same as for literary works they have already been discussed in Chapter 2. Librarians will want to pay special attention to s. 18A of the CDPA, on rental and lending right, which is outlined in that chapter. The Act also makes provision, in ss. 22 to 26, for secondary infringement; that is commercial dealings, broadly defined, in infringing material. Secondary infringement can also be a criminal matter under s. 107: this was also dealt with in Chapter 2.

WHAT IS A 'MUSICAL WORK'?

What exactly is a musical work? Strangely, the Copyright Act 1956 attempted no definition, nor indeed did the previous Copyright Act, of 1911. The 1988 Act does say in s.3(1) that '"musical work" means a work consisting of music' (exclusive of words or action), but that is not very helpful. We probably have to fall back on the definition in the (now repealed) Musical (Summary Proceedings) Copyright Act 1902, s.3. This defined it as 'any combination of melody or harmony, or either of them'. This seems all-embracing (discounting any personal prejudices which might be felt at the inclusion of certain sounds of modern music), though it might exclude some more exotic manifestations of musical talent, like a military drummer's call or the noises produced by a Tibetan monk from a human thigh bone. Moreover, the 1902 definition continues, it must be 'printed, reduced to writing, or otherwise graphically produced or reproduced'. Obviously that needs updating to include methods of fixation which were undreamt of in 1902. It is, however, necessary to keep clear in our minds the distinction between the musical work, that is the actual composition which has been recorded, and on the other hand a sound recording which has been made of it. Two copyrights are involved in, say, a compact disc: the copyright in the musical composition which has been played or sung and recorded on the disc, and the copyright in the actual sounds on the disc. The first copyright is owned by the original composer (or someone to whom the rights have passed), the second by the producer of the recording.

ORIGINALITY

It would be very difficult to prove authorship of anything which has never been put into material form (which, of course, includes electronic recordal), a melody, for example which somebody hums to themself, or an unrecorded and unwritten folk song. Actually, it is not impossible that a modern pop singer might compose and sing a musical work in a pub without any written or recorded version being made. Suppose another singer added this song to his own public repertoire. Would this be infringement? Probably not. *Roberton* v. *Lewis*, 1976 (note the spelling: Roberton, not Robertson) is a complicated but interesting case. Sir Hugh Roberton was a distinguished musician and was for some years conductor of the Glasgow Orpheus Choir. He died in 1952 so the action in question (heard in 1960 though not reported, for some reason, until 1976) was brought by his executors and his publishers. In 1939 the publishers had published for Sir Hugh a song with the title 'Westering Home'. The words were composed by Sir Hugh Roberton, and there was no dispute over these. However, the tune was described as an 'Old dance tune arranged by Hugh Stevenson Roberton'. The song was later, by permission, published on a record by HMV. Then in 1957 one of the defendants wrote new words to the same tune and another defendant, the Decca Record Company, published a record of this song sung by the well-known singer Vera Lynn. The obvious question was whether Sir Hugh Roberton had copyright in his version of this old Scots tune. The plaintiffs relied on the old case of *Walter* v. *Lane*, 1900, (reporters owned copyright in their written record of a politician's extempore speeches). The judge was a bit dubious about this: the plaintiffs could not prove that Sir Hugh really was the first to write the tune down. In any case, after *Walter* v. *Lane* was decided, the 1911 Copyright Act had added the word 'original' to the conditions for copyright in a literary, dramatic or musical work. (It was held in *Express Newspapers* v. *News (UK)*, 1990, that *Walter* v. *Lane* is still good law.) However, the judge did not make a definite decision on this. In fact there was no proof that the defendants had taken the tune directly or indirectly from Sir Hugh Roberton's work: they were able to produce as witnesses pipers from the Scots Guards who had known the tune in the 1930s so there was a different possible line of descent from which the defendants' version could have derived, and the plaintiffs lost their case.

So, what do we learn from this case? First, if someone takes down a hitherto unrecorded and unwritten tune he or she may have copyright in this written or recorded version, though this may depend on the exact circumstances. Secondly, if he or she expends skill and labour on arranging and adapting it this will certainly be a new original work and eligible for copyright protection. Thirdly, it will not be infringement if somebody publishes the same tune, provided that this person has taken it from another source, and not from the first person's work, as the latter has copyright only in his or her own written or recorded version, which is not quite the same (though the difference is subtle) as copyright in the original tune itself.

An earlier case illustrates some of the difficulties which can arise over new versions of old music, *Austin* v. *Columbia Graphophone*, 1923. John Gay (best known for *The Beggars' Opera*) wrote an opera *Polly* which was published in 1729 (though not performed in the author's lifetime). He did not write the music for the songs but this was given in an appendix. When the opera was revived in the early 1920s at the Savoy Theatre it was a great success, and owed a lot to Mr Austin who had worked on, adapted and orchestrated 19 of the original tunes. Wanting to cash in on this the defendant company sent its own musical director to the British Museum Library (now the British Library) armed with a copy of Mr Austin's music. After two brief visits he produced within a few days adaptations of 18 of the original tunes and the defendant soon had records on the market, advertised as 'Columbia records of "Polly"'. The tunes sounded very like the plaintiff's versions. Even though, on a note-by-note comparison, the similarity was not conclusive, the judge held that the general impression to the ear could be taken into account. It was very clear that the defendants had imitated and appropriated the work of Mr Austin. The plaintiff's arrangement of the music amounted to a new work and he was entitled to copyright. He won his case with an injunction, an order for delivery up of infringing copies, and damages.

The question whether the similarities in two musical works are the result of copying can be very tricky. Francis Day and Hunter Ltd, the music publishers, owned copyright in a popular song, 'Little Spanish Town', first published in 1926. Eight bars of another song, 'Why', composed in 1959, were quite similar to part of the first song. The Court of Appeal said that two things had to be proved: similarity; and a causal connection between the two works, in other words that the alleged infringer was familiar with the original work. In this case, *Francis Day and Hunter* v. *Bron*, 1963, the composer of 'Why' admitted no more than that he could possibly have heard 'Spanish Town' when young. The court accepted that subconscious copying might be infringement but it would be necessary to prove that the composer of the offending work was at least familiar with the original. The similiarities between the two pieces were not in themselves sufficient to prove copying; indeed the theme of 'Spanish Town' consisted of a number of quite commonplace elements. The reader who wishes to judge for himself or herself will find the relevant sections of the music set out in the law report, [1963] Ch 591.

With the vast expansion in the musical industry in recent years the question of the copying of pop songs is frequently in the news. One interesting question, not really resolved so far, concerns the technique of 'sampling' where snatches, sometimes very small, of recorded music are put together in a new composite recording, perhaps forming the backing for another vocalist. Whether this is an infringement of copyright would probably depend on whether the court felt that the piece taken was a substantial part of the original. With music, unlike written works, a small segment of the melody can be enough to identify it, and it would doubtless be argued that this is equally enough to constitute infringement. Of course, if a number of small snatches, tiny in themselves, were taken from the same work, there would seem to be a clear case of infringement. Perhaps these questions, interesting though they may be, are hypothetical, for sampling seems to have dropped out of the news, and presumably the pop repertoire, recently as other more dramatic forms of infringement have emerged.

The popular music industry is, as everybody knows, very big business. It can involve very large sums of money and disputes can prove very bitter and hard-fought. A somewhat unusual case which appeared in the newspapers (*The Times*, news items, 15 and 20 March 2001) has been fought not on infringement but on libel. The theme tune for the James Bond films was described to the court, with a degree of hyperbole perhaps, as one of the most famous pieces of music in the world. Credit (and royalties) for the composition had for 35 years been taken by Mr Monty Norman. However, an article appeared in *The Sunday Times* in 1997 stating that Mr Norman was not the real author. Another distinguished composer, Mr John Barry, claimed that he wrote it but made a deal to allow Mr Norman to take the credit. Mr Norman successfully defended his authorship in a libel action and won £30 000 damages. This case is typical of many which appear in the press, though they may not get into the law reports, unusual only in that it fell within the libel field, rather than infringement.

SOUND RECORDINGS

When musical works first entered the copyright regime in the reign of Queen Victoria a work was released to the public either by a public performance or by publication as 'sheet music' on paper. The recording industry grew slowly but by the 1920s and 1930s a large wind-up gramophone and a selection of 78 rpm records, perhaps a dozen or two, in brown paper slips would be found in most homes. It was, however, after the Second World War that the technology advanced, with the electric record player making possible, first, the automatic record changer so that you could listen to a whole symphony, albeit with gaps while the next record dropped onto the turntable, and then the long-play record. In the last decades of the twentieth century the large reel-to-reel tape recorder, which had never found widespread popularity, gave way to the portable cassette recorder. Suddenly a whole new industry in recorded music developed, catering for increasingly affluent youth, and driven by television, radio and pop concerts. Then came the personal stereo from Japan. Back in the 1930s and 1940s, at the fairground or seaside, a minor entrepreneur would set up his cumbersome recording machine and you could take home a record of your own voice to play on your gramophone. Now it was possible, not only to carry your favourite music with you, but also to copy on tape the work of a composer, an artist and a record company, for which you had not paid anything. The age of mass music piracy, commercial and personal, had begun.

Although the 1988 Act treats musical works and sound recordings together, this is an innovation. The old Copyright Act 1956 dealt with primary material in Part I of the Act and relegated secondary material (sound recordings, films, broadcasts and cable programmes) to Part II. Apart from the duration of copyright protection, defined by reference to the composer's lifetime (plus 70 years) in the case of primary works, or by the time of making or release (50 years, as described above) in the case of a recording, the differences in treatment are not very great.

It should be noted, however, that the two major copyright conventions, Berne and the Universal Copyright Convention, do not apply to sound recordings (phonograms). These are separately dealt with in the Rome Convention and the Phonograms Convention (see Chapter 8) which have attracted far fewer signatory states. The international symbol 'P' within a circle, with the date of first issue, is normally placed on recordings or their packaging. This gives notice internationally that protection is claimed. In the original version of the CDPA the 'author' of a sound recording was defined as the person by whom the arrangements necessary for the making of the recording were undertaken. In 1996 this was changed and the author is simply described as the producer: that probably does not change much. All kinds of sound recording are protected; they can be of spoken words, bird song or steam trains as well as music. The 'sound recording' is the actual sounds as recorded and capable of being played back: this is what has the copyright, not the physical tape or disc. All this may sound a bit metaphysical, particularly when we remember that the tune or words, or both, which somebody played or sang or spoke into the recording equipment will also usually have copyright as a musical, dramatic or literary work. What it means is that if someone copies the sounds from the disc or tape onto another tape or disc, that person is infringing copyright in the recording. The original and the magnetic impulses fixed on it are unaffected: they will still play the same sounds but the pirate has captured a reproduction of those sounds on the pirate's own medium for the pirate's own use. In practical terms this means that it is infringement to copy the sounds onto a similar or totally different medium, from disc to disc, or disc to tape, or, indeed, into the memory of a computer. Of course there must be some sort of physical carrier medium, including the computer's hard disk or whatever, for the sounds, otherwise there is no recording. (Note that the American spelling 'disk' has come into general use for a computer disk: for other uses the spelling with 'c' is correct.) A sound recording is defined in s. 5A of the CDPA: essentially this is

> a recording of sounds from which the sounds may be reproduced ... regardless of the medium on which the recording is made or the method by which the sounds are reproduced or produced.

(This section, and s. 5B relating to films, were substituted in 1995 for the original s. 5, but the definition is unchanged.) The definition seems apt to cover anything in current use as a sound recording. It might be a bit doubtful if its application to the perforated roll of an old-style pianola were sought: the notes to be played are recorded, rather than the sounds themselves. Happily this question is not likely to exercise legal brains in the courts of the present day. It is hardly necessary to say, as s. 5A(2) does say, that copyright does not subsist in a sound recording which is a copy of a previous recording.

INFRINGEMENT

Infringement of copyright in sound recordings costs the recording industry (and, of course, composers and artists) a great deal of money in lost royalties. Copying of recordings by individuals is, as everyone knows, widely practised, both copying onto tape or CD for portability and the borrowing of a friend's tape or CD to make an illicit copy. It may be argued that the former is less heinous than the latter, but the law makes no distinction. In 1985, when new copyright legislation to replace the 1956 Act was being discussed, a government Green Paper, *The Recording and Rental of Audio and Video Copyright Material* (Cmnd 9445), gave some alarming figures of the situation at that time. More than 50 million blank tapes were bought annually, 84 per cent of purchasers used them to record music, and of those private recordings 76 per cent were made from records or pre-recorded tapes. Not every illicit recording would mean a lost sale and it would be difficult to quantify the loss, but it must have been very considerable, certainly running into millions of pounds a year. The illicit activity represents, moreover, a cavalier treatment of the property rights of the composers, artists and recording companies.

One solution to the private copying problem has been used successfully in other countries, notably Germany, that is to legalize private copying and compensate the rights owners from funds provided by a levy on the sale of blank tapes. After a lot of uncertainty the government concluded that there was no realistic alternative to this. The principle was supported by bodies representing recording companies and performers. However, there was a great deal of opposition from organizations representing the blind (who would in any case have been exempted from the levy), from legitimate users of blank tapes, and especially from the blank tape manufacturers. The campaign against the levy included dramatic full-page advertisements in the national newspapers (one advertisement contrasted the poor 'innocent' youth with his cassette recorder and the rich capitalist producer). At the same time some people had doubts about the principle of sanctioning the copying of copyright material without the copyright owner's permission (which might, indeed, fall foul of human rights legislation today) even though the copyright owner would be remunerated from the levy. The opposition was so strong that the proposal was dropped and it is still infringement to make a copy of a pre-recorded tape or disc (and the law continues to be flouted on a grand scale). An attempt by the recording industry to strike at the infringer from another direction, by way of the manufacturers of equipment which facilitated his or her nefarious activities, met with no real success. One manufacturer was persuaded to withdraw its high-speed twin-cassette recorder from the market. However, another, Amstrad, was less amenable and sought a declaration from the court that it was doing nothing unlawful by advertising and selling its own high-speed machine (which could copy tapes at double speed). The matter finished up in the House of Lords, *CBS Songs Ltd* v. *Amstrad*, 1988, with a victory for Amstrad. The main point which their Lordships made was that Amstrad were not 'authorizing' infringement, for they had no control over what their customers did with the machines. Private copying of music does not make the headlines as it used to; it has been eclipsed by other forms of infringement, notably downloading from the Internet, but undoubtedly it is still there.

The CDPA did introduce a measure of order into the hiring out of recordings. Section 18(2) made it clear that rental of copies to the public was an act restricted to the copyright owner. This was substituted in 1996 by s. 18A which put in place the European Union Directive on rental right, which has been mentioned in

Chapter 2, and specifically includes films and sound recordings in sub-section (1)(c). Tucked away in Schedule 7, para. 8 of the CDPA is a reminder, amending the Public Libraries and Museums Act 1964, that the provisions of the CDPA relating to rental of sound recordings, films and computer programs apply to public libraries, whether they make a charge or not.

Commercial infringement of sound recordings is, of course, a very serious matter. It is a worldwide plague. The pirates who once haunted the seas of south-east Asia have come ashore, but piracy is also rife in Europe, in the Middle East, and indeed anywhere where there is a market for cut-price pop music. It will be recalled that in the UK the first reported Anton Piller order (search order), actually shortly before the Anton Piller case itself, concerned sound recordings of Indian music, *EMI* v. *Pandit*, 1975. The Anton Piller order, now renamed the search order, has proved a very valuable weapon against the pirate, enabling the copyright owner to gather evidence for civil proceedings.

Commercial dealings in material which the maker, dealer, importer, hirer and so on, knows to be infringing can also be a criminal offence under s. 107 of the CDPA, and this law is most frequently invoked in respect of sound recordings and also videos and computer software. Criminal prosecutions in respect of literary or artistic works are less common. Local trading standards officers have a duty laid upon them to enforce the provisions of s. 107 within their areas and have power to make test purchases and enter premises and seize goods and documents. These provisions are found in s. 107A, added to the Act from a date to be appointed. Apart from prosecutions under s. 107, criminal proceedings are frequently taken under the Trade Descriptions Act 1968 and this Act has proved a useful weapon in dealing with the small-scale dealer in pirated recordings. Commonly action takes the form of a raid by trading standards officers, often on the initiative of FACT, the Federation Against Copyright Theft. The dealer is charged with applying a false trade description, that is, that the recordings or other material are genuine, and (often after some highly imaginative excuses) the dealer is fined £1000 to £2000. It is said that one dealer tried to get around the Act by labelling his stock 'Pirate cassette', thus avoiding the charge of false description, but the story is doubtless apocryphal. In any case, this would not have saved him from prosecution under s. 107.

PUBLIC PERFORMANCE

Copyright in sound recordings is also infringed by their being played in public and the collecting societies (see below) are vigilant to assert their members' rights. Seaside landladies in Skegness had a shock a few years ago when they found that they needed a licence from the appropriate collecting society to cover works heard on the radio relayed to guests' rooms. The question of what constitutes public performance can give some trouble. A number of old cases give some guidance.

These mostly concern copyright in musical works played over the radio rather than recordings but, of course, nowadays nearly all music so played is first recorded, so copyright in the recordings is also at issue. There is an exemption for broadcasts or cable programmes seen or heard by an audience who have not paid, directly or indirectly, to see or hear a sound recording or film included in the broadcast or programme: this does not infringe copyright in the recording or film (or the broadcast or cable programme), CDPA, s. 72. The exemption does not, however, apply to any actual musical composition (or literary, dramatic or artistic work) included, so a licence is still required for this.

The early days of broadcasting are delightfully invoked in *Performing Right Society* v. *Hammond's Bradford Brewery*, 1934. Did the defendants infringe copyright by setting up loudspeakers in the George Hotel, Brighouse, Huddersfield, so that persons in the hotel, not being members of the domestic circle of the person holding the wireless licence, could hear a performance of musical works broadcast by the BBC from the Hammersmith Cinema? The court's answer was yes. *Performing Right Society* v. *Camelo*, 1936, took this a bit further. Mr Giuseppe Camelo and his wife ran a restaurant in the front of 175 City Road, London. The kitchen was at the back of the house, separated from the restaurant by the family sitting room which also served as a passageway. By the open door of the sitting room a wireless set was playing very loudly so that the customers could, and did, listen to it. In the memorable words of Mr Justice Clauson,

> There are persons so constituted that wireless forms a pleasure to them and that while eating their meals in a restaurant they have a pleasure in listening.

This too was a public performance.

A few years later the Performing Right Society was again successful in defending the rights of its members. This concerned broadcasts relayed over loudspeakers to relieve the boredom of workers in a factory, *Performing Right Society* v. *Gillette Industries*, 1943. Although the workers formed a closed group, no outsiders being admitted, the Court of Appeal held this to be a public performance and hence infringement of the copyright of the composers of the music played in the broadcasts.

These cases are now 60 or 70 years old. In those days a wireless set was generally a massive construction in a walnut case as big as a fair-sized TV today. If it were a portable it needed a dry battery nearly a foot square plus a weighty wet battery which had to be topped up regularly with distilled water. An aerial ran from a pole or tree in the garden. A wireless set in the home was not uncommon in the 1930s, but was by no means universal. Nowadays a transistor radio can fill a bar or restaurant with music from a case no bigger than an average book and the copyright owners have a more difficult task enforcing their rights against every infringement by public performance. On the other hand, the principles are still the same and the older cases are still valid. *Gillette* and *Camelo* were both cited in the judgment in *Performing Right Society* v. *Harlequin Record Shops*, 1979. Record shops had started to play music continuously over loudspeakers (instead of confining it to soundproof booths where the customer listened to a record before deciding whether to buy it, as was previously the practice) and the PRS now demanded royalties. The Society was successful: the court held that this was definitely a performance in public.

COLLECTING SOCIETIES

Under copyright law the author (which includes a composer, or the producer of a sound recording) has the sole right to authorize the public performance of the author's work (and hence to demand royalties). Commonly, of course, the rights are licensed by the composer to a music publisher or a recording company. To enforce their rights in practice most composers and music publishers hand over their rights to the Performing Right Society (PRS). The Society then grants licences for the performance or broadcast (including cable) of the works which have been assigned to it. Normally the licences are granted in respect of the premises where musical works are performed, rather than to individual performers, and the fees are standardized according to the kind of premises in question. (Agreements with the broadcasting bodies are naturally different.) The Performing Right Society then works out an estimate of how much each work has been used (exact details are recorded by the broadcasting bodies, samples are taken of other users) and allocates the revenue from the licensing fees accordingly. The PRS has acquired rights in nearly all the pop music composed in this country and a large proportion of other musical works. Through a network of agreements the PRS is linked to similar collecting societies in very many other countries so a composer or publisher will receive payment for performance and broadcasts taking place abroad. The system provides a watchdog guarding the rights of composers and music publishers, taking action in its own name in cases of infringement and ensuring remuneration for use of their works.

The Performing Right Society deals with the rights in the original musical composition. The maker of a sound recording also has rights in that recording and these are handled by a separate collecting society. Most important record companies are members of Phonographic Performance Limited (PPL). They assign their performing and broadcasting rights in their sound recordings to PPL which operates a system of licences broadly similar to that of the PRS. Thus a juke box operator, for example, will need two licences, one from the PRS for the actual works and one from PPL for the recordings of these works. In cases of infringement the appropriate society, as an assignee of rights, will take action, if necessary in the courts, in its own name. The independent government-appointed Copyright Tribunal can adjudicate in a dispute between one of the collecting societies on the one hand, and any organization or individual seeking a licence on the other. The Copyright Tribunal was created by provisions in ss. 145 to 152 of the CDPA. It derives from the old Performing Right Tribunal of the Copyright Act 1956 with its field extended to take in licensing agreements for all kinds of copyright material. One other body may be mentioned at this point although it is not a collecting society. The Mechanical Copyright Protection Society (MCPS) acts for the rights owners, composers and publishers of musical works, in negotiations with broadcasters, film producers, record companies and others, for the use of their works.

LIVE PERFORMANCES

Modern sound recording equipment, particularly the cassette recorder and more recently the video camera, has facilitated a new and profitable kind of piracy – the making and sale of unauthorized recordings of live performances. The explosive growth of the pop music industry has tempted dishonest entrepreneurs to take a share in the profits. In the days when recording equipment was bulky, not very portable and certainly difficult to conceal, piracy was not easy. There was, however, a statute of 1925 and this was updated in 1958 by the Dramatic and Musical Performers' Protection Act. Commercial dealings in illicit recordings of live performances constituted a criminal offence. The original penalty of £50, little more than petty cash for the pirate even taking into account subsequent inflation, was later increased to a maximum of two years imprisonment. The name 'bootlegger' came into vogue for the pirate, deriving from the days of alcohol prohibition in the USA. Whereas bottles of illicit hooch were concealed in the legs of cowboy boots, the modern bootlegger concealed a tape recorder. Although the 1958 Act provided criminal sanctions against the bootlegger, there was no redress for the performer or for the record company which had acquired recording rights for the performance and they had to console themselves with the thought that the bootlegger (in the unlikely event that he received the maximum sentence), would be out of circulation for a couple of years (less remission for good conduct). By the time the bootlegger was caught and convicted he could well have stolen a profitable market from the legitimate producer.

In *RCA* v. *Pollard*, 1982, the plaintiffs had exclusive rights to make recordings of live performances by the well-known American singer, the late Elvis Presley, and brought a civil action against a bootlegger. The defendant was explicitly acknowledged by the Court of Appeal to be a bootlegger, making or selling, or both, recordings of Elvis Presley's live performances. In spite of this, the Court of Appeal found itself compelled, with some regret, to strike out the plaintiffs' statement of claim; that is, to rule that they had no good cause of action, for, as Lord Justice Oliver put it, 'the defendant who makes money out of regular and persistent breaches of the criminal law can scarcely be said to be overburdened with merit'. Not all performers, however, are worried by bootlegging. According to an article in the 'Creative Business' supplement to *The Financial Times*, 20 March 2001, a US rock band, Black Crowes, has for some years allowed fans to tape their shows (as, indeed, have other bands) and is now making their shows available for free downloading from the Internet by those who have purchased their latest CD. It is felt that this legalized 'bootlegging' amounts to worthwhile marketing that creates fan loyalty.

However, the legal situation in the UK has all been changed by the Copyright Designs and Patents Act. Part II of the Act, ss. 180 to 212, deals with rights in performances. The old performers' protection acts are repealed. In an endeavour to tie up all loose ends Part II becomes somewhat wordy. Broadly, however, it gives rights to a performer (or the holder of recording rights) in a live performance (which can be musical or dramatic or a variety act or, indeed, a reading or recitation). These rights are infringed by anyone who makes a recording of a live performance or broadcasts it (including cable) live without permission. Importation or any commercial dealings, including possession in the course of business, also constitute infringement, and so does public performance or broadcasting (including cable) of an infringing recording. Innocent infringement is a partial defence. Making a recording, or importing it purely for private and domestic use, is not infringement. Of course there is nothing to prevent the organizers of a concert or other performance to place a ban on the use of recording equipment in the contract for the sale of a ticket: even a recording for private purposes (assuming you evaded the bouncers at the door) would be a breach of the contract.

Rights in a live performance subsist for 50 years from the end of the year in which the performance took place, or, if a recording is released in that period, 50 years from the end of the year of release. Section 191, dealing with the duration of rights was substituted by an amended version in 1995, with certain additional matter. The usual civil remedies are available. Section 195 allows application to the court for an order for delivery up of illicit recordings, and s. 196 allows the rights owner to enter premises after notice to the police, and to seize illicit recordings provided that the seizure does not take place at the other party's permanent or regular place of business (when s. 195 would be appropriate). As well as the former criminal sanctions, which are retained, it is an offence for someone to represent falsely that he or she is authorized to give recording permission: this means that the mastermind cannot get an innocent person to do the dirty work, by pretending to have authority to permit the other to make a recording. Whilst performers' rights are not the same as copyright (other countries usually bring them into the category of 'neighbouring rights') they are closely analogous. Hence the permitted acts are much the same as for a copyright work. It may be noted that while fair dealing for criticism or review, or for reporting current events, is permitted, there is no exception for research or private study. There are, however, certain concessions for education. Certain libraries also have concessions on lending. The permitted acts are listed in Schedule 2, with a brief reference in s. 189; the library concessions are in para. 6B of the Schedule, and allow that the rights in performances are not infringed by the lending of copies of a recording of a performance by a prescribed library (see s. 37) or archive (other than a public library) which is not conducted for profit.

BROADCASTING AND CABLE

Broadcasts and cable programmes are included in the categories of works attracting copyright in s. 1(1)(b) of the Copyright, Designs and Patents Act, where they are brought together with sound recordings and films. A broadcast is defined in s. 6(1) as

> a transmission by wireless telegraphy of visual images, sounds or other information which – (a) is capable of being lawfully received by members of the public, or (b) is transmitted for presentation to the public.

This is pretty clear and will cover radio, TV and viewdata services. Note that the transmission is by wireless telegraphy. Encrypted transmissions are included if decoding equipment has been made available to the public; s. 6(2). The author, and hence first owner of copyright, is the person who transmits the programme, if that person has responsibility to any extent for its contents, and any person who makes arrangements for the transmission with the person transmitting it (ss. 9(2)(b) and 6(3)).

A cable programme is defined as any item included in a cable programme service, which in turn is defined as a service consisting

> wholly or mainly in sending visual images, sounds or other information by means of a telecommunications system, other than by wireless telegraphy

for reception at more than one place, or for public presentation, s. 7(1). A number of exceptions is given in s. 7(2): broadly these exclude from the definition of a cable programme service any service providing two-way communication, and any private service operated exclusively within a business, or by a private individual for domestic purposes only. The duration of copyright is 50 years from the end of the year in which a broadcast was made or a cable programme was included in a cable programme service, s. 14(2). There is no extension for repeats, s. 14(5).

Copyright infringement is constituted by the same sort of acts as with other copyright material, namely copying the broadcast or cable programme, issuing copies to the public, showing or playing it in public (except to a non-paying audience, and it is not possible to avoid the Act by making a concealed charge), re-broadcasting it or including it in a cable programme service. Commercial dealings, including possession in the course of business, and importation (except for private use), are caught by the usual civil and criminal sanctions. It should be remembered, of course, that copyright usually subsists in the original material included in a broadcast or cable programme. Thus there can be copyright simultaneously in, say, a musical work, a recording of that work, and a broadcast of that recording. The broadcaster or person making the cable programme will have to clear copyright with the owners of rights in the musical composition and the recording. However, incidental inclusion will not breach copyright. Fair dealing for the purpose of criticism or review and news reporting is permissible, but the research or private study exception does not apply to broadcasts or cable programmes. Private recording of a broadcast or cable programme for the purpose of viewing or listening to it at a more convenient time ('time-shifting') does not infringe copyright in the broadcast or cable programme or any work contained in it, s. 70.

Broadcasting is subject to a good deal of regulation under a number of statutes which we cannot consider in detail. The Independent Broadcasting Authority (IBA), established as the Independent Television Authority, was required by statute to provide (through contractors) high-quality TV and sound broadcasting services and had extensive duties relating to programme content. The IBA was disbanded under the Broadcasting Act 1990 and two new regulatory bodies emerged, the Radio Authority and the Independent Television Commission. The Broadcasting Complaints Commission (BCC) handles certain complaints. Two cases which have reached the courts are *Wilson* v. *Independent Broadcasting Authority (No 2)*, 1988, where representatives of the Scottish National Party failed to get declarators (a Scottish legal term, in effect a declaration) that the allocation of broadcasting time to the Party was unfair, and *R.* v. *Broadcasting Complaints Commission, ex parte Owen*, 1985. In the latter case the Social Democrat leader sought, and was refused, judicial review of the refusal by the BCC to entertain a complaint that his party received disproportionately little coverage in BBC and IBA news programmes.

Cable services are not a new idea. Rediffusion of wireless broadcasts from a central receiver to subscribers in a limited area was in operation in some towns by the 1940s, providing trouble-free reception in the days when the domestic wireless set was still at an early stage of development and broadcast transmissions were not wholly reliable. With the advance in cable technology in recent years cable programme services have taken off. They are subject to controls on unsuitable programme content. Concern that programmes would be overweighted with cheap foreign (namely North American) material imposed a duty to ensure that a reasonable proportion of content came from the EEC (as it then was).

FILMS AND VIDEOS

Cinematographic films can be immensely expensive to make so the producer of a major feature film wants to maximize the box office takings of the production. At the same time they may be copied reasonably easily by a pirate who has access to the reels and some fairly basic copying equipment. Before the 1956 Copyright Act came into force, although the cinema industry was nearly half a century old, and the golden years of films were already fading, copyright for films had to be deduced by analogy with other forms of material. The 1956 Act introduced specific protection for cinematograph films in s. 13, but not for those which were made before the Act came into force on 1 June 1957. Thus older films continued to be protected as original dramatic works, provided that they could be regarded as such, and this position was retained by Schedule 1, para. 7, of the CDPA. Photographs forming part of a film attracted copyright as photographs. Obviously the provisions with regard to old films will become less and less important as time goes by. It seems that the oblique protection as dramatic works given to films by the Copyright Act 1911 was sufficient to satisfy the requirements of the Berne Convention which had added cinematograph productions to the categories of protected works, by the Berlin revisions of 1908. It is noteworthy that films could be brought into the Convention so early, given the difficulties which some Civil Law countries, notably France, have experienced in trying to reconcile protection of films with the strictly personal nature of *droit d'auteur*.

In the CDPA 1988, sound recordings, films, broadcasts and cable programmes are brought together in s. 1(1)(b) among the descriptions of work in which copyright subsists. The qualifications for copyright protection are similar to those for other types of copyright material. Infringement is constituted by making a copy of the film or issuing copies to the public, broadcasting it or including it in a cable programme. Section 16 lists the restricted acts in relation to copyright in general, that is the acts where the right to do them is restricted to the copyright owner, and these are expanded in ss. 17 to 20. Section 21 should be noted: making an adaptation is a restricted act in relation to literary, dramatic or musical works, films (also artistic works) are not included. This did make sense when making an adaptation of a film or artistic work involved substituting completely new images for the original. It seems to leave a loophole now that images can be manipulated by computer to produce a distortion, rather than an adaptation, of the original film. What is the position with regard to 'colourized' versions of black and white films? In a French case, *Huston c/ Turner Entertainment*, 1991, the heirs of an American film director, John Huston, were able to stop the showing of a colourized version of his film *Asphalt Jungle*, on the ground that it infringed his moral right of the integrity of his work, even though this version had been produced lawfully in the United States.

A film is defined in s. 5B(1) as 'a recording on any medium from which a moving

69

image may by any means be produced'. Thus a video recording comes within the definition and it would cover digitally recorded moving images: it is difficult to envisage anything which foreseeable technological advance could produce which would be outside the definition. The definition of the 'author' was changed in 1996 by amendment of s. 9 by the Copyright and Related Rights Regulations. In the original version of s. 9 the author was the person who made the arrangements for making the film. Now, the author is the producer and the principal director, a partial step towards the Civil Law recognition of creative input as the source of *droit d'auteur*. A film is now a work of joint authorship (unless the producer and principal director are the same person), s. 10(1A). The duration of copyright is for 70 years from the end of the year of death of the latest to die of the principal director, the author of the screenplay, the author of the dialogue or the author of music specially created for and used in the film. The director is entitled to moral rights.

Section 85 gives a right of privacy in a film (or photograph) to the person who commissions it for private and domestic purposes. So, for example, a professional photographer engaged to make a video (or photographs) of a wedding cannot pass it on to a TV journalist (or otherwise make it public) when, a few years later, the happy bride is convicted of murdering her husband. (This does not affect the copyright in the film or photographs, which remains with the 'author', the photographer.) Rental right has already been mentioned in connection with sound recordings: it applies equally to films and videos.

There is a flourishing trade in pirate videos, despite the running battle fought by the film companies aided by the Federation Against Copyright Theft (FACT) and local trading standards officers. Pirates are often able to get the video on the market before release of the film or genuine video in this country. These may be made from genuine videos or from a 'borrowed' copy of the original film. The case of *R. v. Lloyd and ors*, 1984, was mentioned in Chapter 1. Lloyd, a cinema projectionist, would borrow a film and rush it to his confederates for copying. Although the defendants argued successfully on appeal that simply borrowing was not theft, film distributors have their civil remedies for infringement, and trading activities in infringing videos would fall foul of the penal provisions of s. 107 of the CDPA. Pirate videos are sometimes made with a hand-held video camera pointed at the screen during the showing of a film. Such a video is usually of poor quality but the unsuspecting purchaser does not realize this until after getting the video home: the packaging may be very convincing. Whilst the little local retailers may be caught, it is often difficult to track down large-scale pirates. (It is now common practice to mark uniquely each copy of a feature film on release, making it rather easier to track down the source on infringing copies which appear on the market.)

CENSORSHIP OF FILMS

Contrary to popular belief, there is no general censorship of films in this country, that is to say, nationwide pre-showing censorship. It is a criminal offence under the Obscene Publications Act 1959 to 'publish' an obscene film, or even to possess it for gain (to oneself or to someone else). 'Publish' includes showing the film, but also selling it or hiring it out, or offering to do so, or even giving or lending it. The danger of morality crusaders harassing cinemas is met by a requirement that a prosecution in respect of a feature film (that is one in 16 mm or larger format) needs the consent of the Director of Public Prosecutions. The Protection of Children Act 1978, which forbids the taking of indecent photographs of children under 16, and any distribution or showing of such photographs, also applies to films. However, these statutes provide for prosecution *ex post facto* for an offence which has already been committed, they do not provide a mechanism by which censors may act to stop a film, short of court action. There is no way in which a film producer may guarantee that the law will accept a film as suitable for showing.

To a large extent the uncertainty is taken away by the British Board of Film Classification (BBFC) (known until 1985 as the British Board of Film Censors). This is an independent body, established in 1912 with the object that proper national standards are maintained in films which are put out for public showing. The film industry submits its products voluntarily to the Board which has a body of men and women who act as examiners. The Board will grant a certificate if it thinks that the film is suitable, though sometimes cuts are required before a certificate is granted, and the Board may refuse a certificate altogether. The five categories of certificate are familiar to filmgoers: U for unrestricted viewing by anyone over the age of five, PG where parental guidance is advised, 15 is not for showing to children under that age, 18 for adults only, and Restricted 18 for adults only in licensed cinema clubs. It is virtually certain that no prosecution would follow the appropriate showing or distribution of a film granted a certificate by the BBFC. The Board is an independent body financed by the fees charged for examination of films, but the Home Office, film trade and local authority representative associations are consulted before the president and secretary are appointed.

Film censorship is enforced in a rather oblique fashion by the Cinemas Act 1985 (not to be confused with the Films Act 1985) which consolidates a number of earlier statutes. The Act provides that any premises used for showing films must get a licence from the local authority as licensing authority. When granting a licence the authority has a statutory duty to impose restrictions regarding the admission of children. In practice this means that the licence of the BBFC is usually accepted as the standard. However, it is open for a local authority to impose its own standards so a film could be refused (or permitted) in one area but not in a neighbouring one. Cinema licensing is ostensibly concerned more with safety and public order than with censorship, and the police and fire authorities have to be notified of an application for a licence. As might be expected a licence is not required for a showing at a private house to which the public is not admitted and other rather complicated exemptions apply when the showing is for instructional or advertising purposes when the public is not admitted, or the show is free. In fact the system, or lack of system, of film censorship in the UK seems to work fairly well. Generally the Board's decisions seem sensible enough to satisfy most people's ideas of what ought, or ought not, to be shown.

VIDEO RECORDINGS

It is logical to treat a video as a film and it comes within the definition in s. 5B(1). However, in some ways it does present different problems. Compared with a conventional motion picture film a video is very much easier to make, needing no complicated processing. It can be copied and multiplied easily and it can be shown on an ordinary TV screen. The video has proved a great temptation to the commercial pirate and even to the private copier. It has also worried people because of the ease with which pornographic and other undesirable material may be produced and made available, particularly to children. The Video Recordings Act 1984 lays down a form of censorship. This is done by the BBFC and the categories (general viewing, without or with parental guidance, unsuitable for children or young persons under a certain age, or supply only in a licensed sex shop) are similar to those applied to films. However, the Video Recordings Act has teeth, which no provision for film censorship has. It is a criminal offence, punishable with a fine up to £20 000 to supply or offer to supply a video which has no certificate. It is also an offence to supply (or offer) a video to a child who has not reached the age specified in the certificate, or to supply (or offer) one certified for sex shops only anywhere other than in a sex shop. There are limited defences for innocent breach of the Act. There are also certain exemptions, for example if the video is not supplied for reward or in the course of business. Supplying a video to those who took part in events recorded in it is exempted, so a good clean video of a wedding can be supplied to the participants (but not if it contains sex or violence!). Certain kinds of videos are totally exempt from the Act (but not if they include violence to humans or animals, or human sex). These are educational, informative or instructional works, video games, and any concerned with sport, religion or music.

4 The work of the artist, designer and photographer

We pass now to artistic works, broadly defined. Artistic works are within the copyright regime in s. 1 of the Copyright, Designs and Patents Act 1988, together with literary, dramatic and musical works, and there is not a great deal of difference in the treatment of these different categories of copyright material. Industrial designs are dealt with separately and the 1988 Act made some considerable changes to the law protecting these. Although design protection is different from copyright it is convenient to include it in this chapter. To start with, however, let us look at artistic works.

ARTISTIC WORKS

The expression 'artistic work' is defined broadly enough in the Act to give protection to practically any two- or three-dimensional work which human imagination can produce or a computer can generate, so long as it is original. An artistic work means a graphic work, photograph, sculpture or collage, a work of architecture (that is a building (which includes any fixed structure) or part of it, or a model for a building), or a work of artistic craftsmanship (s. 4). A graphic work has a broad definition which would seem to cover any two-dimensional product of an artist's capability. It includes any painting, drawing, diagram, map, chart or plan, and any engraving, etching, lithograph, woodcut or similar work. This will obviously include computer graphics. The word photograph has a definition which was obviously drafted with future, as well as present, technology in mind. It means

> a recording of light or other radiation on any medium on which an image is produced or from which an image may by any means be produced, and which is not part of a film.

This will take in an X-ray image, but what about the record of an ultrasound scan produced by hospital equipment? Fortunately, that seems a rather unlikely candidate for litigation. It would, in any case, probably be covered as a diagram, chart or plan. The definition would seem capable, without any real straining of the words, of coping with digital photography.

SKILL AND LABOUR

A graphic work, photograph, sculpture or collage must, of course, be original (and we shall return to this matter shortly). Fortunately it is subject to copyright 'irrespective of artistic quality' saving the court from the hopeless task of making aesthetic judgements. A child's drawing is as much entitled to copyright as a work hung at the Royal Academy. On the other hand the courts will expect a certain amount of skill and labour to have been expended in the creation of the work. A pop star wore very simple facial make-up, basically some coloured stripes and was photographed in his make-up for publicity purposes. The defendants published a picture of him with roughly the same pattern on his face. The court felt that this was too ephemeral and insufficiently original to attract copyright, *Merchandising Corporation of America* v. *Harpbond Ltd*, 1983.

It is not easy to say what is substantial enough to attract copyright: in some cases fairly insubstantial items have passed the test in the courts. In one case copyright and trade marks overlapped: a German association, Werbegemeinschaft Inlettweber GmbH, successfully claimed copyright in a simple device of the words 'Karo Step' distinctively lettered, surrounded by four concave-sided triangles. Mrs Brigette Bishop, who imported duvets and covers from Germany, registered the same device as a trade mark in the UK. If the German body had previously registered the trade mark themselves then a trade mark infringement action would have been possible. However, the court held that copyright subsisted in this simple device and (for this and other reasons) ordered that Mrs Bishop's registration be removed from the trade mark register, *Karo Step Trade Mark*, 1977. It seems that there may be a lower threshhold for substantiality in artistic, as compared with literary, copyright. As instanced earlier, Exxon Corporation failed when asserting literary copyright in the single word 'Exxon', *Exxon Corporation* v. *Exxon Insurance Consultants*, 1982. A tie-on parcel label was not much more substantial than the Karo Step mark but it too was held to be covered by copyright, *Walker (Charles) and Co. Ltd* v. *British Picker Co. Ltd*, 1961. The two companies, who made 'pickers' for textile machinery, the former from leather and the latter from buffalo hide, were originally associated. After they parted in 1956 the defendants continued to use the label, slightly modified, adopted by Walker in 1949. It was a simple utilitarian design (there is an illustration in the Patent Reports, [1961] RPC, 57 at 58) but the court decided that it was sufficiently original and distinctive to attract copyright.

ORIGINALITY

Artistic works, like literary, dramatic and musical works, must be original to attract copyright protection. In a number of cases the courts have applied the test of originality to artistic works. Mr Justice Wills' judgment in *Kenrick* v. *Lawrence*, 1890, goes into flights of judicial fancy at the prospect of a time when 'all the remaining ignorance, male and female, [women did not get the vote on equal terms with men until nearly 40 years later] of the three kingdoms shall be swept into the electoral field' thus putting immense power into the hands of the owner of copyright in a simple sketch of a hand with a pencil marking a ballot paper. A million copies of this aid or inducement for the illiterate voter had been sold since 1885. The judge admitted that an identical reproduction of the plaintiffs' drawing might attract protection, though he felt it absurd to call it a work of art. However, the defendants' almost, but not quite, identical version of the same subject did not infringe. There was no copyright in the subject or, as we might say, following the principles of literary copyright, in the idea. His Lordship seemed not uninfluenced by the thought of the monopoly power in this simple device falling into the hands of some unsuitable person (or, indeed, of one political party). However, his conclusion was undoubtedly sound. In *Bernstein* v. *Murray*, 1981, the defendants contended that there was no originality in the plaintiffs' sketches for a dress as they simply used known style features. Nonetheless, the court held, these were used in a novel way, involving sufficient originality to confer copyright on the drawings.

Originality can be a tricky problem. Two artists who paint, say, Westminster Abbey from the same viewpoint may well produce very similar pictures but each will have copyright in his or her version. But suppose that one artist painted the abbey in the studio, drawing inspiration from the other's painting. Would this be infringement? Or, to bring the hypothesis up to date, the artist viewed a copyright work on the Internet and painted his or her own interpretation of the same theme. *Bauman* v. *Fussell*, 1953 (but not reported until 1978), gives some guidance. The plaintiff had taken a very dramatic photograph of two fighting cocks in Cuba and it was subsequently published in the illustrated magazine *Picture Post*. The defendant cut it out of the magazine and stuck it up on his studio wall. He freely admitted that he was inspired by the photograph when he painted a picture of the same subject. Expert evidence from four distinguished figures in the art world was heard at the trial. As expert witnesses their function was to draw the court's attention to similarities and differences, not to say that the work actually was a copy: that was for the court to decide. (The function of an expert witness in any field, whether a handwriting specialist, for example, or a computer expert, an accountant or an engineer, is to help the judge to decide the question at issue, not to decide the question for the judge.) The Court of Appeal, by a 2–1 majority, held that the artist's work was original. It did not reproduce a substantial part of the photograph and did not infringe the photographer's copyright. However, one of the judges, Lord Justice Romer, dissented, basing his view on what the painter had included from the photograph, rather than on what he had left out. The lesson to be learned from *Bauman* is that originality is a defence to a claim of copying, though the court has to decide how original the alleged copy is.

Towards the end of the nineteenth century there was a vogue for reproducing famous paintings on the theatre stage as *tableaux vivants* with live persons posed within a frame against a painted background. Hanfstaengl, the well-known Munich art publisher, attempted in a series of actions to restrain this alleged infringement of copyright in the paintings, but without success. The plaintiff had some limited success with regard to the painted backgrounds of two tableaux but lost his case with regard to the posed figures. Lord Justice Lindley, in the Court of Appeal, regarded the plaintiff's contention as a construction of the Fine Arts Copyright Act 1862 (the relevant statute at the time) which was never dreamed of when it was passed, *Hanfstaengl* v. *Empire Palace*, 1894. A further twist came when the House of Lords rejected Hanfstaengl's claim that sketches of the *tableaux vivants* published in the *Daily Graphic* infringed copyright in the original pictures: the sketches could not be said to be copies of the original pictures, *Hanfstaengl* v. *Baines*, 1895.

What if an artistic work is based on an existing object, a meticulous drawing of a plant, for example? This was settled over 250 years ago in *Blackwell* v. *Harper*, 1742. Mrs Blackwell made engravings of 300 medicinal plants. Obviously at a time when most medicines were concocted from herbs it was important for identification that the engravings should reproduce accurately the appearance of each plant and its parts. The defendant contended that as copies of existing (natural) objects the engravings were not protected by the legislation in force, but the court rejected that defence. Although the statute which applied at that time was repealed a very long time ago, the principle in *Blackwell* still stands.

RIGHTS OF THE ARTIST

If the artist is a 'qualifying person' according to s. 154 and the artistic work qualifies with regard to country of origin, s. 155, then he or she has rights which are very much the same as the rights in literary, dramatic or musical works. These matters have already been discussed in Chapter 2 with particular reference to written works: the regime is practically the same for artistic works so it is unnecessary to repeat it here.

It is infringement to copy the work, that is to reproduce it in any material form, including making a three-dimensional copy of a two-dimensional work or vice versa. It is infringement to broadcast it by television (or in a cable programme) or to issue copies to the public, (which, of course, does not mean subsequently distributing copies already put into circulation). However, showing an artistic work in public (which would be infringement of the copyright in a film) is not infringement. Making an 'adaptation' is a restricted act in relation to literary, dramatic and musical works, but not artistic works. (The term 'restricted act' means an act which only the copyright owner, or someone granted the owner's permission, may do.) This produces the rather odd result that it would not apparently be infringement to make a pencil sketch of an oil painting, which would count as an adaptation, but it would be infringement to reproduce it as a sculpture. The restriction on three-dimensional copying of two-dimensional works has had a practical application in respect of the reproduction of industrial products from the original engineering drawings. Another curious result of this rule is that it is infringement to adapt a story (a literary work) into pictures, but not to adapt the pictures as a story. Storing an artistic work in any medium by electronic means counts as reproducing it in a material form, which constitutes infringement.

The first owner of copyright in an artistic work is normally the person who made it, that is the original 'author'. (As we have seen, the statute uses the word 'author' very broadly to mean a writer, artist, and so on.) The author can, of course, pass the ownership of the work on to somebody else, as when the painting is sold, but that does not transfer the copyright without a further agreement to do so. There is one important exception to the artist's entitlement to copyright, namely, as with a literary work, if a work is made in the course of the author's employment (which includes apprenticeship) the copyright belongs to the employer (subject to any agreement to the contrary). Moral rights also apply to artistic works and the author has the right to be identified as the author whenever the work is published commercially or exhibited in public or broadcast or shown in a film. This also applies when a graphic work or photograph depicting a work of architecture or of artistic craftsmanship, or a sculpture, is issued to the public. The right must be asserted in the manner given in s. 78. There is a number of exceptions in s. 79 to the right to be identified, the most important being a typeface design, a computer-generated work, and a work made, or made available, for publication in a periodical or collective reference work. The moral rights extend also to objecting to derogatory treatment, and the right not to have somebody else's work falsely attributed to oneself. Derogatory treatment is dealt with in s. 80 and infringement of the moral right is centred on making the mutilated version public in any one of a number of specified ways. In the nature of things there are some differences between derogatory treatment of an artistic work and of any other copyright work. Artistic works are covered in subsection (4) and literary, dramatic and musical works in subsection (3). Perhaps artistic works are more susceptible to derogatory treatment than other copyright works: it is easy enough to imagine such cases, putting a moustache on the Mona Lisa would doubtless qualify if the painting were still in copyright. It would be unworkable for the owner of a building to seek the architect's approval for every change to its appearance, perhaps long after it was built, so the right does not apply to a work of architecture, but where the architect is identified on the building he or she may insist on the identification's being removed. There is a special right of privacy (in s. 85) in a photograph or film (including a video) which has been commissioned for private and domestic purposes: it must not be made public without the consent of the person who commissioned it. So a photographer who sells copies of the video or photographs commissioned by the bride's father for a society wedding, or shows them in public or on TV, would infringe the right.

DROIT DE SUITE

In some countries, notably France, an artist has long had the so-called *droit de suite*, that is the right to some recompense on future sales of a work after the artist had disposed of it. So, if the artist, starving in a Paris garret, sells a picture for a loaf of bread and a bottle of wine, he or she is entitled to a percentage when it is auctioned for a million francs after fame has come. The UK has resisted European Union attempts to introduce this to all countries in the Union. One major concern is the effect of what is tantamount to a sales tax on the very important London art market and the likelihood that trade would migrate to London's chief rival, New York.

EXCEPTIONS TO ARTISTS' RIGHTS

There are statutory exceptions which protect a person using copyright artistic material for certain valid purposes. These closely parallel the exceptions available in the case of literary, dramatic and musical works, discussed in Chapter 2, though with differences and additions which stem from the obviously different nature of the material. The fair dealing exemptions in ss. 29 and 30, for research or private study and for criticism, review and news reporting, apply as for other copyright works, except that there is no exemption for use of a photograph for reporting current events. If fair dealing may be difficult to define in relation to a written work, it would seem even more difficult when it involves an artistic work. Sections 45 and 46 allowing copying for the purpose of Parliamentary or judicial proceedings and Royal Commissions or statutory inquiries and reporting them, also apply. The solemn pages of the law reports are not generally enlivened by pictures. However, illustrations of trade marks or drawings from patent specifications do appear quite frequently in the Reports of Patent Cases, and charts or diagrams may sometimes be seen in some other specialized series.

A fairly obvious exeption in s. 31 permits the incidental inclusion of an artistic (or indeed any other) work in another artistic work, a film, broadcast or cable programme. It would be ridiculous if an artist could sue for infringement because a painting happened to get within range of a TV camera. It is also permissible to draw or paint, photograph or film, or include in a broadcast or cable programme, a building or (provided that it is permanently situated in a public place) a sculpture, a model for a building or a work of artistic craftsmanship, or to issue copies to the public, s. 62. If the artist has disposed of the copyright he or she may still copy the original work in making another work provided that the main design of the original is not repeated or imitated, s. 64.

ARTISTIC CRAFTSMANSHIP

A 'work of artistic craftsmanship' is included in the definition of an artistic work in s. 4 of the 1988 Copyright, Designs and Patents Act. This category, which appears earlier in the Copyright Acts of 1911 and 1956, was obviously intended to bring under copyright protection the sort of production which is not a 'pure' work of art, nor yet simply a work of craftsmanship. We may, perhaps, think of such items as a piece of fine jewellery, or a one-off craftsman-built piece of furniture or a wrought iron gate. There has been a surprising dearth of reported cases: the few that we have deal with rather grey areas where it is not obvious whether the work in question is one of artistic craftsmanship or not. In a case in the 1930s the judge seemed to accept that an haute couture dress could possibly be a work of artistic craftsmanship, though in the case before him he did not agree that the craftsmen (actually women) who made up that dress from the designer's drawings were 'artistic craftsmen', one factor influencing him being that the designer and the makers were not one and the same person, *Burke* v. *Spicer*, 1936. A rain cape to cover mother and baby, admittedly a much more utilitarian garment than Mrs Burke's dress, was not a work of artistic craftsmanship in the eyes of the court, *Merlet* v. *Mothercare*, 1986. Cuisenaire rods, wooden rods of various lengths and colours used to teach mathematics to children, lacked any element of craftsmanship, *Cuisenaire* v. *Reed*, 1963 (an Australian case), and a Canadian judge held that they were not artistic, *Cuisenaire* v. *South West Imports*, 1969. In *Shelley Films* v. *Rex Features*, 1994, on an interlocutory (interim) application the court held that it was at least arguable that an artistically arranged set for an historical film could be a work of artistic craftsmanship.

The leading case, *Hensher* v. *Restawile*, 1976, which reached the House of Lords, tries to give some help but their Lordships, whilst all agreeing that the three-piece suite at issue was not a work of artistic craftsmanship, were not very clear what the words really meant. In fact, the case concerned the original prototype (not the furniture as marketed, for that was produced in quantity and could not claim to be works of craftsmanship), and Lord Reid and Lord Morris of Borth-y-Gest expressed some doubt whether the prototype, a flimsy mock-up, was itself a work of craftsmanship. Their Lordships were at least agreed that they should not make an aesthetic judgement but could hear evidence as to the question of artistic character, but they were divided as to whether the artistic character should be judged objectively, or whether the intent of the author was relevant, or the effect on the ultimate purchaser, or whether both the intent and the result should be considered. The 'Atlantic', one version of the plaintiffs' suite, was described by the buyer for a large furniture company: 'It is a wonderful suite; it's horrible, it's vulgar and it's brash, but I am afraid unfortunately the young people will go for it.' It was, as another witness said, slightly vulgar but a good commercial design. That was not enough to constitute a work of artistic craftsmanship and the plaintiffs lost their case for infringement of copyright. So we are left with no clear guidance as to what a work of artistic craftsmanship really is.

The reason why there is little authority on this subject is probably, at least in part, that it overlaps with other categories. A garden ornament could qualify as a sculpture, a garden seat is likely to be an industrial design, many works of craftsmanship have original drawings behind them which can form the basis of a copyright claim. If the work is mass-produced it ceases to be a work of craftsmanship and it is very dubious if the prototype comes within the definition unless it has real qualities of both craftsmanship and artistic character. It has been suggested that the assemblages of house bricks or evaporated milk cans which appear ever more frequently in the art galleries (and the Sunday newspapers) might be works of artistic craftsmanship: this is not very convincing, since they would seem to have more the character of sculpture in line with, say, the assemblages of scrap iron which are generally accepted as such. However, although few cases have reached the law reports, the provision of copyright for works of artistic craftsmanship must form a useful potential weapon to protect such original works as jewellery, luxury bookbindings, fine silver or embroidery, to take a few examples at random.

PHOTOGRAPHS

The CDPA made some changes in the copyright regime relating to photographs. Most important is that the copyright owner is now the person who created the photograph: formerly it was, rather strangely, the owner of the material on which the photograph was taken. The duration of copyright is, as for other artistic works, 70 years *pma* (following the amendment introduced by the Duration of Copyright and Rights in Performances Regulations 1995). There is a limited surviving complication which can give a longer period to certain unpublished photographs taken between 1 June 1957 and the commencement of the 1988 Act, 50 years from first publication, but this is of very limited scope. The right of privacy in a photograph commissioned for private and domestic purposes has already been mentioned. In general, however, a photograph is treated in the same way as any other artistic work.

TYPEFACES

Most people, when they read a book, a periodical or other text, are not very aware of the typeface in which it is set. Yet both utilitarian and aesthetic considerations have led to a proliferation of newly-designed typefaces in recent years which can do much to improve the appearance or legibility (or both) of printed matter. A typeface is a work of artistic creativity and, if successful, it can be a valuable piece of 'intellectual' property. The design of a typeface attracts copyright as an artistic work but some special provisions apply. These are found in s. 55. Fairly obviously it is not infringement to use a typeface in the ordinary course of typing, composing text, typesetting or printing, to possess an article for that purpose or to do anything with the material produced. This applies even if the article used is an infringing copy. However, importing, dealing with or possessing for the purpose of dealing with articles designed or adapted to produce material in a particular typeface, constitutes both a civil wrong or, in certain circumstances, a criminal offence, to be dealt with under the appropriate sections of the Act which deal with copyright infringement. Once the copyright owner has marketed (or someone else has, with the owner's licence) articles for producing materials in that typeface the owner's monopoly lasts for 25 years (reckoned, as usual, from the end of the year), after which anyone may produce and use such articles. The two sections are a bit cumbersome and should be referred to for exact details. Now that metal punches, matrices and type have given way to computer-generated images, there could be some difficult questions as to what exactly constitutes an 'article' for producing materials in the typeface. Presumably a disk carrying the appropriate computer software would qualify, but what about the program itself as opposed to the physical carrier medium? The moral right of integrity, not to be treated in a derogatory manner, applies to typeface, but the right to have the designer's name acknowledged obviously does not. Copyright in 'the typographical arrangement of a published edition', the image on the page, has already been mentioned in Chapter 2.

There is an international convention, the Vienna Agreement (1973) for the Protection of Typefaces envisaging 15 or 25 years protection by means of a state's design or copyright law, or by a registered deposit system, with provision for use by a printer who has legitimately acquired the typeface, and this was in mind when the right was introduced in the CDPA.

THREE-DIMENSIONAL COPIES

The acts constituting infringement of copyright in an artistic work do not include 'adaptation' as such (unlike the situation with literary, dramatic and musical works). However, it is infringement of copyright in a two-dimensional work to reproduce it in three dimensions, or *vice versa*, s. 17(3). A graphic work does not have to have artistic quality as commonly understood for the purposes of artistic copyright so a diagram, map, chart or plan can attract copyright. This provision assumes some importance in the manufacturing sphere where a three-dimensional industrial product might well infringe copyright in the original two-dimensional engineering or design drawings. The Copyright, Designs and Patents Act 1988 has made considerable changes in the relevant law but it is interesting and instructive to look back at some very important earlier cases which are still valid even though the *British Leyland* case (discussed below) and the 1988 Act have shifted the emphasis.

LB (Plastics) Ltd designed and manufactured a very successful knock-down plastic drawer system. The defendants, Swish Products Ltd, in a case which went right up to the House of Lords, had developed drawers which bore a resemblance to the plaintiffs' products. The drawers themselves did not come within the scope of artistic copyright, they were certainly not works of artistic craftsmanship, and they did not qualify either for protection as industrial designs (which we shall look at later). The only possible approach for the plaintiffs was to contend that the defendants' drawers were three-dimensional copies of the plaintiffs' drawings. In fact, the defendants had never seen the actual drawings, but their Lordships were prepared to hold that copyright in the plaintiffs' drawings was indeed infringed by the defendants' product, *LB (Plastics) v. Swish Products*, 1979.

Nichols Advanced Vehicle Systems v. Rees, 1979, involved a tale of devious doings in the Formula One car racing world. Nichols Advanced Vehicle Systems (NAVS) were developing a car to be raced by their team, The Shadows. Certain employees of NAVS concocted a plan to force the company into liquidation, the intention being to buy the plant and cars. This Plan A failed so the defectors put Plan B into operation. They set up a new company and they persuaded a large part of the workforce to leave NAVS and join them. These included the chief designer who had meanwhile passed on a considerable number of drawings for the NAVS car to the new company where they were doctored by removing the NAVS name, reference numbers and dates, and substituting new ones. Now, it was vital for the new company to get their racing team, The Arrows, on the track by late January 1978 in order to qualify for the Formula One association. By using some 170 of the NAVS drawings they achieved this. By this time the owner of NAVS was very suspicious. He obtained an Anton Piller order (search order) against the other company and this produced indisputable evidence of infringement of NAVS drawings. In the ensuing trial the judge was shown a selection of the drawings and the parts made from them and he had no hesitation in identifying the parts as three-dimensional copies. An attempt by the defendants to assert that the former chief designer owned copyright in the drawings (he did some of his work at home) failed in the face of his letter of appointment produced in evidence by the plaintiffs. This showed clearly that he was an employee, not a self-employed designer, so his employers,

NAVS, owned the copyright. The judge felt that in the circumstances a moderate extra sum by way of extra (or punitive) damages was appropriate. An injunction to stop further infringement (including racing the car) was given and an order for delivery up of the infringing parts and drawings. The defendants had a choice in this last order. His Lordship put it thus: 'Whether they say "Oh well, this is hopeless; take the car away", or whether they take a sledge-hammer or a couple of screwdrivers and set to work to find the bits, I don't know … One thing I want to be clear about is that this car is not to be driven.'

The *British Leyland* case

In 1986, after a 21-day hearing the House of Lords decided a case which, as Lord Bridge of Harwich pointed out, would have far-reaching consequences for all sections of industry whose products needed replacement parts which derive from original drawings. The case, *British Leyland* v. *Armstrong Patents*, 1986, involved the exhaust pipe of the Marina motor car but it was really a test case affecting the whole of the £800 million a year market in spares for British Leyland cars. (British Leyland has had a number of reorganizations and name changes, its direct heir today being Rover: at that time it held a dominant, if not the dominant, position in the British motor industry.) Since 1973 British Leyland had managed to persuade most of the spares industry that they needed to be licensed by BL if they made spare parts for BL cars. Armstrong stood out against this and continued to manufacture car exhausts without a licence. They had not seen British Leyland's original drawings but had examined and measured actual examples and made their exhausts on the basis of those data, a process sometimes called reverse engineering. The situation was similar to *LB (Plastics)* v. *Swish Products*, also a House of Lords case, and their Lordships were not prepared to depart from that. So far, so good, Armstrong were clearly infringing BL's copyright in their design drawings. But their Lordships did not leave it there. They went on to reject British Leyland's case on grounds which had little to do with copyright law and much to do, the cynical would say, with public policy. They recognized the right of the owner of a BL car to repair it and if that involved purchasing spares from a manufacturer other than BL, so be it. In other words, they found a 'spare parts exception' to the general rule. One Law Lord, Lord Griffiths, was unable to go along with the others. He felt, however, that indirect copying without reference to the original drawing was not what the Copyright Act 1956 intended to be infringement and was prepared to depart from *LB (Plastics)*. On that ground he also decided in Armstrong's favour, although expressing strong reservations to the spare parts exception. The British Leyland case was a landmark. In fact the 1988 Act has made some changes to the law and, in effect, given statutory sanction to the spare parts exception. This stems from the revision of the law on industrial designs and its relation to copyright. We shall now look at the law on designs.

DESIGNS

One area of protection for works of an artistic nature is of considerable commercial importance, that relating to designs which are used for industrial production. This originated around 200 years ago, at first to protect textile designs for a limited period only. The modern law is contained in the CDPA. Prior to the 1988 Act protection was available for 15 years by registration under the Registered Designs Act 1949 and was available for those features of industrial designs which had aesthetic, not functional, purpose. Litigation arose over articles incorporating designs as diverse as stacking chairs (*Benchairs* v. *Chair Centre*, 1973), shirts for the England football team (*Cook and Hurst's Application*, 1979), the underside of a shower bath tray (*Gardex* v. *Sorata*, 1986) and the shell of a chocolate egg (*Ferrero's Application*, 1978).

The situation now is that there are two kind of protection for industrial designs. Protection for the purely aesthetic features can still be obtained by registration under the 1949 Act as amended. The whole of the 1949 Act as amended is reproduced as Schedule 4 to the CDPA. But the CDPA introduced a new 'design right', defined in s. 213. This is automatic as soon as an article is made to the design or it is expressed in a 'design document' (which may be drawn, written or in electronic form).

Registered designs are dealt with by the Designs Registry which is part of the Patent Office. The design must be new and original and must consist of features which appeal to and are judged by the eye. The features may be of shape, configuration, pattern or ornament, applied by an industrial process but not dictated by construction or function. Certain things are excluded, sculptures (unless intended to be multiplied by an industrial process), wall plaques, medallions and printed matter like calendars and greeting cards. Protection extends up to 25 years.

Design right, introduced by the 1988 Act, is different. It is automatic, not involving registration or other formalities. It protects any aspect of shape or configuration of an article, internal or external, but not surface decoration. It must be original, not commonplace. Protection against copying lasts for 15 years from when it is first made or recorded or 10 years from the time when it is first marketed, whichever expires earlier.

There are two important exceptions to design right giving statutory force, in effect, to the 'spare parts' exception of *British Leyland* v. *Armstrong Patents*. If the design takes a particular shape so that it 'must fit' against another article so that either may perform its function, it is not protected. This will cover the car exhaust in *British Leyland*. Also if the shape 'must match' the appearance of another article of which it forms an integral part (for example, a car body panel), again it is not protected.

The relation between copyright and these rights are spelled out in ss. 51 and 52. Section 51 says in effect that the owner of an (unregistered) design right may defend his right if anybody makes articles to the owner's design, only by asserting the design right, not copyright. Section 52 applies where an artistic work has been exploited by the owner (or with the owner's licence) by making copies by an industrial process and marketing them. It is not infringement of copyright in the artistic work after 25 years from first marketing the articles to make articles or doing anything with them. In other words, copyright cannot be used to extend registered design right beyond its duration of 25 years.

5　Electronic data

THE INTERNET

Probably the first thing to remember about the Internet is that it is very largely a phenomenon of the richer, developed part of the world. This is hardly surprising, of course. In 1997, 96 per cent of Internet hosts were located in the 27 (now 29) countries of the Organization for Economic Cooperation and Development (OECD), according to V Keenan, *Guardian*, 13 May 1997, cited by Williams and Nicholas (2001). Also noteworthy is the dominance of the English (including American) language. Around 90 per cent of the computers connected to the Internet are in English-speaking countries. More than half (60 per cent) of the messages now passed are in English (though that is down from 85 per cent in 1996), and eighty per cent of home pages are in English. (These figures were given in *The Times*, 19 March 2001.) Obviously the situation will change, and probably fairly quickly. In particular, the vast home and overseas Chinese population will bring Chinese into the statistics (it is easy enough to input data in the Chinese script). However, for the time being at any rate, it would seem likely that the problems of the Internet are seen very largely through Western eyes, and the solutions are likely to be those which would occur to people brought up in the Western, and specifically British or US, legal traditions. It cannot be too strongly stressed that what applies to copyright in material distributed in other forms, applies equally to material distributed on the Internet. The special problems arise over enforcement.

The Internet is still in its infancy. Books on Internet law have been appearing for the past few years, indeed long enough for the earlier ones to get out of date. Two things need to be remembered about Internet law. First, a crime, or a civil wrong, is just the same crime or wrong if it is committed over the Internet as if it is committed over the telephone, or face to face with the other party. Secondly, the Internet is not like some albatross soaring for ever over the southern oceans and rarely if ever touching the land: the Internet starts from earth and all the actors have a base somewhere on earth.

This chapter is too short to deal comprehensively with the law of the Internet and the questions which it poses now and which it will pose in the future, but some of the interesting matters which are already arousing attention are highlighted below.

NAPSTER AND YAHOO!

It is useful to start off by looking at two foreign cases which attracted a good deal of attention in 2000 to 2001. One concerned copyright infringement, and the other control of illegal material on the Internet.

Napster

A company in the USA, Napster Inc., was founded by Shawn Fanning who had devised file-sharing software which allows users to swap music files stored on their computers. In simple terms, a user could search the music collections on all other users' hard disks and, having located a piece of music, download it to his or her own computer for present and future enjoyment. This was facilitated by what is known as MP3 technology which compresses files and enables them to be downloaded rapidly, particularly if the user has a high-speed Internet connection. This proved extremely popular, particularly with young people: it made an enormous amount of music, the complete holdings on the computers of all the users, including rare or discontinued recordings, available at no cost to the user, and with no significant loss of quality in the recordings. Over nine thousand million downloads are said to have been made via Napster in the year 2000. There are many different MP3 players on the market to which the music can be transferred. Alternatively, with the aid of a writeable CD-ROM drive, which plugs into the computer, it is possible to make your own CD of the downloaded music.

Not surprisingly, the recording companies were seriously worried, even though Napster's defenders claimed that, having been able to 'sample' a recording, the user would be more inclined to go out and buy a legitimate copy; a specious argument, one would think. Alternatively, these believers in the high moral standards of music fans suggested that a recording taken would be one which the user already owned but wanted available in a more convenient format, perhaps a composite album of the user's favourite pieces. A group of more than a dozen companies, led by A & M Records Inc., brought an action against Napster. It was, of course, the fact that Napster's involvement was limited to provision of its server and system and only made possible the swapping of recordings between users, 'peer to peer' (P2P) as it was called: Napster was not downloading the music itself. This made it different from the case of another US company, MP3.com, which launched a service in January 2000 called MyMP3.com, making copies of 80 000 compact discs and storing them on its own computers for downloading via the Internet. Whilst most of the music companies whose works had been taken by MP3.com settled for appropriate royalties, the largest of all, Universal Music Group, secured a federal court ruling of copyright infringement.

In the Napster case the music companies brought their action on the grounds of 'contributory infringement' and 'vicarious infringement'. (It would seem that Napster's actions could be caught, if in the UK, by s. 24 of the CDPA, secondary infringement:

> Copyright in a work is infringed by a person who, without the licence of the copyright owner-
> (a) makes …
> (c) possesses in the course of a business …
> an article specifically designed or adapted for making copies of that work, knowing or having reason to believe that it is to be used to make infringing copies.

What happened in the Napster case was that the District Court of the Northern District of California issued a preliminary injunction, having found that the record companies were likely to be able to prove Napster's contributory and vicarious liability for the direct copyright infringement by its users. Napster appealed to the Court of Appeals of the Ninth Circuit which agreed with the lower court but said that the injunction was too broad as it stood, and remitted the case to the District Court. In the end, or at least in March 2001, Napster capitulated, with an offer of a US$ 1000 million (£700 million) royalties over five years (which was rejected by the big music companies), and acceptance of a court order to block its users from sharing copyright material within three days of receiving lists of the music in question from the companies. Furthermore, Napster entered negotiations with the eCommerce unit of Bertelsmann, the German media group, to form a legitimate service with non-copyright music which is available to Napster added to Bertelsmann's own catalogue.

Yahoo!

Yahoo! (the exclamation mark is part of the name) is a US-based Internet service provider. The case involved online auctions of Nazi memorabilia on Yahoo!'s web site. In May 2000 the International League Against Racism and Anti-Semitism (LICRA), the Union of French Jewish Students (UEJF) and a third anti-racist organization, brought an action against Yahoo!, arguing that the inclusion of Nazi material breached French law which bans the sale or exhibition of Nazi uniforms, insignia or emblems. The court in Paris ordered Yahoo! to block access in France to the offending pages. The practicalities were examined by a commission of three experts, one French, one British and one American, who proposed a filter which would identify keywords and the nationality of the surfer, which would not be perfect but would enforce the ban as regards some 70 to 90 per cent of those seeking to evade it, and the court confirmed its original order. Yahoo! protested but in a partial capitulation agreed to block the sites, because of its 'overall concern about violence and hatred' (*Jewish Chronicle*, 5 January 2001), whilst seeking a US court decision that the judgment was not enforceable in the USA, and reserving a decision whether to appeal in France. The case has aroused debate, although there have already been less publicized decisions to rather similar effect in Germany and Australia. On the one hand it is said that a state has the right to enforce its laws within its boundaries, on the other that to act thus with regard to a foreign entity exceeds its legitimate jurisdiction. In the debate a measure of, perhaps justifiable, French chauvinism over the insidious Americanization of French society may be detected on the one hand, and on the other a feeling that, while America may not rule the world, it can at least rule the Internet. Yahoo! was doing nothing wrong under US law.

COPYRIGHT

The Napster case indicates that copyright can exist in that mythical zone known as cyberspace. The first two practical difficulties involve deciding where it happened and who made it happen. In Napster it was fairly easy. Napster was based in the USA and it was clearly Napster which facilitated the infringement. The aggrieved music companies were also based there. The companies sued in the USA and the decision could be enforced by a court which was located in the USA. (Leaving aside the question of the jurisdiction of the different states of the USA, copyright, in any case, is now mainly a federal matter.) But other practicalities are the real problem. As mentioned previously, some years ago a small book by the author on an Indian religion was scanned into a computer in the USA and placed on the Internet. The book has little commercial value, it was written to inform adherents and enquirers about that religion and the infringer believed that he was doing a service by making it more widely available. However, suppose that were not the case, what could the author do? First, it would be necessary to locate the infringer, a reasonably easy task when a paper-based work is distributed through terrestrial channels, but not easy on the Internet. Suppose it were worth pursuing in the US courts and an order is obtained to remove it from the infringer's website. By that time it had circled the world many times, and probably been downloaded in a dozen different countries ... But it is tedious and unnecessary to go on. The law is clear (if you can decide which country's law applies) but the practical problems are immense.

The European Union struggled for three years with a draft Directive on copyright in the information society. A compromise deal in February 2001 allowed consumers to reproduce material they already own but not to sell copies or distribute them in large numbers. The Directive, among other provisions, requires adequate legal protection against circumvention of technological measures to protect copyright. (This was already provided by s. 296 of the CDPA, though perhaps not to the standard required by the Directive.)

DEFAMATION

Defamation on the Internet is horribly easy and can have serious consequences. Whilst copyright law is broadly the same in most countries, defamation law is not. It may be very difficult tracking down the person who actually placed a defamatory statement on the Internet. How far is it possible to bring an action against one of the intermediaries in the process of making the statement available on the net? A recent case, *Godfrey* v. *Demon Internet*, 1999, is reminiscent of the older case of *Byrne* v. *Deane*, 1937. In the latter case an anonymous defamatory statement was posted up in a golf club. The writer could not be traced but the club secretary was sued for allowing the notice to stay there. (See Chapter 9 for the details.) In *Godfrey* v. *Demon Internet* an obscene message purporting to come from the claimant was posted to a newsgroup site. It was accepted that this was defamatory of the claimant. The claimant had notified Demon, the Internet Service Provider (ISP), that this was a forgery and asked for it to be removed but the ISP did not comply. It was held that as Demon controlled the software for the transmission of the message, they were the publisher. Demon might have had a defence under s. 1(1)(c) of the Defamation Act 1996 if 'he [*scilicet* 'they' (Demon)] did not know, and had no reason to believe, that what he did caused or contributed to the publication of a defamatory statement.' However, the defence was clearly not open to the defendants in view of the notice given to them. It is unlikely that the last word has been said by the British courts on the question of the liability of intermediaries.

OBSCENITY AND CRIME

A British trial in February 2001 was the culmination of an international investigation of paedophile pornography on the Internet. Seven members of the 'Wonderland Club' who had exchanged pornographic pictures of the cruel sexual abuse of nearly 1300 children received prison sentences. The defendants were perhaps fortunate in one way, for the maximum sentence for possession and distribution of child pornography was raised on 11 January 2001 from three to 10 years when an amendment to the Protection of Children Act 1978 came into force, after their crimes were committed. (*The Times*, leading article, 14 February 2001.) This demonstrates another way in which control of the Internet is exercised by the law, by striking at the end user. Under the law of the UK, and of other countries, simple possession of an indecent image of a child is a crime. This provides a very powerful weapon in the struggle against 'child abuse' (an unfortunately vague term) which has in recent years taken over from homosexual practices as the 'sexual' behaviour most detested by society.

In cases of this nature the end user can often be easily identified and dealt with: prosecutions for downloading such images are commonplace. How about other areas of the criminal law? Can the end user of material to inflame racial hatred, or terrorist material, or illegal weapons or drugs, be tackled in the same way? Crime on the Internet is a slippery area. In Napster (though that was a civil, not a criminal, matter) the law struck at the facilitator, in Yahoo! at the perpetrator, in *Godfrey* (another civil case) at the ISP, in the pornography cases at the end user. The Internet is international, or perhaps supranational, but international enforcement faces the fact that there are probably few crimes which are regarded with the same seriousness and urgency in all, or most, countries.

REGULATION

> [The] distinction between applicability and enforceability is fundamental to the future development of Internet law. It is a comparatively easy task for a legislator to draft a law which applies to a particular activity undertaken via the Internet, but much more difficult to frame the law so that it is enforceable in practice. Reed (2000), 252.

In October 2000 the American Bar Association suggested the creation of a multinational 'global online standards commission'. The Internet will undoubtedly undergo more, and more effective, policing: whether it can ever, or should ever, be brought completely under control are open questions.

ELECTRONIC COMMERCE

E-commerce is somewhat outside the scope of this book but it is of such great, and growing, importance that one or two matters may be interesting enough to the reader to receive brief consideration in this chapter. What most people probably think of as electronic commerce involves commercial transactions carried out over an electronic network, from computer to computer, by business organizations and/or individuals. Thus the law of e-commerce is essentially one aspect of the law of the Internet. Commercial transactions involve primarily the law of contract. As already explained, a contract is formed, in English law, when one party makes an offer, the other accepts it, and the 'consideration' (on one side the price, on the other the goods or services to be supplied) is agreed. (It is presumed that both parties have the intention to form a legal relationship.) Many contracts are made face to face, for example the purchase of goods in a shop. Others are by correspondence on paper, or on the telephone. If questions of the parties' identity arise they are generally easy to solve: in a business-to-business (B2B) transaction the parties' identities and intentions are probably authenticated by official stationery and a written signature. When we enter the Internet, however, the problems of confirming identity and authenticity become much more challenging.

AUTHENTICATION AND ENCRYPTION

Electronic signatures can be produced by various biometric techniques, or even by scanning on screen an actual written signature. However, encryption techniques are widely used to send secure messages, not only contractual documents, over the Net and they provide a method of identifying the sender without doubt. The idea is simple; its operation is also simple given the appropriate software; but the actual construction by a highly skilled software engineer is formidably complicated. Single key encryption is really a very sophisticated electronic development from the manual codes used by armies in the Second World War. It involves the sender's applying the key, which is a fairly lengthy series of numbers, to the whole of the message, or perhaps only part of it to form the 'signature'. This encrypts the message in an unreadable form. The message is then sent. The recipient has a copy of the key and can decrypt the message with it and knows with certainty that only the holder of that key could have sent it. Of course both parties must have the key. The alternative is public key encryption. Here there are two different keys. The sender has a secret key. There is also a public key, also belonging to the sender (and probably identified as belonging to him by some independent certifying body). Anybody can use the public key to decrypt the message but it will do so only with messages encrypted by the sender's secret key, thus providing a guarantee of the identity of the message's sender. If the recipient wants to reply, the reply can be encrypted with the public key, and only the secret key can decrypt the message.

For centuries the law courts have had to grapple with problems of the authenticity of documents and the integrity of their contents. In medieval England authenticity and integrity were generally guaranteed by the attachment of the wax seal of the originator. Another method was the chirograph: two copies were made on a single sheet of parchment, the word *chirographum* was written between them and the two halves separated by a jagged line and taken by the two parties. If the two halves fitted together then authenticity was proved. On the Continent a public notary, granted his authority by the ruler, drew up (and still does) in formal (and longwinded) language certified copies of legal documents which were acceptable to the courts. Judges could examine such documents and accept them as proof of a claimant's case: the science of palaeography originated in the law courts, not in the historian's study.

Cryptography is the modern answer for the electronic world. Section 7(1) of the Electronic Communications Act 2000 reads like this

(1) In any legal proceedings–
(a) an electronic signature incorporated into or logically associated with a particular electronic communication or particular electronic data, and
(b) the certification by any person of such a signature,
    shall each be admissible in evidence in relation to any question as to the authenticity of the communication or data or as to the integrity of the communication or data.

The Act provides, in s. 1, for the Secretary of State to establish and maintain a register of approved providers of cryptography support services. Such services are defined in s. 6, essentially they involve facilitating the use of cryptographic techniques which ensure that communications can be accessed only by certain persons, and that their authenticity or integrity can be ascertained. In July 2000 in the USA the President signed the Electronic Signatures in Global and National Commerce Act with a swipe of a smart card holding his electronic signature. The Act makes an electronic signature legally binding. (It may be a little while before Her Majesty, in the UK, abandons the practice of approving a new Act of Parliament with the traditional 'La Reine le veult' in Anglo-Norman French!)

One matter which attracted much debate was whether legislation should require people to allow the government access to encryption keys. This was hard-fought and the government had to back down. Section 14 prohibits any Minister (and certain others) from imposing a requirement on any person to deposit a key for electronic data with another person (except the intended recipient of encrypted data). However, the Minister or other can require that arrangements must be made to ensure that information which must be kept under any enactment would not become inaccessible if the key is lost or becomes unusable.

HACKING

Hacking, that is to say, unauthorized access to computer files without causing damage or loss, was not illegal in the 1980s. This was decided by the House of Lords in *R. v. Gold and Schifreen*, 1988. Stephen Gold and Robert Schifreen obtained access to a British Telecoms computer by using passwords which they were not authorized to use. Ingenious arguments by the prosecution led to their conviction under the Forgery and Counterfeiting Act 1981. However, the Court of Appeal quashed the conviction, and this decision was upheld by the House of Lords. It would have been different if they had been proved to have caused actual damage. In *Cox v. Riley*, 1986, the defendant erased the program on the circuit card of a computer-operated saw and was convicted under the Criminal Damage Act 1971. The Mad Hacker, as Nicholas Whiteley, a teenager, called himself, caused £25 000 of damage when he broke into the computer systems of three universities. Unable to resist boasting about it, he also was convicted under the same Act and served a prison sentence (*R v. Whiteley*, 1991).

Following a Law Commission Report, *Criminal Law: Computer Misuse*, Cm 819, The Computer Misuse Act 1990 was enacted. Three offences are created by the Act. First, it is an offence to cause a computer to perform any function with intent to gain unauthorized access, knowing that it is unauthorized, s. 1. Secondly, it is an offence to commit the offence in s. 1 with intent to commit or facilitate a further serious offence, s. 2. Thirdly, it is an offence to do anything intentionally and knowingly to cause an unauthorized modification of a computer which will impair its operation, hinder access to any program or data, or impair the operation of the program or the reliability of the data, s. 3. Unauthorized access *per se*, under s. 1, is the least serious offence attracting up to six months imprisonment and a fine. The other two can carry up to five years imprisonment and a fine.

Whilst the Act is a valuable reminder to the hacker that his (the hacker is usually young and male) activities are not just harmless good fun but can have very serious consequences, there have been few convictions. The main difficulty, of course, is proof. Of its very nature hacking is a quiet and surreptitious crime, the hacker is often a 'loner' and, unless *in flagrante delicto*, he has a very good chance of evading capture.

DATA PROTECTION

(Note: 'data' is a plural noun, singular 'datum'.)

Information about individuals has always been held by government and private organizations, but the advent of the computer created a much greater threat to an individual's privacy, as well as a much greater likelihood that the individual will suffer detriment as a result of inaccuracy or disclosure of information. The operations of government and large-scale business have expanded into new and ever wider areas, causing concern about the possibility of misuse of the increasing amount of information held in files, and particularly computer files, not accessible to the people about whom the information is held. As a result, after long debate and various government reports, particularly those of the Younger Committee on Privacy (1972) and the Lindop Comittee on Data Protection (1978), the UK followed the example of several other countries and enacted the Data Protection Act 1984. Sweden was the first country to legislate in this field, in 1973, though the State of Hesse in West Germany had a data protection law as early as 1970. Other west European countries followed, France in 1978, Denmark, Luxembourg and the German Federal Republic (West Germany, before reunification) by 1980, and others have followed. A significant abstainer, however, was the USA. Impetus was given to the UK legislation by the probability that these countries would create legal barriers to the transfer of computer-held data to countries which did not have adequate data protection laws. This could have had serious repercussions in the UK where the processing, in one way or another, of electronic data transmitted from oversea has considerable commercial importance.

INTERNATIONAL

In the international field two bodies concerned themselves with data protection. The Organization for Economic Cooperation and Development (OECD) which brings together a number (29 in 2001) of the developed nations of the world, adopted non-mandatory guidelines on the protection of privacy and transborder flows of personal data in 1980. A more formal arrangement is the Data Protection Convention of the Council of Europe. The Council of Europe (not, of course, to be confused with the European Union) represented at that time the non-communist states of Europe, though its membership has now taken in a number of east European states, bringing the current total to 40. The Convention was opened for signature in 1981.

Unlike the OECD guidelines, the Council of Europe Convention is binding on those states which have signed and ratified it. The UK ratified in 1987 when the last provisions of the Data Protection Act 1984 had come into force. Both these international instruments seek to balance freedom of information and free flows of information with personal privacy. The provisions of the UK Data Protection Act 1984 closely followed the Convention. In 1995 the European Union passed the 'Directive on the protection of individuals with regard to the processing of personal data and on the free movement of such data', a somewhat cumbersome title for a document which starts off with a preamble beginning, as is usual in EU Directives, 'Whereas ...' and continues with no fewer than 72 preliminary paragraphs. Data protection varied considerably among the member states and the aim of the Directive was to harmonize the laws. (A further Directive of 1997 addressed the particular problems of privacy in relation to the telecommunications sector.) As the manner of implementation is left to individual states, many of the requirements are couched in general terms. The Directive applies not only to computer-held personal data but also to data which are processed other than by automatic means and which form part of a filing system, Art. 3. The data subject (individual whom the data concern) must give unambiguous consent to processing of personal data, unless certain important reasons for processing are present, Art. 7. Data on some sensitive matters are subject to special restrictions, Art. 8. There are provisions on confidentiality, security and access for the data subject. Article 25 forbids transfer of personal data for processing to countries which do not provide adequate protection. This has been a difficulty with the USA which relies on self-regulation. A 'safe harbor' (*sic*) agreement between the EU and the USA was negotiated in the year 2000, under which a list of companies and other organizations in the USA would pledge themselves to provide protection adequate to meet the EU demands. However, take-up by US companies was negligible in the first year, and the EU rules aroused strong hostility in the USA.

DATA PROTECTION ACT 1998

The Directive was brought into UK law by the Data Protection Act 1998 which came into force on 1 March 2000. Although the 1984 Act is totally repealed by the new Act, the latter follows the form, and much of the content, of the Data Protection Act 1984. Under the 1998 Act the Data Protection Registrar, who had wide responsibilities for the implementation and enforcement of the previous Act, acquired the grander title of Data Protection Commissioner. From 30 January 2001 the incumbent took on responsibility additionally for freedom of information and is now known as the Information Commissioner. There are a few other changes in the designation of persons concerned with personal data. A 'data controller' is a person who is in control of the data, commonly within an organization of one sort or another: a data controller determines the purposes for which data are processed. In the old Act a data controller was called a 'data user'. Often a company or other body will outsource its data processing, have it done by an outside company or person: that person is now known as a data processor (formerly this was a 'computer bureau'). One designation is unchanged, a 'data subject' is an individual who is the subject of personal data, the person for whose benefit the law was passed. Incidentally, some people have difficulty in understanding the difference between data and information. Data are the actual words, figures or whatever, which you have in your record; information is the knowledge which you can derive from them.

Manual data

The Data Protection Act 1998 is concerned with personal data, which means data which relate to a living individual who is identifiable from those data (or from those data and other information in, or likely to come into, the data controller's possession), s. 1. There is also a category of 'sensitive personal data' which relate to the data subject's ethnic origin, political opinions, religious or similar beliefs, trade union membership, physical or mental health, sex life, or criminal record. The 1984 Act was concerned only with data held on computer: there is an important change in the new Act, it applies also to data in a 'relevant filing system'. This is explained, not very clearly, in s. 1(1) as a set of information structured by reference to individuals or to criteria relating to individuals so that information relating to specific individuals is readily accessible. This seems to mean that if your filing cabinet or card index is neatly arranged by names, or trade or some such category, then it is within the Act: if it is just an unsorted lot of papers dumped in a drawer, then you are exempt. A booklet from the Data Protection Registrar (now Commissioner), comments,

> It is not wholly clear how this definition translates in practical terms in all conceivable situations. The Commissioner can only give general guidance: the final decision in cases of dispute is a question for the Courts. Whether or not manual information falls within this definition will be a matter of fact in each case. *The Data Protection Act 1998: An Introduction.* 1998. pp.3–4.

There was a lot of argument as to whether manual data should be included. The French, whose law is much more concerned with privacy than ours, included manual data in their own data protection law a long time ago.

Data Protection Principles

The Act hinges on the data protection principles set out in Schedule 1: Section 4(4) of the Act says,

> Subject to section 27(1) [which introduces exemptions], it shall be the duty of a data controller to comply with the data protection principles in relation to all personal data with respect to which he is the data controller.

There are eight principles, changed to a small extent from the data protection principles in the 1984 Act. Personal data shall be

1. processed fairly and lawfully, and not unless the data subject has consented, or it is necessary for a contract, a legal obligation on the controller, the vital interests of the subject, the administration of justice, or the legitimate interests of the controller or the person to whom data are disclosed;
2. obtained only for specified lawful purposes and shall not be processed in a manner incompatible with those purposes;
3. adequate, relevant and not excessive;
4. accurate and kept up-to date;
5. not kept longer than necessary;
6. processed in accordance with the rights of data subjects under the Act.
7. Measures shall be taken to prevent unauthorized or unlawful processing, or accidental loss, destruction or damage;
8. Personal data shall not be transferred to a country outside the European Economic Area (the European Union states plus Norway, Iceland and Liechtenstein) unless that country ensures adequate protection.

Rights of the data subject

The rights of the data subject are given in some detail in ss. 7 to 14. These rights can be enforced in the High Court or County Court. They are, the right to be informed by a data controller if any data on the data subject are held, and if so to receive the data (a fee may be charged), s. 7; the right to prevent processing which is likely to cause damage or distress, s. 10; the right to prevent processing for the purpose of direct marketing, s. 11; the right to stop automated decision-taking on matters which significantly affect the data subject, s. 12; the right to have inaccurate or incomplete data corrected, or the illicit holding of exempt data stopped, s. 12A.

Exemptions

A number of exemptions are given where certain provisions of the Act do not apply. These exempt the data controller from complying with the non-disclosure provisions, or from subject access, depending on the case. Areas in which exemptions apply in certain situations are national security, s. 28; crime and taxation, s. 29; health, education and social work, s. 30; regulation of financial malpractice, charities and health and safety at work, s. 31. There are also exemptions in certain circumstances from a number of the requirements of the Act when data processing takes place for the special purposes of journalism, literature or art, s. 32. Needless to say, personal data processed by an individual for family or household affairs are exempt from the important parts of the Act, s. 36. A further group of miscellaneous exemptions appears in Schedule 7. Particularly important, as it was a major concern of those who opposed the inclusion of manual data, is the exemption for a confidential education or job reference, para. 1 of the Schedule.

Administration and enforcement

The Data Protection Commissioner, renamed from 30 January 2001 as the Information Commissioner, holds a prestigious office and is appointed by the Queen by Letters Patent (an administrative document under the Great Seal, used nowadays only for certain important matters of state). The Information Tribunal (formerly Data Protection Tribunal) has a Chairman and Deputy Chairmen who are senior lawyers appointed by the Lord Chancellor, with other members to represent the interests of data subjects and data controllers. The Commissioner has the general duty to promote good practice and conformity with the Act by data controllers and to disseminate information, and is the authority in the UK for the purposes of the Council of Europe Convention and the EU Directive. The Commissioner maintains the register (see below) and has extensive duties of assessment of complaints and enforcement: appeals are to the Information Tribunal. Failure to comply with an enforcement notice is an offence. The 1984 Act required registration by any data user (now called data controller), which involved submitting a complicated form. Information as to who held data was placed on a register which was available for public reference. The process is now called notification and is dealt with in ss. 16 to 26. It is an offence to process personal data without registering, ss. 17 and 21. It is to be hoped that the new system will be a little simpler. The new register, like the old, is available for anyone to find out if someone is holding personal data. So, if you want to know if Company X may have data on you, you can, as a first stage, consult the register to check if Company X has notified that it holds personal data, and to obtain its address and other particulars. You can then ask the company in writing if they hold data on you personally and require them to provide the data. A fee (subject to a maximum) may be charged by the company. A typical fee would be £10 but a big organization, like a university, may have more registrations than one for different branches of its operations. (Four £10 fees to cover all four registrations by a university might cynically be calculated to deter the whole student body from flooding the university administration with applications to see their files.)

FREEDOM OF INFORMATION

Governments are by nature secretive, often with good reason. The Official Secrets Acts impose criminal sanctions on anyone who reveals official secrets, and are discussed in Chapter 9. What we are concerned with here is 'open government' and the right of the citizen, in effect, to penetrate the files of government departments and other public bodies and obtain the information which is stored there. Most, probably, of the information in question is not held as electronic data, though doubtless it will increasingly be so held. However, this chapter is the most appropriate place to give a summary of the Freedom of Information Act. The Act is wordy and complex. However, the key to its provisions may be found in s. 1(1).

> 1. General right of access to information held by public authorities.
>   (1) Any person making a request for information to a public authority is entitled–
>   (a) to be informed in writing by the public authority whether it holds information of the description specified in the request, and
>   (b) if that is the case, to have that information communicated to him.

A 'public authority' means, basically, a body appearing in the list in Schedule 1 (and it is a very long list), or a publicly-owned company (one owned by the Crown or by, with certain omissions, a public authority). Not surprisingly there is a lengthy list in Part II of the Act of exempt information ranging from information likely to prejudice defence, s. 25, or law enforcement, s. 30, to the honours list, s. 36. The Data Protection Commissioner's title is changed to Information Commissioner, and the functions of that office correspondingly widened to promote the observance of the Act. The Commissioner also has powers to make a decision (with a right of appeal by the complainant or the authority to the Information Tribunal) on a complaint that a public authority has failed in its duty and, if so, to issue an enforcement notice. Failure to obey an enforcement notice has the ultimate sanction of a court finding of contempt of court. Fees may be charged for the provision of information, and there are provisions to restrain vexatious applications or applications as part of a campaign by a number of persons.

PROTECTION OF SOFTWARE

COPYRIGHT AND *SUI GENERIS* PROTECTION

In the early 1980s, when a new copyright law to replace the 30-year old Copyright Act of 1956 was coming under consideration, the protection of computer programs from infringement was a grey area. In a couple of court cases the judge was prepared to assume that they were protected by copyright but these were only interlocutory (interim) matters: there was no fully-argued case on the issue. It was clear that programs had to be brought unambiguously into the intellectual property system, but there was debate as to the most appropriate form of protection. There were two alternatives, either to treat a program as a literary work, with the full protection of copyright, or to apply *sui generis* protection specific to programs. Strong arguments were advanced for each solution. This was, in fact, a worldwide problem: in Japan it pitted two powerful government ministries against one another, each championing one solution. In the UK a working party of the Society for Computers and Law came down on the side of *sui generis* protection. It was argued that the useful life of a piece of software was so short that it was unnecessary to grant it copyright for 50 years or more, by the end of which time it would have been completely out of date for many years. Moreover, as one piece of software is almost always developed from earlier work, with any programmer standing on the shoulders of predecessors, copyright could tie up use of a particular line of development for an inordinate time. The advocates of protection by copyright were able to put forward, among other arguments, that there already was a fully-fledged, worldwide system of copyright, to which computer software could be added with no great difficulty. In the event, copyright won the day, and a short statute of only four sections, the Copyright (Computer Software) Amendment Act 1985, laid down that the Copyright Act 1956, then current, shall apply to a computer program as it does to a literary work. Many, perhaps most, countries, including Japan, adopted the same solution, and there was a wave of amending legislation around that time. The French had some difficulty fitting the idea of *le logiciel* (program) into the concept of an *oeuvre de l'esprit* and the Law of 3 July 1985 which amended the Law of 11 March 1957 (the main statute on author's right) established a somewhat different regime for programs, with a much more limited period of protection of 25 years. (The term of protection is now the same as for other works.) In Germany the Bundesgerichtshof (BGH), the highest appeal court, recognized computer programs as literary works or illustrations of a scientific or technical nature, *Inkasso Programm*, 1985. An Amendment in 1985 added computer programs to the list of protected works in the 1965 copyright law.

When the CDPA was passed in the UK in 1988 computer programs were included within the definition of literary works in s. 3(1)(a). This was expanded in 1992 by adding the preparatory design material for a computer program, as subsection (1)(c). So the position is that computer software is treated just like a literary work, and further has protection in other countries under the international conventions (subject to the law of the country concerned).

The real problems which emerged were, and still are, concerned not so much with straightforward copying of a computer program as with improvements or changes made by another programmer. It can be very difficult to decide whether one program is an original work or whether it is a slightly changed, but substantially infringing, copy of the original. The role of the expert witness, who can unravel the complexities for the guidance of the court, can be very important in software infringement cases. Quite often a program may look quite different from another when the source code is examined, yet it may be simply a disguised copy of the other. The courts in the USA were early faced with problems of software infringement. One case was *SAS Institute* v. *S & H Computer Systems*, 1983. The court made it clear that the basic idea is not protectable: it is, of course, axiomatic that there is no copyright in ideas. The court went on to look at certain key elements in the alleged copy and found that these had been taken from the original, and that there was infringement. The US courts have been prepared to consider the 'look and feel' of the program, or the 'structure, sequence and organization', in order to assess whether there has been copying, for example *Whelan Associates* v. *Jaslow Dental Laboratory*, 1987. (This interesting case, which involved software for running a dental laboratory, is reported in the Fleet Street Reports, making it available to those who do not have access to the US reports.) In the UK the American approach was first followed in *MS Associates* v. *Power*, 1988, and then in *John Richardson* v. *Flanders*, 1993. However, in *Ibcos Computers* v. *Barclays Mercantile Highland Finance*, 1994, Jacob J criticized the reliance on American precedents in British courts, given the differences in copyright law in the two countries, and paid attention to the degree of over-borrowing of the skill and labour of the original programmer.

MORAL RIGHTS

There was some controversy over whether moral rights should apply to computer software. There would seem to be, in theory, no reason why the author of a program should not be given the rights to be acknowledged as author of the work and to object to derogatory treatment. These are provided for, in relation to literary and other works, in ss. 77 and 80 of the CDPA. However, computer programs and computer-generated works are specifically excluded, ss. 79 and 81. The third moral right, not to have a work falsely attributed to oneself, does apply, s. 84. In fact, an action for passing off would probably succeed in this case.

THE SOFTWARE DIRECTIVE

Harmonization of legal protection of computer software across the European Union has been achieved by Directive 91/250 on computer programs. Although a number of member states of the European Community, including the UK, had enacted legislation on this issue, the situation varied from country to country, and there was a lot of hard discussion and bargaining before agreement was reached. The Directive, first of all, required states to protect programs by copyright as literary works within the meaning of the Berne Convention, Art. 1(1). Secondly, protection applies to the expression, in any form, of the program, not to ideas or principles, 1(2), and a program will be protected only if it is original in the sense that it is the author's own intellectual creation, 1(3). The Directive was implemented in UK law by the Copyright (Computer Programs) Regulations, SI 1992/3233, which introduced certain essential amendments to the CDPA 1988. Section 50A provides that it is not infringement for a lawful user to make a back-up copy of a program, and any term or condition in an agreement to restrict this right is void, s. 296A. Next, it is not fair dealing to convert a program from a low-level language into a version expressed in a higher level language or incidentally to copy it in the course of doing so, s. 29(4). However, s. 50B does allow such conversion and copying (decompiling the program) if it is done solely to obtain information to create an independent program which can be operated with the decompiled program or another program, and subject to certain restrictive conditions in subsection (3). Again, any agreement to restrict the right is void under s. 296A. In addition, s. 50C allows copying or adaptation by a lawful user if it is necessary for lawful use, and particularly for correcting errors in the program, provided that there is no agreement forbidding it.

PATENTABILITY OF PROGRAMS

Copyright provides a very long period of protection for computer software. However, it does not provide a monopoly right and it is by no means impossible for two programmers working quite independently to come up with the same, or very closely similar, programs. Each would, of course, have copyright in his or her own version, even if it is virtually the same as the other. The situation is very close to that in the old case of *Bailey* v. *Taylor*, 1830, mentioned in Chapter 2. A patent, on the other hand, has a limited duration of 20 years but does give a complete monopoly to the first person to file an application. However, in s. 1(2) of the Patents Act 1977, derived from the European Patent Convention (not a European Community instrument), Art. 52 specifically excludes a computer program 'as such' from patentability. Those words 'as such' are uncertain enough to leave a loophole and there have been various attempts to exploit it and gain the advantage of monopoly rights.

Essentially, in order to obtain patent protection for a computer program it is necessary to show that the program must produce a new technical effect. This is seen in the 1985 guidelines of the European Patent Office (EPO). *Vicom's Application*, 1987, is the leading EPO case. It concerned digital enhancement of images, and the patent was granted because the application was held to be for the invention which the program was used to perform, that is, a technical effect, indeed an industrial application, not for the program as such. In the UK *Merrill Lynch's Application*, 1988, failed in the Court of Appeal. The applicants sought a patent for a system for automated trading in stocks and shares. The only technical result was simply a method of doing business, and that is in itself excluded from patentability by s. 1(2) of the 1977 Act. A different attempt to circumvent the restriction is seen in *Gale's Application*, 1991. This case also went to the Court of Appeal. The applicant's invention was a new method of calculating square roots. This clearly is not patentable as such, but he hoped that by embodying it in the ROM (Read Only Memory) of a computer he bypassed the restriction. The Court could not accept a distinction between a program on a disk and one on ROM, and rejected his application.

OTHER PROTECTION

It should be remembered that any written documentation for a computer program is separately covered by copyright as a literary work. If it is simply a pirated version of a piece of commercially available software, the manual will probably have been photocopied by the pirate and supplied with the fake program. It may well be easier to prove infringement of the documentation than of the actual program. Moreover, the existence of a pirated manual would probably be evidence that the accompanying program is a pirated copy. Obtaining evidence for copyright infringement has been greatly helped by the development of the Anton Piller (search order, explained in Chapter 1). A search order may well include the requirement that the prospective defendant should display and print out documents held in computer readable form. If the program or its packaging bears a registered trade mark which has been falsely applied by the pirate the draconian penalties of s. 92 of the Trade Marks Act 1994 could lead to up to 10 years imprisonment.

PROTECTION OF DATABASES: THE 1997 LAW

When we use the word database we think automatically of data held in the memory of a computer. Indeed the word is a modern coinage, coeval with the rise of electronic data processing. However, s. 3A of the CDPA, added in 1997, defines a database as a collection of independent works, data or other material which are individually accessible by electronic or other means. So data which are held, for example, on paper in a filing cabinet constitute a database (provided that they are arranged in a systematic or methodical way, as s. 3A also requires). That is why the new law of 1997 on the protection of databases has been dealt with in Chapter 2, with only this short mention here.

SEMICONDUCTORS

The microchip, or semiconductor, is at the heart of a vast range of electronic devices. A semiconductor chip is a very small item but is built up of a number of layers each of which contains complicated circuits to operate programs. The design of these chips is a highly skilled and very expensive matter which may involve thousands of hours of work but, like so many other forms of intellectual property, the design can be copied and identical chips produced at relatively low cost. The technique for copying involves photographing the several layers through the translucent material by very precise adjustment of the focus of a special camera, a difficult but, given the right equipment, reasonably straightforward operation. Pirating semiconductor chips is a lucrative industry in some parts of the world.

When the chip industry reached the stage of mass production, concern was expressed by manufacturers about illicit copying. Various suggestions were canvassed regarding legal protection. A patent could be the answer where the chip was of totally novel design, but this was not the usual position. Registered design protection covered aesthetic qualities only. Copyright, probably in the original drawings for each layer, was the last possibility but also had some disadvantages. In the end it was decided to introduce *sui generis* protection. The USA led the way with the Semiconductor Chip Act 1984 (popularly known as the Chip Act, which does not sound so funny in the USA where potato chips are known as 'French fries'). Japan also got in early. The European Community produced a Directive in response to US threats of denial of protection to foreign manufacturers whose countries did not provide reciprocal protection. The UK complied with the Directive and then, when the CDPA, Part III, had introduced (unregistered) Design Right (separate, of course, from the existing Registered Design Right) in 1988, the Design Right (Semiconductor Topographies) Regulations 1989, SI 1989/1100, more or less assimilated chip protection to Design Right. To make sense of the new provisions it is necessary to read Part III alongside the Regulations, as the modifications to Design Right where it concerns semiconductors have not been actually incorporated into the CDPA. The designer is the first owner of Design Right in a semiconductor topography unless it is commissioned or produced by an employee in the course of employment, when it belongs to the commissioner or employer (subject to agreement to the contrary). The right lasts for 10 years from the time when the semiconductor chip is first made available for sale or hire, or 15 years from when it was first designed or made (time running as usual from the end of the year). Private non-commercial reproduction is permitted. One important provision is that it is not infringement to reproduce the design for the purpose of analysing or evaluating it, or analysing, evaluating or teaching the concepts, processes, systems or techniques embodied in it; or as a result to create another original semiconductor topography. This is known as reverse engineering.

6 Patents and other industrial property

This book is concerned with the law relating to information in its widest sense, that is to say relating to the material which is handled by the information specialist, and naturally the law of copyright is of prime concern. However, in the wider world an equally important area of intellectual property is that of patents. (Patent should be pronounced with a short 'a' as in Pat, not pate.) Patents in general, and patent law, are relevant to the work of the information specialist, and indeed to very many people whose work involves using or handling business or scientific or technical information. A patent can be an extremely valuable piece of property and owners of patent rights fight hard to prevent anyone else from muscling in on those rights. But patents have a further value which is of great importance. Every country keeps records of patents applied for, and granted, and these records are a very important source of information for scientists, for inventors, and for companies whose business lies, directly or indirectly, in the development of new products, whether pharmaceutical drugs, machinery, household products, electronic inventions, or indeed virtually anything where scientific or technical innovation can turn a profit. Patent records can alert the scientist or inventor to the latest developments in their field, can confirm, or otherwise, that an invention really has not been thought of before, and for a business can show what competitors are doing, and point the way to further advances. In one of its guidance leaflets the Patent Office says 'If you don't access patent documentation, you are cutting yourself off from THE WORLD'S RICHEST STORE OF TECHNICAL INFORMATION'.

The term 'intellectual property' covers a wide field, but patents, with some other matters, are often described as 'industrial property' (though industrial property sometimes is loosely defined to include copyright as well). Trade marks, trade secrets and industrial designs are the other types of industrial property. Trade secrets fit in well with other confidential information so they will be discussed in Chapter 9; industrial designs have already been dealt with in Chapter 4 as they relate to the work of the artist. Most of this chapter will be concerned with patents but trade marks do deserve a mention, as does the protective regime for plant varieties, if only for the sake of interest and completeness.

PATENTS

'Letters patent' meant originally an open ('patent') letter from the Crown (being different from 'letters close' which were closed up, sealed and addressed to a particular individual). This was one of the commonest forms of government documents used in the Middle Ages for conveying administrative instructions, granting rights and privileges, and so on, where the matter in question was of public, rather than purely individual, concern. Letters patent were written in formal language, formerly in Latin of course, were addressed with some such formula as *Omnibus ad quos presentes littere pervenerint* ..., 'To all to whom these present letters shall come ...', and were authenticated by the attachment of the sovereign's Great Seal. They are still used to a limited extent for certain important formal acts of state. From early times letters patent were used to confirm the grant of trade or industrial monopolies to a favoured person, and it was natural that, as the practice developed of allowing an inventor a head start in the exploitation of his invention by forbidding others to make use of it, the inventor's privilege should be confirmed by the issue of letters patent. This continued right up to 1978 (though the Great Seal had been replaced by the less impressive seal of the Patent Office in the late nineteenth century), but now a laconic certificate that the patent has been granted is all that the patentee (the person to whom the patent is granted) gets.

The grant of a commercial monopoly was, particularly in the sixteenth century, a source of income for the crown, for it would not, of course, be granted gratis unless to someone whom the sovereign wished to reward for services rendered or simply for friendship. Abuse of the system led to the Statute of Monopolies of 1623 forbidding the grant of monopolies unless authorized by parliament, with the exception of a 14-year grant to an inventor to exploit a new invention. This was the genesis of the patent system as we know it today. The aim was, as it still is, to encourage invention by giving the inventor a clear run, now of 20 years, to profit without competition. Some see this as a social contract whereby society's encouragement in the early years is balanced by free use of the invention after the patent expires.

There are considerable differences between copyright and patents. Copyright in the UK (and in nearly all countries) is automatic; a patent is granted only after application and a lengthy official process. Copyright lasts, with only a few exceptions, until 70 years after the author's death, whilst a patent lasts for 20 years only. Copyright is not infringed by anyone who produces a similar work quite independently; a patent gives a complete monopoly in the exploitation of the invention concerned.

The principal statute is the Patents Act 1977 which came into force on 1 June 1978, replacing the Patents Act 1949. Some provisions of the 1949 Act continued to apply to patents granted before June 1978 but these are now of historical interest only. Some amendments to the 1977 Act were made by the Patents, Designs and Trade Marks Act 1986 and quite a lot more by Part VI, ss. 287–295, of the Copyright, Designs and Patents Act 1988. Larger textbooks will include the amended text of the Act as an appendix. There is a very large, and growing, literature on patents: *Terrell on the Law of Patents*, the standard practitioners' handbook, was first published in 1884 and has now reached its 15th edition. Reports of important cases are given in the Reports of Patent Cases and the Fleet Street Reports, and not infrequently appear in the general series of law reports as well as in relevant journals.

Patents are administered by the Patent Office in Newport, South Wales, under the Comptroller-General of Patents, Designs and Trade Marks, supported by a large staff. (Note the distinctive spelling of Comptroller.) Lawsuits on patents are heard in the Patents Court in the Chancery Division of the High Court, or in the Patents County Court. (Note that it is *Patent* Office, but *Patents* Court.) Section 287 of the Copyright, Designs and Patents Act 1988 empowers the Lord Chancellor to designate any County Court as a patents county court with jurisdiction over patents and designs. Judges with special knowledge of intellectual property are assigned to these courts. Patents Court business is heard under the multi-track procedure. The Comptroller-General (or a senior officer of the Patent Office) hears many cases on patent matters in what are in effect judicial hearings: these are quite often reported in the Reports of Patents Cases. Appeal lies from a Patent Office decision to the Patents Court.

CRITERIA FOR PATENTABILITY

A patent is granted for an 'invention'. Whilst everyone knows what an invention is, it is not easy to define. The 1977 Act sidesteps this difficulty by laying down in s. 1(1) the conditions which the (undefined) invention must satisfy, and then in s. 1(2) listing certain things which (amongst others) are not to be regarded as inventions. To qualify for a patent an invention (a) must be new, (b) must involve an inventive step, and (c) it must be capable of industrial application.

The requirement that an invention be new means that it does not form part of the 'state of the art', which includes all matter which has been available to the public before the date on which the patent application is received at the Patent Office. Although a search is made by the Patent Office before a patent is granted it is impossible to be sure that this covers every possible source where the invention might have been anticipated. Hence a defence to an action for infringement not infrequently takes the line that the invention was not really new, so the patent should not have been granted in the first place.

This defence succeeded in *Windsurfing* v. *Tabur Marine*, 1985. The plaintiff's surfboard with a sail had been anticipated a number of years earlier by a twelve-year-old boy who had made a crude sort of sailboard which he had sailed on summer weekends. However, the defendant in another case was not able to convince the court that the well-known Workmate workbench lacked novelty simply because the vice arrangement on it bore some resemblance to an old bookbinder's press, *Hickman* v. *Andrews*, 1983. The inventor does have to be very careful that no information about the invention gets out before the 'priority date' when the Patent Office has received the patent application, for any prior communication to the public will be enough to defeat the claim that the invention is new. The exceptions to this are very limited indeed. It may happen that the inventor does not realize the commercial possibilities of the invention, or is simply ignorant of the law and makes it public in a scientific journal or lecture before applying for a patent. This is quite enough to defeat the claim to novelty. If two or more people, or companies, are working along the same lines, the first to file an application for a patent gets the priority. This 'first to file' system is operated in most countries and has the merit of allocating indisputable priority in a simple way. Some countries, notably the USA, prefer a 'first to invent' system which depends on proving which of two or more inventors actually invented the invention first.

To acquire a patent an invention must be, first, new and, secondly, it must involve an 'inventive step'. This means that the invention would not be obvious to a person skilled in that particular field. If it would be obvious to a skilled technician familiar with the relevant literature but unimaginative and lacking in inventive capacity, then no inventive step is involved. Thus, there was no inventive step in bonding together a reflective sheet and a transparent one for car number plates, to take a straightforward example, *Jamesigns' Application*, 1983. In the *Windsurfing* case Lord Justice Oliver used the following analysis: first, identify the inventive concept in the patent; secondly, decide what the unimaginative skilled technician would have known at the relevant date; thirdly, decide what differences exist between the invention and what was already known; fourthly, decide whether the differences would have been obvious to that technician or whether they really were an invention.

Thirdly, a patentable invention must be capable of industrial application, in other words it can be made or used in industry (including agriculture). Patents are meant to protect practical inventions, not theories. This is brought out in the list in s. 1(2) of things which cannot be patented as such. These include a discovery, scientific theory or mathematical method, the rules or method for performing a mental act, playing a game or doing business. The actual presentation of information is excluded and so, naturally, are aesthetic creations or other things of the kinds covered by copyright. Computer programs are specifically excluded (they are, of course, protected by copyright): this provision has given rise to a lot of difficulties.

110

The words 'as such' in s. 1(2) means that the apparatus for, say, playing a game could be patentable (but not the method), and a computer programmed to perform a particular task might be patentable though the actual program is not, *Merrill Lynch's Application*, 1988. (Quite a lot of patent (and trade mark) cases involve an appeal to the court against a refusal by the Patent Office of an application for a patent (or trade mark): the case will generally be headed '*So-and-so's Application*' in the law report.) This is still a rather uncertain area: substantial numbers of what are certainly software patents are granted by the European Patent Office and in the USA it is possible to patent computer software. Also excluded is a method of treatment or diagnosis for humans or animals, s. 4(2). This certainly does not mean that a new drug cannot be patented: the pharmaceutical companies depend very heavily on patent protection to earn a return on their vast research investment. A known drug put to a new use can also be protected. So, for example, a drug or machine to treat lumbago can be patented, but not a method of massage or manipulation for the same purpose. Plant and animal varieties, or biological processes for producing them, are not patentable, but microbiological processes are patentable. Plant varieties have their own legislation, the Plant Varieties and Seeds Act 1964.

Needless to say, a patent will not be granted for anything which might encourage offensive, immoral or anti-social behaviour. It is difficult to imagine what sort of thing an inventor might try to patent which would be caught by this provision. There are a couple of old cases (when the law was differently worded) in which the question arose whether certain coin-in-the slot machines were excluded as gambling machines. In addition, if an application for a patent contains anything which the Patent Office considers may prejudice the defence of the realm or public safety it may prohibit or restrict publication or communication.

HOW A PATENT IS OBTAINED

The first thing an inventor has to think of when considering protection for an invention is whether it is desirable at all to go for a patent. It is going to cost quite a lot of money, taking into account the Patent Office fees, professional fees of a patent agent or other advisers, the expenses of preparing the application and so on, it is going to run into thousands of pounds. The fees of the Patent Office are reasonably modest, currently (January 2001) £200 for search and examination. There is also an annual renewal fee after four years to keep the patent alive, starting at £50 and rising each year to £400 for the final (twentieth) year. The professional fees of a highly-skilled patent agent will add considerably to this. If the inventor is more ambitious and wants protection in the major industrial countries the cost is multiplied. One saving consideration is that the inventor can drop out at an early stage if it becomes clear that the invention is not going to be a commercial success after all. If the decision is to go for a patent all the details will have to be revealed to the public, with the risk that someone else will take the idea, follow it up, improve on it sufficiently to escape the charge of infringement and take the market away from its originator. Other companies, scientists and engineers will be watching patent applications like hawks to see what their competitors are doing and how they can profit from that knowledge. However, the inventor may decide to keep it secret in which case there is the risk that somebody else has been working along the same lines and decides to apply for a patent. The other possibility is to make the invention public and rely on a headstart to keep in front of competitors.

It is possible for an individual to make an application for a patent without expert help. The Patent Office publishes useful guidance but does warn that obtaining a commercially useful patent requires a high level of expertise, and advises that anyone who is not thoroughly experienced in patent matters should employ a patent agent. Registered patent agents are normally science or technology graduates who have passed the examinations of the Chartered Institute of Patent Agents and fulfilled requirements of on-the-job training. Formerly they had a monopoly but this was abolished by the Copyright Designs and Patents Act 1988. Many patent agents are in private practice, sometimes combining the work with that of trade mark agents, and also dealing with registered designs, but large industrial companies employ their own in-house experts. Professional assistance will include searches of the relevant scientific and technical literature and patents granted or pending to determine (as far as possible) if the inventor really has come up with something new, as well as advice on the commercial possibilities and on whether to apply for a patent or not. The patent agent will prepare the application, see it through all stages to grant, and after grant monitor possible infringements and advise on the necessary action.

A great deal of thought and care must be given to the original application. It is not possible to put in a vague description and fill in the details later. A full description ('specification') of the invention, with drawings if necessary, prepared in the standard manner as laid down by the Patent Office, must be provided. The applicant must state the claims defining the distinctive features which make the subject a new invention: the claims must be carefully drafted to ensure that the novel features are fully covered. A short abstract summarizing the specification is also necessary. As soon as the application (with the necessary form) is received at the Patent Office it will have a filing date. The date of filing an application for a patent is described as the priority date: there is still a long way to go but the inventor now has priority over anybody else who tries to patent the same thing.

The next stage is the preliminary examination and search, which must be applied for (on the appropriate form with a fee) within 12 months: if you are dilatory a one-month extension will cost you another £135. The application will be examined by Patent Office officials who will check that it complies with the rules and will send the applicant a report on a search of prior patents and other sources for anything which could be relevant to the novelty or obviousness of the invention. The Patent Office search is no guarantee that every possibility has been explored, but it may be sufficiently disappointing for the applicant to drop out at this stage. Otherwise the Patent Office will now publish the application and copies will be on sale to the public. It will also be available to subscribers to online services. It normally takes 18 months from first application to reach this stage. Now that the invention has been made public it is open to anybody to send in comments on its patentability to the Comptroller and these will be passed on to the applicant.

There is now another form and another fee to be sent within six months before the final hurdle, the substantive examination. If everything is in order, and the invention is, as far as the examiner can see, really new and not obvious, the patent is finally granted. If it fails the examination you will have an opportunity to dispute the examiner's findings or to make necessary amendments if possible. The whole procedure may be completed within about three years; it must be completed within four and a half years.

PATENTEE'S MONOPOLY

As mentioned above, a patent gives a monopoly in the exploitation of an invention to the patentee (who may be the inventor in person or someone to whom the inventor has passed on the rights) for 20 years from the filing date, subject to the formality of annual renewal after the first four years. The patentee's monopoly is qualified to a limited extent by the provision in s. 48(1) of the Patents Act 1977 that (to simplify the somewhat complicated provisions) if the patentee is not fully exploiting the patent in the UK when it has been in force for three years anybody else may apply to the Comptroller to require the patentee to grant a licence to use the patent to the person applying (subject, of course, to satisfactory remuneration for the patentee). The justification for a compulsory licence is that, if the patentee does not satisfy the public demand for the invention, somebody else should be allowed to do so.

Whilst the period of 20 years is normally sufficient to allow the patentee to exploit an invention, there were many complaints from the pharmaceutical industry that it was too short in the special case of pharmaceutical products. Developing and testing a new drug and ensuring that it is safe can easily take a dozen years, leaving the manufacturer only a few years to recoup the enormous sums of money expended to bring a new drug to the market. An amelioration of the situation was brought in by an EEC Regulation in 1992 allowing for Supplementary Protection Certificates to be issued by national authorities in respect of a medicine, extending the period of patent protection by a maximum of five years. A Regulation from the European Union, formerly EEC, has direct effect in Member States (unlike a

Directive which must be re-enacted in each Member State) so this applies in the UK.

INFRINGEMENT

Section 60 of the 1977 Act sets out the actions which constitute infringement of a patent. In trying to tie up all loose ends the section becomes wordy and complicated. It relates to actions done in the UK, while the patent is in force, and without the consent of the proprietor of the patent. It is infringement to make, dispose of (or offer to dispose of), use, import or even keep, the invention. This applies where the invention is a product, and where the invention is a process rather than a product it applies also to a product directly obtained by means of the process. Where the invention is a process it is infringement to use it (or offer it for use) in the UK, but only if the infringer knows (or it would be obvious) that this would be infringement. Needless to say, a patent owner who hears of infringement will take immediate steps to ensure that the infringer knows about the patent. Of course the proprietor's lack of consent is crucial. Something which is done privately and for non-commercial purposes is permissible and is not infringement. There are a few other exemptions, certain experiments, preparation of a medicine from a prescription in a pharmacy, or use of the invention aboard a ship, aircraft, hovercraft or vehicle, which is temporarily in the UK or territorial waters. In other words, any ordinary commercial use is likely to be infringement, even if (with the exceptions detailed) it is quite innocent. Certain provisions have been added to the Act in s. 28 and a new s. 28A, dealing with anything done during the time when a patent has lapsed for non-payment of fees and before it is subsequently restored. A new s. 64, substituted for the original version in the Act, concerns the continuation of acts done in good faith before the priority date of the patent. These provisions are rather complicated and details may be sought in the amended sections. They will not, of course, be found in the original version of the Act.

Sometimes cases of infringement are cut and dried: it is clear on examination that the defendant's product or process is (or is not) the same as the claimant's, or overlapping it. Generally the courts interpret the patent claims strictly, which is one reason why they have to be drafted with great care in the first place: any vagueness is likely to be decided against the patentee. However, a measure of common-sense may be acceptable in interpretation of the patent: an infringer cannot expect to get away with it simply by making unimportant variations. The words 'secured essentially upright' (used of the blades of 'grass' in a patent for plastic turf) did not have to mean that the blades were very near vertical: the defendants' turf which had a distinct lay from the vertical still infringed copyright in *Monsanto* v. *Maxwell Hart*, 1981.

The leading case, in which the House of Lords defined the approach to be taken by the courts, came a couple of years later (*Catnic Components* v. *Hill and Smith*, 1983). The plaintiffs' patent was for a steel lintel to span the tops of doorways and other openings when building a wall. The lintel was hollow and the rear plate was described in the patent as 'extending vertically'. The defendants produced a very similar lintel but with the rear plate six to eight degrees off the vertical: did that infringe? Their Lordships took a pragmatic view: 'A patent specification should be given a purposive construction rather than a purely literal one derived from applying to it the kind of meticulous verbal analysis in which lawyers are too often tempted by their training to indulge.' The words 'extending vertically' could not be taken to exclude a back plate which was nearly, but not quite, vertical, otherwise the whole purpose of the patent would have been lost. So, a variant which does not affect the way in which the invention works is no defence to an infringement action: obviously it would be otherwise if the defendant has introduced a variant which would have a material effect on the working of the invention.

It can happen that the defendant has taken the 'pith and marrow', the essential claims, of the invention but has carried them out by improved, perhaps more up-to-date, technology. This could still be infringement. To suggest a rather imaginative example, if the inventor of a novel machine had worked it by steam it could still be infringement if the defendant had built the same machine but had changed the motive power to electricity. Section 125 of the Patents Act 1977 reproduces more wordily Art. 69 of the European Patent Convention. The latter says that a patent shall be taken to be as specified in the patentee's claims, interpreted by the description and drawings. A Protocol explaining Art. 69 says that a middle way between taking the literal meaning of the claims, or using them only as guidelines, should be adopted which will provide fair protection for the patentee, with reasonable certainty for a third party in understanding the patent.

A high proportion of the reported infringement cases are extremely technical involving, for example, complicated chemical compounds or electronic components, and needing highly specialized expert analysis to isolate the issues for the court. Patent infringement actions can, therefore, be very lengthy and extremely costly. The plastic grass case mentioned above was spread over 19 court days, so if you multiply that by the fees of counsel and solicitors in court, add counsel's opinion before trial, solicitors' costs in preparing the case, and fees of expert witnesses perhaps, it can be seen how the costs mount up. One solicitor's standard question to any patentee contemplating bringing an action against a big company for infringement of a patent is 'Can you afford to lose £100 000?' Quite apart from lawyers' fees for the very skilled practitioners in this field, expert witnesses do not come cheap, though the recent reforms in civil procedure include an attempt to reduce the burden of expert evidence, where possible to the use of a single court-appointed expert. Only a small proportion of actions commenced are pursued to the stage of a court hearing (as, indeed, in other fields of civil litigation): the parties usually agree some settlement, or one gives in, beforehand. Frequently, where the claim is for an injunction to stop infringement, an interim (formerly called 'interlocutory') injunction at a preliminary stage of the proceedings is enough to convince the infringer that there is nothing to be gained by fighting on. Legal opinion varies as to how far alternative dispute resolution, arbitration or mediation, canvassed in the latest civil justice reforms, can be applied to intellectual property issues. It is most apt for the resolution of contractual issues, which are less likely to arise in this field, but it is not unlikely that we shall see an increase in the use of these less expensive methods of resolving disputes.

THREATS, REMEDIES AND OFFENCES

It is by no means unknown for somebody who owns a patent (or, indeed, somebody who does not own it) to threaten legal proceedings against a competitor when there are no grounds for the threat. The Patents Act 1977, s. 70, gives the person threatened a cause of action against the threatener, but not if he or she is the actual manufacturer or importer rather than a distributor or other later link in the chain. The action is also available to somebody who is indirectly threatened, for example a distributor whose customers are threatened. It is, of course, a good defence to show that the acts complained of really are infringement, or that the supposed threat was not really a threat. This provision (which can result in a declaration from the court that the threats are unjustified, an injunction and perhaps damages) has parallels in the law of designs and registered trade marks, but not copyright. (Perhaps the nearest equivalent in respect of copyright is an action for a declaration that the claimant's acts do not constitute infringement. This is what happened in *Amstrad* v. *BPI*, 1986. When Amstrad faced criticism of their double-speed twin-cassette recorder from the representative body of the recording industry who were afraid that it would facilitate piracy they put the ball in their opponents' court by seeking a declaration that they were doing nothing illicit in marketing their machine. Section 71 of the Patents Act 1977 does provide a largely similar procedure in respect of patents.)

The civil remedies in patent cases are similar to those available in copyright cases: an injunction to stop the infringement; a declaration that the patent is valid and has been infringed; and damages or an account of the infringer's ill-gotten gains. However, the defendant's not knowing nor having reasonable grounds for knowing of the patent will prevent the claimant from claiming damages or an account, even if the word 'Patent' or similar words are on the product unless the patent number is also shown.

Patent law again parts company with copyright in the area of criminal law. There is no equivalent in the Patents Act of the penal section in the Copyright, Designs and Patents Act 1988 which makes commercial dealing in materials infringing copyright a criminal offence with, in certain cases, quite substantial penalties. In the Patents Act a small group of offences are created by ss. 109–112: they penalize selling goods as patented when they are not, falsifying patent records and misusing the name of the Patent Office.

ALTERNATIVE ROUTES TO A PATENT

If an inventor wants patent protection in other countries he or she can make a separate application in each of those countries. Alternatively there are two routes which can simplify the process by block applications covering a number of different countries. One depends on the European Patent Convention, and the other on the Patent Cooperation Treaty. Note that, for reasons of national security, any UK resident who intends to apply for a patent abroad must first seek Patent Office approval unless the applicant has already applied for a UK patent for the same invention.

European Patent Convention

This Convention, which began operations in 1978, simplifies obtaining a patent in most West European countries and a small number of others, 20 states in all. A single application is made at the Patent Office or at the European Patent Office (in Munich or The Hague) designating the countries where protection is required. The procedure is similar to that for a UK application and if all goes well the applicant will be granted a European patent. This is in effect a bundle of national patents for the designated countries and each will be subject to the patent law of the particular country. The official fees are kept fairly low: a European patent covering 10 countries would cost around £3000, but of course the other expenses involved would add significantly to this. The European Patent Convention is not a European Union instrument, although in fact all members of the EU are among the signatory states to the Convention, as are Cyprus, Liechtenstein, Monaco and Switzerland.

Patent Cooperation Treaty (PCT)

This Treaty has now been signed by nearly 100 states, ranging from Albania to Zimbabwe. It is administered by the World Intellectual Property Organization (WIPO) (see Chapter 8) in Geneva. The Treaty came into effect in 1978 but was slow in being accepted. Eventually the numbers of signatories built up and usage grew considerably. By the year 2000 there were 109 signatories who filed just under 91 000 applications in that year, nearly half of which came from the USA, as compared with 6 per cent from the UK, and only 3.5 per cent from developing countries. The PCT procedure involves two stages. In the first, international, stage a single application is made at one of the Receiving Offices which are located in certain countries: in the UK this will be the Patent Office. The countries for which a patent is required are designated in the single application. The application is passed to one of the five International Searching Authorities which will conduct an international search and preliminary examination. The report on these will be published by WIPO and sent to the national patent offices of the countries which the applicant designated. The official fees for this first stage will amount to around £2000 for 10 countries.

There is now a second, national, stage. Each national patent office deals with the application according to its own procedure. The applicant will have to pay the fees set by each office and will have to provide a translation (which will probably be expensive) if required. The result will be a national patent in each of the designated countries, assuming that all goes well. The advantages are that a single application in a single language and following a single set of rules will cover the early stages for all the states which the applicant has designated. The applicant is able to drop out after this stage if the international search and preliminary examination are unfavourable, or if further consideration has changed the applicant's mind. It also gives the opportunity to put off the expenses of the national applications for up to two years.

Community Patent Convention

The idea of a European Community (European Union) patent was conceived more than 40 years ago but is still undergoing what has proved an immensely long gestation. Although the Convention was signed by the EEC states in 1980, disagreements between the states have delayed its implementation. When (or if) it comes into force it will be possible to obtain a single Community patent valid in all the countries of the European Union.

PETTY PATENTS

Readers may be confused if they meet the term 'petty patent'. A number of foreign countries make provision for something rather like the UK's (unregistered) design right, giving 'second tier' protection to functional designs or in some countries to a wider range of industrial products or processes. Registration is necessary but without a full examination and with a lesser degree of inventiveness necessary than for a full patent. Lacking examination before grant, a petty patent is more open to challenge from a holder of prior rights, offsetting the advantages of speed, simplicity and cheapness. The duration of protection is limited, commonly 10 years or less, rarely up to 15. The conditions vary from country to country, as does the nomenclature: petty patent, utility model, patent of short duration, *brevet de courte durée* (Belgium), *modelo de utilidade* (Portugal), *Gebrauchsmuster* (Germany).

PATENT INFORMATION AND SEARCHING

Patent Office

As we mentioned at the beginning of this chapter, patent records form an invaluable source of technical and business information and a brief note may help to set this in context for those who are new to patents. The Patent Office says in its helpful leaflet on the Patent Search Service (from which this information is taken),

> The commercial and technical knowledge stored in patents has a significant role to play in a broad range of business activities from basic research through to product marketing.

It can avoid duplication of effort in research and development where ideas have already been tried out by others, help solve technical problems, inform you on competitors' products and markets, assist you in protecting your own inventions, and keep you updated about new processes and products and fresh markets.

The Patent Office Search and Advisory Service is staffed by highly skilled specialists who have access to over four million patents, not only from the UK but also filings with the European Patent Office and under the Patent Cooperation Cooperation Treaty. They also have access to every major online patent database and to databases on the Internet. With these formidable resources the Service can offer information for the would-be patentee, for the owner of a patent who wants to keep a watchful eye on developments in a particular field, and much more. Searches may cost from upwards of £500 to upwards of £2000 according to requirements, and a report in 10 working days is the aim.

British Library

After the British Library moved to its new site by London's St Pancras station what was formerly known as the Science Reference and Information Service, and before that as the Patent Office Library, was transferred from Chancery Lane to the St Pancras site. Apart from housing the national patent collection, the British Library claims to have the world's most comprehensive patent library. The services provided include reading room access, free enquiry and fee-based search services, and other information services. In addition training courses for users of patent information such as librarians and other information professionals, legal staff, technologists or researchers, are run regularly on such topics as an introduction to patents information, online patents databases for beginners, or patent information on the Internet. A one-day course costs at this date around £200.

Online

A leading player in the patent information field is Derwent Information. Derwent World Patents Index (Derwent WPI) is described as the world's most comprehensive database of international patent information with over 10 million inventions containing 20 million patent documents, growing at a rate of more than 27 000 documents every week. Information is gathered from 40 patenting authorities, going back in many cases to 1963. Titles and abstracts are given in English, and technical diagrams are often included. The Derwent classification system facilitates searching by keyword, subject, name, frequency and other requirements. Specialist trainers run regular training sessions in the UK and elsewhere. Searching on the Internet is now possible and Derwent also has a document supply service for patent documents including older ones.

TRADE MARKS

Although distinctive marks had long been used by merchants and manufacturers it was not until the Trade Marks Registration Act 1875 that provision was made for central registration of trade marks. Registration was opened on 1 January 1876 and the first trade mark to be registered was for beers, the famous Bass red triangle. The current statute is the Trade Marks Act 1994 (TMA) which repealed the Trade Marks Act 1938 and brought the law into line with the EEC Directive to approximate the trade mark law of Member States of 1988.

Trade marks are different from the other principal forms of intellectual property for there is often (but by no means always) very little, if any, intellectual input. (Sometimes, however, an immense amount of research is required, particularly if the mark is to be used in many countries: the Chinese character for 'four' needs to be avoided, for example, for it is pronounced the same as the character for 'death'; 'eight' on the other hand connotes good luck; Rolls Royce, it is said, considered naming one of its models 'Silver Mist' until they discovered that 'Mist' means a bad smell in German. The visual and psychological impact must be considered, and extensive search is necessary to avoid infringement of existing marks.) This is a fascinating field but peripheral to the subject of this book, so only a brief sketch will be given here.

DEFINITION

A trade mark 'means any sign capable of being represented graphically which is capable of distinguishing goods or services of one undertaking from those of other undertakings.' This is the definition in s. 1(1) of the Trade Marks Act 1994. It goes on, 'A trade mark may, in particular, consist of words (including personal names), designs, letters, numerals or the shape of goods or their packaging.' This does not really leave much out, unless it is incapable of being represented graphically: a sound, a colour, even a scent, can be defined in musical notation, descriptive words, a formula, or other accepted written or diagrammatic form.

Arms and logos

It must be noted, however, that the definition refers to a mark used in trade. If an individual wants some personal distinguishing mark to decorate his or her writing paper which can (at least in theory) be defended in law against another user the best thing is to petition the College of Arms for a grant of a family coat of arms. This will be much more expensive and not automatically awarded, but does confer a certain social prestige. In 1955 the High Court of Chivalry emerged from two centuries in abeyance to protect Manchester Corporation's right to restrain the use of its arms by a local theatre, *Manchester Corporation* v. *Manchester Palace of Varieties*, 1955. (A respectable corporate body may, of course, also be granted arms. Tesco, the supermarket chain, successfully petitioned the College of Arms for a grant.) However, it was made clear at the Manchester Corporation trial that only exceptional circumstances would justify convening the High Court of Chivalry again in the future. In any case that Court would not protect the strange 'logos' now used by many public bodies in place of their elegant armorial bearings, and they could not be protected as trade marks unless the owners were using them in trade. Curiously enough, some universities and like corporate bodies have gained some protection of their souvenir trade by registering various renderings of their arms as trade marks. In Scotland protection of armorial bearings is taken much more seriously and Lord Lyon King of Arms will take action against misuse.

REGISTRATION

Trade marks are dealt with by the Patents Office: the Comptroller-General's full title is Comptroller-General of Patents, Designs and Trade Marks. An application must bear a representation of the mark and must specify the class or classes of goods or services and in detail the actual goods and services which the applicant intends to trade in. The 42 classes can make strange reading. Class 3 includes bleaches, cleaning, scouring and abrasive preparations, but also cosmetics and toothpaste. The office fee is £200 plus £50 for each additional class. If examination shows that the mark is acceptable and does not come within the excluded categories, it will be advertised in the weekly *Trade Marks Journal*. Anybody who has cause to oppose registration has three months to do so (and companies or individuals with an interest in a mark may find it necessary to scan the Journal regularly). All being well, the mark will then soon be registered. If the mark is not accepted the applicant may have a formal hearing before a senior officer, and appeal to the court is possible. Many of the reported cases concern refusal by the Patent Office to register a mark. The Patent Office has a Search and Advisory Service available (for a fee) to a would-be applicant, and it is also possible for an individual to search the register, which is held on computer, in the Patent Office search rooms in Newport and London.

Unacceptable marks

Obviously a mark will not be registered if it is similar to an existing one for the same or similar goods or services. It must be distinctive: a common surname would be ruled out, as would an everyday term likely to be used by other traders. It must not be descriptive of the goods or services in terms of quality, purpose, geographical origin or the like. In an old case *Perfection*, 1910, for soap was refused, but *Chunky*, 1978, dog meat scraped through. *York* (referring to York in Canada) was allowed only as part of a complete mark, not by itself, for trailers, *York Trailer Holdings* v. *Registrar of Trade Marks*, 1982. Emblems or portraits relating to the Royal family are unacceptable, so are the Red Cross and the Olympic symbol. There are restrictions on depictions of national flags and emblems and the flags and emblems of international organizations. Those are the main exclusions, but obviously anything offensive or against the law will not be registered, *Hallelujah*, 1976, was refused for women's clothing as likely to offend. *Jardex* disinfectant was not in the same class as *Jardox* meat extract but was refused because of the obvious danger of confusion (*Edwards*, 1945). It will be seen that, although registration is fairly speedy and inexpensive, it is not automatic (and fees are non-returnable).

INFRINGEMENT

Section 10 of the TMA defines infringement very broadly. To simplify drastically, it is infringement to use in the course of trade an identical or similar mark for identical or similar goods or services for which it is registered. There are some common-sense exceptions: it is not infringement for a person to use his or her own name or address, and words describing goods or services which happen to overlap with the trade mark do not infringe. Nor does honest use of the mark to indicate the purpose of spare parts or the like.

In a civil action for infringement the claimant can be awarded the usual remedies, injunction, damages, account, as well as an order for erasure of the infringing mark or delivery up of infringing material. There are also severe criminal penalties for unauthorized use of a trade mark; up to 10 years imprisonment and a fine. Counterfeiting of branded clothing, computer software, sound and video recordings and other products is a serious matter and these penalties were introduced to try to put a stop to a growing dishonest trade. Prosecutions are frequent, often after raids by trading standards officers or at the instance of producers' associations, but the courts seem reluctant to impose the highest penalties.

COLLECTIVE AND CERTIFICATION MARKS

A trade association may now register a 'collective mark': the application must state the regulations governing members' use of the mark, conditions of membership and other information. An authorized user may call on the association to take action against an infringer, and if the association fails to act the user may take proceedings in his or her own name.

Stilton cheese, made only in the Melton Mowbray area of Leicestershire is well known to connoisseurs. (Stilton was the staging post on the road to delivery in London, not the place of manufacture.) The Stilton cheese makers of Melton Mowbray were successful in 1967 in getting the word 'Stilton' registered as what is known as a 'certification mark'. This means that only cheese which complies with certain conditions of method and place of manufacture can be described as Stilton cheese. Well-known certification trade marks include the word 'Sheffield' on cutlery, the British Standards 'kite' mark and the 'Woolmark' representing in a simplified way skeins of wool.

PASSING OFF

Passing off falls more in the sphere of competition law than intellectual property but a claim that a defendant is passing off his goods as those of the claimant will often succeed where there is no infringement of a trade mark, and indeed a passing off claim is often added to a trade mark infringement action as a fall-back position. Claims have succeeded on the Coca-Cola bottle, *Coca-Cola* v. *Barr*, 1961, get-up of buses, *London General Omnibus Co* v. *Felton*, 1901, and tranquillizer capsules, *Hoffman-La Roche* v. *DDSA Pharmaceuticals*, 1965. However, the manufacturers of *Toofy's* bubble gum shaped like a set of false teeth failed to restrain competitors from marketing their own gum in the same revolting shape, *Blundell* v. *Margolis*, 1951.

COMMUNITY TRADE MARK

While the EEC Directive served to harmonize the trade mark laws of what is now the European Union, a parallel Regulation established a Community Trade Mark (CTM) valid across the whole European Union. The office, curiously named the Office for the Harmonization of the Internal Market (trade marks and designs), is in Alicante, Spain, and applications for a Community Trade Mark are made there. A limited search is made before grant, with some possibility of national searches as well. One advantage of the CTM procedure is that application may be made in any of the EU official languages and other proceedings may be in one of the five official languages of the Office. Unlike the long delayed Community Patent, the CTM has proved successful.

PLANT VARIETIES: UPOV

As a final note to round off the subject of industrial property, mention may be made of the Union pour la Protection des Obtentions Végétales (UPOV), or in English the Union for the Protection of New Varieties of Plants, dating from 1961. This is the international body, to which a limited number of states belong, concerned with the rights of the plant breeder. The member states agree to provide, by patent or otherwise, exclusive rights for the producer of a new plant variety. In the UK, where plant varieties cannot be patented, the system is administered by the Plant Variety Rights Office, under the Plant Variety and Seeds Act 1964. A European Community Plant Variety Right was also created by a Regulation of 1994.

7 Copyright abroad

Although the international conventions require certain minimum standards of protection to be provided by all their signatories, the approach to protection of literary, artistic and musical works can vary quite considerably from one country to another. In the UK copyright has long been treated almost as a commodity: the law is concerned above all with the economic exploitation of a piece of property, and copyright extends beyond works of authorship to what in some countries are not regarded as subjects for copyright but are described as 'related rights' or 'neighbouring rights', such as sound recordings, films or broadcasts. True, the particular qualities of intellectual property require that it cannot be treated in exactly the same way as a pound of sugar or a piece of furniture, but it is only grudgingly and recently, in the Copyright, Designs and Patents Act 1988, that the law has admitted moral rights for the writer, artist or composer, over and above the purely economic rights. By and large, the other Common Law countries, those countries which derive their legal systems from the English Common Law, most of the Commonwealth, as well as the USA, have tended to take the same approach. This chapter will illustrate the different ways in which the copyright laws operate in a few selected countries.

In the countries of the Civil Law tradition (those countries whose legal systems derive, directly or indirectly, from Roman law) authorship involves far more than the production of a piece of saleable property. The author has rights in his or her creation which are seen as almost sacred or spiritual. The work is the author's child, the law talks about the right of paternity; the author's reputation in relation to the work is safeguarded even long after death. The position in France is described first, as in no other country are the sacred rights of authorship so strongly asserted. Germany provides another example of the Civil Law approach. It is worth glancing at another approach, that which prevailed in the socialist states of Eastern Europe, though now subject to the dramatic changes which overcame them on the collapse of communism. In Asia the protection of intellectual property has had a chequered history and, despite having recently entered the world copyright community, China is still regarded circumspectly by Western owners of copyrights. Japan has a long tradition of copyright protection. Singapore, nearly 50 years from colonial status, has partially redeemed a rather tarnished reputation with a well-regarded copyright act and strong measures against infringers. South Africa is interesting as a country which blends a distinguished Civil Law tradition with an overlay of the Common Law. Lastly, the USA, a Common Law jurisdiction, plays a very important role in international intellectual property affairs. The European Union has emerged from what was originally expected to be no more than a European Economic Community and has, not always happily for the UK, made radical changes in the intellectual property laws of the Member States, in the interest of harmonization: this is important and will be looked at where it fits more appropriately, in Chapter 8.

CIVIL LAW COUNTRIES

FRANCE

Whilst the UK may be seen as the originator of the Common Law approach to copyright, France offers perhaps the best example of the very different approach of the Civil Law countries. Used in this sense, usually with capital letters, the Civil Law refers to those legal systems which derive ultimately from the revival of Roman law in the Middle Ages, the legal systems of the states of continental Europe and of many of the areas of Asia and the Americas which they first controlled. For reasons which will be familiar to historians England remained relatively untouched by this revival and the Common Law of England developed on idiosyncratic lines, characterized particularly by an obsessive attention to the minutiae of correct legal procedure and by reliance on the sacrosanct precedents set by former decisions of the judges. By contrast, the decisions of even the highest French courts have no formal authority in a later similar case, though earlier judicial reasoning may have strong persuasive value in the courts, equally with the considered opinions of legal writers, when a comparable situation falls for adjudication again. It is certainly not true to say that precedents are unimportant, but readers of French works on intellectual property will immediately notice that the cases cited are fewer than in English books, and they have more the character of illustrations than of authorities. Case law is referred to in French as *jurisprudence*, a little confusingly for the English reader for whom the word means legal theory.

Although royal grants of monopoly rights in an edition of any particular work were made in France as far back as the beginning of the sixteenth century, these were accorded to printers and publishers. Only very exceptionally were they made to authors and then normally with the intention that they be transferred to the publisher. Thus, as in England, the early history of copyright was bound up with the purely economic aspect of publishing. It was only in the latter part of the eighteenth century, when the ideas of the Enlightenment were strong, that the rights of the author assumed the importance which has characterized French law ever since, and only after the French Revolution was legislation passed to protect them. Two laws, of 1791 and 1793, protected the exclusive right of authors, composers and artists in the dissemination of their works, for their own lifetime and, originally, for only a few years afterwards. With relatively small amendments and additions these laws were to govern authors' rights in France for over 150 years, though amplified by the conclusions of the judges and textbook writers, until they were replaced in 1957. The whole law of intellectual property is now codified in the *Code de la Propriété Intellectuelle*, which came into force on 1 July 1992, replacing, so far as the rights of authors are concerned, the Laws of 11 March 1957 and 3 July 1985, and which has subsequently been amended in detail.

The French term *droit d'auteur* is commonly translated as copyright, but the underlying meaning is not the same. Whilst copyright derives from the economic property right in the printer's 'copy', the idea of *droit d'auteur* subsumes far more than purely pecuniary rights. The *droit d'auteur* is something personal, almost sacred, comprising not only the right to the exclusive economic exploitation of the material in question but also the right to the integrity of the author's creation. In the often-quoted words of the report to the Assembly which passed the law of 1791, '*la plus sacrée, la plus personnelle de toutes les propriétés est l'ouvrage, fruit de la pensée d'un écrivain.*' Thus the author enjoys, personally, perpetually and inalienably, his or her moral rights in a work, the right to be recognized as author, to publish (or not), to prevent mutilation or distortion, and even to withdraw from contracts for publication (for example if the author's views have changed, though with due compensation to the publisher or other to whom the economic rights have been passed). Although the author's economic rights cease 70 years after the author's death, the moral rights endure (at least in theory) for ever. Indeed an attempt by the writers' association to defend the moral right of an author, Choderlos de Laclos, dead for more than 150 years, nearly succeeded when the title of his very readable but rather scandalous novel *Les liaisons dangéreuses* was used in the 1960s for a film directed by Roger Vadim and very loosely based on the original. It went right up to the *Cour de cassation* (the highest court) and failed only because the writers' association was held to lack standing to bring an action in the matter. There was a good deal of sympathy for defending the long-dead author's right and it is likely that the courts would have granted protection had there been some person or body with the legal standing to pursue the claim.

Because French law weights the balance in favour of the author the exceptions for what in the UK is called fair dealing are limited broadly to a copy or representation of the work strictly for private or family use, and to short citations, parodies or press reviews. The idea of compulsory licensing is repugnant. As, usually, the author is economically the weaker party certain safeguards are built into the law to prevent unfair exploitation by a publisher and to allow, particularly, revision of an unfavourable contract. An artist enjoys the *droit de suite*, a right to receive three per cent of the price of a subsequent sale of his or her work.

Difficulty does, however, arise at times from the French emphasis on the individual author's right. What happens when there are several authors of a work? Distinction is made between a 'composite work', a 'collective work' and a 'work of collaboration'. A composite work incorporates some pre-existing work, as with a translation, an anthology, an arrangement of a piece of music, a copy of an artistic work. A collective work is one where the contributions of various contributors are merged indistinguishably, as for example in a three-volume sailing manual put together by a nautical institution. In such cases there is an identifiable individual (or body) who (or which) owns rights in the work. In this particular case the Centre nautique des Glénans allocated the work to authors, determined the format and so on. Philippe Harle had been coordinator of Volume I but that did not give him rights in the collective work, *Harle contre Centre nautique des Glénans*, 1970. The idea of a collective work with a corporate author, by nature incapable of intellectual creativity, is alien to the French concept of the personal, almost sacred, nature of an author's creation, to *l'esprit humanistique* of the law in this area. The courts, as well as legal writers, have argued not infrequently for a restrictive interpretation of this category, or even for its abolition. (In the UK, by contrast, we see no serious problem in the exercise of an author's rights by a collective body.)

A 'work of collaboration' is one in which several people have taken part: the co-authors exercise their rights in common (and can go to the courts if they disagree). Each, however, retains rights in his or her own personal work and can usually exploit them (unless agreed otherwise) provided that this does not prejudice the exploitation of the common undertaking. Thus, for example, the author of the words of a song could allow them to be read as a poem without consulting the composer of the music, and the latter could authorize the use of the music in a film.

The difference between the copyright and *droit d'auteur* approaches is seen most clearly in an 'audiovisual work' (the expression introduced by the 1985 Law to signify a cinematographic film or television production). In the UK the situation is simple: one person (or most probably a company) buys the right to make a film from, say, a book, employs scriptwriters, actors and so on, produces the film, and then owns the total rights in the finished product. In France it is not so straightforward. Once again the emphasis is on the individual and personal rights of the originator of a creative work. A film or TV production will have many co-authors. Certain people are presumed to be co-authors unless proved otherwise:

the authors of the scenario, of the adaptation, the spoken text, the music and songs, together with, of course, the director. But in addition anyone who has made any creative intellectual contribution may have the quality and rights of a co-author. This may (but may not) include the producer: it depends whether the contribution is simply that of a business entrepreneur, or if the producer does take a creative part. Many others can (but not automatically) be included – cameramen, dubbers, cutters, creators of scenery and costumes – provided that their work exemplifies personal creative endeavour.

The co-authors retain their moral rights in respect of the work. The result is that once the film or TV production has reached its final form the agreement of the co-authors is, in the final resort, necessary before any modification of this version may be made, whether by addition, cutting or changing any part of it. Although it is assumed that the contract between the producer and the co-authors cedes to the producer all rights of exploitation (with limited exceptions), the co-authors receive their due share of the proceeds of future exploitation. The matrix or original copy may not be destroyed. However, transfer to another form, such as videocassette, needs only consultation with the director.

The Law of 3 July 1985 made some important changes to the 1957 Law. It introduced *droits voisins*, neighbouring rights, giving rights to performers. It requires the authorization of the performer for any fixation, reproduction or public communication of a performance. Although this is closely analogous to *droit d'auteur*, the legislator stopped short of including performers' rights in that category (as, indeed is the case in the UK where performers' rights are treated separately in the Copyright, Designs and Patents Act 1988). The same Law brought computer programs within the scope of the law but with one very important derogation from the French concept of author's right. The 1985 Law provides that, unless otherwise agreed, a program created by one or more employees in the exercise of their functions belongs to their employer. The author of a program may not object to adaptation, nor may the author withdraw from any agreement to cede his or her rights in it. One other provision of the 1985 Law is worth mentioning, the extension of the duration of protection for musical works to 70 years *pma* from the 50 years then current. The slow rate of return on music (classical rather than pop) was the reason for this.

Droit de personnalité

In the French approach to intellectual property one may see a reflection of the more general concern with the individual's right of *personnalité*. Art. 9, added to the Civil Code in 1970, enshrines the individual's right to respect for his or her private life, a right only recently given full and formal recognition in the UK in the Human Rights Act. The seriousness with which this right is regarded is indicated by the number of relevant court cases. These have tackled publication of an individual's address in the press, or telephone number, or a photograph, or state of health. The privacy of the medical history of a deceased person given in a book was invoked in 1996 on behalf of his wife and children. Pictures of the daily life of mentally handicapped in an institution infringed their right of privacy (1993). An individual's *personnalité* is also protected by Art. 226 of the Penal Code with severe penalties for such offences as surreptitiously recording an individual's private conversation, or photographing a person without permission in a private place.

A well-known music hall artiste was able to stop the newspaper *France-Dimanche* from publishing an article with details of the birth of her baby and a photograph of her in an advanced stage of pregnancy, *Soc Edi7 contre Dame Chancel*, 1985. The leading actress in the soap opera 'Chateauvallon' was photographed in a wheelchair by telephoto lens from a hospital roof after an accident. She recovered substantial damages following publication of the pictures, *Dame B ... contre Soc VSD*, 1986. (The use of the honorific 'Dame' before a female litigant's name is a legal convention.) Needless to say, persons in the public eye have brought most of the reported actions. Brigitte Bardot was one: *SA 'La Dernière Heure' contre Dame Bardot et autre*, 1986. (For those whose knowledge of commercial French is sketchy, a company is *une société* and *Société Anonyme* (SA) denotes a limited company.) However, lower down the scale of media interest, two prison officers obtained an order that their faces should be blocked out in all unsold copies of a journal which published a clandestine photograph of them with a well-known prisoner in the prison exercise yard, *Soc VSD et autre contre CL et autre*, 1986.

GERMANY

Germany is firmly within the Civil Law tradition. With regard to intellectual property, the author's right approach, as in France, holds sway, rather than the copyright approach of the Common Law countries: the German word *Urheberrecht* means 'author's right'. The full rights of an author can be obtained only through the author's own individual creation, until they pass to someone else on the author's death, but a licence may be granted to another to utilize the work within the limits of the licence. A legal person, that is a company or other institution, cannot be the owner of an author's rights, even if the author is an employee, but a contract of employment implies that the employee has granted an exclusive licence to the employer to use any work produced in the course of his or her employment. This provision preserves the Civil Law concept of the rights of the individual creator of a work, whilst allowing an employer to benefit from the work for which the employer employs personnel. (Rights in an industrial design, *Geschmacksmuster*, or 'design patent', created in the course of employment belong to the employer: this is an important difference between author's right and design law.) However,

German law escapes the difficulties of the extreme *droit d'auteur* approach, with the multiplicity of rights involved in a film, for example, or the need to bend the concept of an author's rights in order to accommodate a performer's rights in a performance which is only secondary to the original author's script. This is achieved by acceptance of the idea of neighbouring rights, or related rights, related to author's right but flexible enough to cope with very different requirements.

Moral rights are protected by the law. These are the right of an author of a work to recognition as such, the right to prohibit any distortion or mutilation of the work which would prejudice the author's intellectual or personal interests in it, and the right to decide whether, and how, the work is to be disseminated. An author may also demand access to the original, or a copy, of the work which is held by another person if the author needs to make a reproduction or adaptation. *Droit de suite* (in German, *Folgerecht*) enables an artist to claim, but only through a collecting society, five per cent of the sale price if a work is resold through an art dealer or auctioneer.

The law is contained in the *Urheberrechtgesetz*, the Law on Author's Right and Related Rights of 1965, amended a number of times, particularly in 1985 and 1994. Rights of property were guaranteed by the Constitution of the German Federal Republic before reunification, and the courts ruled that an author's intellectual property came under this protection. The acknowledgment of intellectual property as 'property' in the strict sense may perhaps be reflected in the fact that an amendment introduced by the 1985 Act increased the maximum penalties for commercial dealings in infringing materials to the same level as those provided by the law against theft of material property, namely five years imprisonment or a fine. Other illicit exploitation of an author's right or related rights without the owner's consent attracts up to one year in prison or a fine.

The duration of protection by author's right was set at 70 years *post mortem auctoris* and when the term was harmonized throughout the European Union the longer German period was chosen rather than the Berne Convention norm of 50 years *pma*. Certain neighbouring rights are protected for 25 to 50 years. Some computer programs were given author's right protection by the Law of 1985, but rather grudgingly, and it was not until 1993 that, following an EC Directive, the scope was widened to cover most programs. The requirement that works protected by the Act must be personal intellectual creations was a stumbling block to full recognition for computer software.

Perhaps the most important addition to the law by the amending Act of 1985 was the provision of remuneration to an author for photocopying of his or her works. The making of a photocopy of a work (other than a musical work in print or manuscript, a computer program or an essentially complete copy of a book or periodical) for defined private or personal uses became permissible, while the author is remunerated from the photocopying levy. Two forms of levy are collected by the collecting society and distributed to owners of rights. First, there is a once-

131

for-all levy on the first sale or hire of photocopiers. Secondly, where copiers are installed in educational or research institutions, public libraries or copy shops, a small copying levy is collected in respect of each copy made. Copying of sound or video recordings for private use is permissible under the 1965 Law. Originally the rights owners were remunerated (through the collecting society GEMA) from a levy of five per cent of the wholesale price of recording equipment only. However, with the dramatic fall in the price of recording equipment the returns fell and a levy on blank audio and video tape was added by the 1985 Law (calculated per hour of playing time). (A blank tape levy was proposed in the UK before the 1988 Act was drafted but met a good deal of opposition from tape manufacturers and others, and was not proceeded with.)

Germany has acceded to the major intellectual property conventions, including Berne and the Universal Copyright Convention (UCC). Incidentally, Germany has, in the Max Planck Institute in Munich, what is probably Europe's most distinguished research institute in the field of intellectual property.

COPYRIGHT IN A SOCIALIST ENVIRONMENT

A brief note on the way in which the concept of an author's rights in his or her creation was treated in a socialist system before the collapse of communism in eastern Europe is appropriate at this point. The Soviet Union acceded to the Universal Copyright Convention (UCC) in 1973 (having signed the Paris Convention for the Protection of Industrial Property eight years previously). Accession was preceded by a certain amount of soul-searching as to whether membership of such an organization was compatible with socialist principles on the rights of authorship. Lenin, in the early years of the twentieth century, expressed himself strongly on the position of the author in a capitalist society. 'Freedom of the bourgeois writer, painter or actress is only masked dependence on a moneybag, bribe or keep.' Thus economic conditions in bourgeois society will force the author to sell his work to a publisher, nearly always he loses his copyright, and royalties are calculated solely from economic factors. Copyright therefore becomes concentrated in the hands of capitalist monopolies. The theory of Soviet copyright law required that the personal interests of the author were blended with the interests of the whole of society. The aim was to stimulate the creation and distribution of scientific, literary and artistic works. The term 'intellectual property' did not really fit in with the Soviet concept of author's right. The author was seen as receiving a wage for his or her creative work, even though this may be paid only when the work had been completed, rather than receiving a price for the sale of a piece of merchandise or (intellectual) property. There was a special tax category for writers and artists, equating them broadly to factory and office workers rather than to professionals in private practice. Moral rights were recognized; the right to claim authorship and the right to integrity of the work. When the Soviet Union signed the UCC it was necessary to extend an author's rights, previously available only during the author's lifetime, to the UCC minimum of 25 years *pma*. The Russian Federation, successor state to the Soviet Union, joined the Berne Convention in 1995.

To take one other example, author's right in socialist Czechoslovakia contrasted markedly with that of the USSR. The western part of Czechoslovakia, now the Czech Republic, for many centuries formed part of the Holy Roman Empire – indeed Prague was for a time the imperial capital – and the country has a historical affinity with the Civil Law systems. The individual creativity of the author remained in the socialist state, which emerged in 1948, as the essential prerequisite for author's rights. Hence only an actual physical person, not a corporation, could be an author and the first owner of copyright. This led to difficulties and the copyright law of 1965 paid lip service to an author's rights but said that a socialist organization (other than one engaged in publishing) could use without permission a scientific or artistic work created by an employee in the course of employment, in the fulfilment of its own tasks. Thus the theory of the individuality of copyright was harmonized with a socialist economic structure. At a time when rights in computer programs were first coming to public attention the Copyright and Industrial Property Institute of the prestigious and ancient Charles University of Prague conducted a detailed study and concluded that the lack of individual creativity in a computer program prevented its acquiring author's rights. Czechoslovakia was generally regarded as the most 'westernized' of the communist states, and this seems to be reflected in the author's rights law. Membership of the Berne Convention dates back to 1921, soon after the emergence of the new state of Czechoslovakia, and the country was an early signatory of the UCC in 1960. Incidentally, Czechoslovakia favoured special copyright concessions to developing countries envisaged in the 1967 Stockholm revision to the Berne Convention: it may be surmised that, unlike the works of authors in the more popular languages such as French and English, those in Czech or Slovak would be little disadvantaged by the concessions.

ASIA

JAPAN

A Publishing Ordinance of 1887, enacted only 19 years after the Meiji Restoration which marked her emergence as a modern state, may be taken as the beginning of copyright law in Japan. The Ordinance revised an earlier one which was particularly concerned to control the publishing of books, requiring a government licence to publish but granting monopoly rights to the publisher. Modern Japanese law follows the Civil Law tradition and when the first full copyright law was enacted in 1899, designed to comply with Berne requirements, it was based largely on the German model. Japan acceded to the Berne Convention in 1899 and was also one of the early signatories, in 1956, of the Universal Copyright Convention, and has since joined the other major conventions in this field.

The law of 1899 survived until 1970 when the current Copyright Act was passed, and this, with several updates to 1996, remains the current law. It opens with a statement of purpose, to secure, by providing for the rights of authors with respect to their works, the protection of these rights 'having regard to a just and fair exploitation of these cultural products, and thereby to contribute to the development of culture', Art. 1. The inclusion of the wider cultural issues is interesting and somewhat reminiscent of the moral tone of copyright legislation in communist countries. Performances, phonograms and broadcasts are also mentioned: these are treated separately from 'works', in the later articles of the statute. There is a definition of a work in Art. 2(1)(i):

> work means a production in which thoughts or sentiments are expressed in a creative way and which falls within the literary, scientific, artistic or musical domain.

The concept of taking the creation of a work back to the author's thoughts and sentiments is unusual, perhaps almost unique as an approach to copyright legislation, though in sentiment it is not all that far from the French approach to the sacred rights of an author in a work. The definition seems to have limitations in that it does appear to exclude more prosaic products. Does a telephone directory, for example, express thoughts and sentiments in a creative way? A case under the old law (which included no definition) did uphold copyright in a telephone directory, *Sakimura* v. *Yashiro*, 1919. On the other hand, in *Kotani* v. *Japan Lines*, 1964, the court found 'no expression of the plaintiff's thoughts' in the form for a shipping document, and denied it copyright. The definition of a work, incidentally, does not require fixation: a speech would be protected, and a lecture is specifically included as eligible for copyright protection in Art. 10(1)(i).

The Japanese term for copyright is romanized as *chosakuken* and is written with three characters. (Although Japanese is a completely different language from Chinese it is written with Chinese characters supplemented by two phonetic syllabic 'alphabets'.) The first two characters (*cho saku*) signify 'a (literary) work' or 'authorship' and the last (*ken*) means 'power'. (The term is of modern coinage.) Thus it translates more closely to the French *droit d'auteur* than to the English idea of copyright. Indeed the author's right approach of the Civil Law countries is very evident in the Copyright Law. Moral rights receive some emphasis: the author's right to make the work public (which includes the right to discontinue publication if the author's views have changed, with due compensation to the publisher), the right to claim authorship, and, thirdly, the right to preserve the integrity of the work against distortion or modification. This last right is subject to some limitations, in particular a work reproduced as a school textbook may be subject to modifications deemed unavoidable for school education. Any other exploitation of a work 'prejudicial to the honour and reputation of the author' is also infringement of moral rights.

In the same Civil Law tradition, neighbouring rights (that is, the rights of performers, of producers of phonograms (sound recordings) and of broadcasting organizations) are clearly distinguished from the rights of authors. (Cinematographic works are protected by author's right.) The duration of protection, formerly only 20 years, has been extended to 50 years. Moral rights do not extend to performers but there is an alternative, to sue in tort under the Civil Code. Performers and phonogram producers have a right to reasonable remuneration for commercial lending but a right analogous to British Public Lending Right for books and journals was deferred.

The exemptions to copyright permit fairly generous use by educational institutions, subject in certain cases to payment to the author. Libraries also have privileges, for example to supply copies for a user's research. In line with the law of some other countries copying is permitted of a copyright work by the user for personal, family or similar limited use. This precludes copying by another for the user.

The year 1985 was a vintage year for copyright amendment as a number of countries amended their legislation to provide for the protection of computer works. Japan passed an amending law which extended copyright protection to computer programs. There had been a struggle over this between two powerful government ministries, one of which favoured copyright and the other *sui generis* protection for a much shorter term. This reflected similar argument in other countries, including the UK, but in the end, as elsewhere, the supporters of copyright won the day.

Both civil and criminal remedies are available for infringement, with the latter bringing up to three years imprisonment or a fine up to three million Yen (around £17 000 at the rate of exchange current in February 2001). However, Japanese law makes no provision for exemplary damages in civil cases. The first successful criminal prosecution for software infringement by an organization came in 1999 and resulted in fines between ¥300 000 and ¥500 000 on five individuals who had developed software for their company from an illegally copied program of their previous employer (*IP Asia*, September 1999, 14). Software piracy is a serious problem in Japan resulting in huge losses for legitimate producers and the Copyright Council has called for maximum fines to be increased at least to ¥100 million (*IP Asia*, February 2000, 5).

SINGAPORE

Singapore's constitutional history is relevant to the subject of copyright. Singapore was administered as a British colony, being linked with Malacca and Penang in the Straits Settlements. After the Second World War Penang and Malacca joined the Federation of Malaya which became independent in 1957 but Singapore did not become part of Malaysia (as it was now named) until 1963, and two years later, in 1965, left to become an independent and sovereign republic within the Commonwealth.

This situation was at the heart of a notable lawsuit, *Butterworth* v. *Ng Sui Nam*, 1987. Singapore, it must be admitted, had acquired an unenviable reputation for book piracy. The UK Copyright Act 1911 had been extended to Singapore in 1912. When the 1956 Copyright Act repealed the 1911 Act in 1956 it was provided that the 1911 Act remained in force in those countries (including Singapore) to which the Act had been extended. In the new republic existing laws were continued in force. So, there was no doubt that the 1911 UK Act continued to be part of the law of Singapore. But, and this was the crucial question, did it protect works published outside Singapore, in the UK?

When Butterworths and other book and music publishers brought actions for infringement of copyright against the defendant bookseller, the defendant argued that on Singapore's independence this Act became a Singapore Act, a totally different law deriving its force from the sovereign power of Singapore. The Act could not be extended to the UK because Singapore had no power to extend its laws to any other country. The Singapore Court of Appeal rejected this argument and held that the 1911 Act still extended to countries which were originally 'His Majesty's Dominions' (if they had not subsequently repealed it) even if they were now independent of each other, so British works were still protected in Singapore.

Although the *Butterworth* decision was received with a welcome sigh of relief by British publishers, strong arguments have been put forward in Singapore against what is often seen as excessive protection of foreign publishers and authors. At that time Taiwan was one major source of pirated English language books of the sort in which Mr Ng traded. Mr Ng himself submitted a memorandum to the Select Committee on a new Copyright Bill (some months before his appeal was heard by the Court of Appeal). He argued that the extent of piracy was much exaggerated. Moreover, he said, with respect to any textbook almost invariably 80 to 90 per cent of its content was copied from earlier works, and he cited an American court case (without giving any reference): A published a textbook. B published another textbook a year later. A sued B alleging that B had copied up to 80 per cent of A's book. B did not deny this but he pointed out that 80 per cent of A's book was copied from other books! The court dismissed A's claim. An argument which does arouse sympathy in developing countries generally (though it is arguable whether

Singapore could still be regarded as a developing country) was put forward by Mr Ng. Textbooks, as a vehicle of development, are vital to national development. The prices of UK and US textbooks are normally beyond the reach of an average student, so second-hand, pirated and photocopied copies help to solve the problem rather than being an impediment to national development. (An argument which carries some echoes of this is currently (2002) being put forward in certain developing countries to justify the production of cheap versions of patented drugs, in defiance of the original patentees' rights (this issue is examined in Chapter 10).)

It is important to realize that this attitude to copyright is widely and sincerely held, though perhaps the students' union of the National University of Singapore expressed it rather awkwardly when they said in their submission to the Select Committee, 'The actual purchase of reference books is an alternative to photocopying', an expensive alternative as they proceeded to show, giving as an example the costs of the basic texts to a third-year law student. At that time a student could borrow a library book, take it to one of the many copy shops and collect a complete photocopy bound in a neat blue wrapper a couple of hours later. It may be mentioned that locally published works by Singapore academics and other authors suffered as well as foreign ones.

In view of Singapore's history, her copyright law is firmly within the Common Law tradition, though moral rights are recognized. The law was completely updated by the Copyright Act 1987, a comprehensive piece of legislation drawing heavily on the Australian Copyright Act of 1968. The vexed question of photocopying is dealt with in quite liberal provisions. Fair dealing is permitted for research (which excludes industrial research or research by non-governmental corporate bodies and the like) or private study, and some guidelines are given as to the factors to be taken into account to determine whether any dealing is 'fair'. A library which provides photocopying machines for use by readers is covered against an accusation of authorizing infringement provided that a notice in A4 size as prescribed in the Copyright Regulations is placed near the machine. (This provision follows closely an amendment to the Australian Copyright Act, made in 1980 in the wake of *Moorhouse* v. *University of New South Wales*, 1976, referred to in Chapter 2.) Perhaps the most generous provision in the Act allows a non-profit-making library to supply (on a signed undertaking by the person requesting the material, that he or she requires it for private study or non-commercial research, and for a charge, if any, not more than the cost of making the copy) a copy of one or more articles in a periodical or, and this is the interesting provision, the whole or part of a published literary, dramatic or musical work which is in the library collection. In fact this concession may be less generous in practice. In most cases it would be difficult for a student to certify honestly (and convincingly) that he or she needs a copy of a whole book. A few years ago at least one major library in Singapore was restricting copying to a maximum of 50 per cent of a book.

137

The Act also allows multiple copying of insubstantial portions of works in the course of education in an educational institution, or even (subject to limitations and the payment of a royalty if requested) of larger portions, including the whole, or a substantial part, of a published work if copies cannot be obtained in reasonable time at a reasonable price. One further provision of the Act needs to be mentioned in this regard. The Copyright Act contains provisions similar to the concessions for developing countries in the 1971 Paris Act of the international copyright conventions. When a work is not available in Singapore at a price reasonably related to Singapore prices, any person may apply to the Copyright Tribunal for a compulsory licence to publish an edition of it for the purpose of systematic instructional activities. Under rather similar conditions a licence may be obtained to publish a translation into one of the official languages (Chinese (Mandarin), English, Malay, Tamil). There are several restrictive conditions. The publisher seeking a licence must have sought, but failed to obtain, a licence from the copyright owner. Moreover, newly published works are excluded for a period of three years from first publication in the case of scientific and technological works, seven years for fiction and the like, and five years for other categories. In any case, a reasonable royalty must be paid to the copyright owner.

It will be seen that the provisions outlined above represent a compromise between the advocates of complete freedom and those with a vested interest in protection. Severe penalties were set for commercial dealings in infringing materials, a fine up to S$100000 (about £28000 at the 1987 exchange rate) and imprisonment for up to five years, though some concern has been expressed by bodies representing copyright owners that no minimum penalties are prescribed. There have been many well-publicized prosecutions of counterfeiters. Attempts to raise awareness of intellectual property issues have included an exhibition 'IP 2000' staged in a popular shopping mall. Nevertheless, protection for foreign works is rather limited and Singapore has yet to shake off its dubious reputation as a pirate haven, particularly of dealers in counterfeit computer software. A recent amendment to the Copyright Act has legalized the position of parallel imports, works legitimately published under the copyright law of another country but without the permission of the copyright owner from another country.

Singapore's main copyright requirements, protection without registration and a 50 year *pma* duration, comply with the Berne Convention, and Singapore joined Berne in 1998 but is not a member of the Universal Copyright Convention. Bilateral agreements have been concluded with the UK, the USA and Australia. Moreover, copyright subsisting under the 1911 Act at the commencement date of the new Act shall continue. In view of the decision in *Butterworth* v. *Ng Sui Nam* this means that British works published before the 1987 Act came into force retain copyright protection.

CHINA

The two interlinked technologies essential for the wide diffusion of human knowledge both originated in China. The writing system, although a trial to the adult foreign learner (as the present author can testify), has among its various advantages over the pseudo-phonetic Roman script, an economy in expressing a whole concept with one or two characters, well-suited to printing with moveable type. Absolutely essential to wide diffusion of the printed word – or ideograph – is a relatively inexpensive medium on which to print: Gutenberg's reinvention would have remained an intellectual curio had he not been able also to utilize another Chinese invention, paper. There have been attempts, not entirely convincing, to trace a concept of copyright back to the Song dynasty (960–1279 AD) but it was not until the early twentieth century that a copyright law was passed and that did not survive the establishment of the People's Republic in 1949. With the breakdown of China's isolation from the non-communist world from the late 1970s copyright was once more on the agenda, not least because the USA linked it to improving trade relations. Eventually, after a very long gestation the Copyright Act finally emerged in 1990 and came into force in the following year.

The Chinese expression for copyright is *banquan*, the right (*quan*) in the printing plate (*ban*), analogous to the English right in the printer's copy, but another expression, *zhuzuoquan*, has equal authority. *Zhuzuo* means writings and this is perhaps closer to author's right. (For those unfamiliar with the *pinyin* romanization of Chinese, the letter *q* is pronounced like English *ch* and *zh* is near enough to English *j*.)

The ideological thinking behind the Copyright Law appears in Art. 1:

> This law is formulated in accordance with the Constitution in order to protect the copyrights and neighbouring rights and interests of authors of literary, artistic and scientific works, to encourage the creation and propagation of works that are beneficial to the development of socialist spiritual and material civilisation, and to promote the development of a flourishing socialist scientific and cultural environment.

China is undergoing rapid metamorphosis but it is still, a decade later, a socialist society, though whether Art.1 in its present form will survive a future update of the law is an interesting question. The legal system is based in the Civil Law and the use of judicial precedent in the courts lacks authority, even if it is possible to locate previous decisions given the paucity of reported copyright cases. As a signatory to the Berne Convention China does not require registration to ensure copyright. However, there is a voluntary registration scheme which is valuable to provide proof of copyright ownership in a dispute, particularly for a foreigner.

Works protected include literary, artistic, natural science, social science and engineering technical works, Art. 3. Among the various forms which these may take are oral works, presumably speeches and lectures. Folk art forms (*quyi*) such as ballads and storytelling get special mention. Cinematographic films are covered by copyright, as are computer programs which are protected for 25 years, renewable for a further 25. Copyright does not apply to laws or judicial documents, or administrative documents, news and certain forms and tables. Moreover, the fair dealing exemptions in Art. 22 are extensive, giving, for example, the right to use a previously published work for study, research or enjoyment, and a blanket exemption for use by state entities. An employee has, broadly speaking, copyright in a work created by him or her in the course of employment, but the employer has priority in use of the work, Art. 16. The duration of rights is in general 50 years *pma*, but moral rights are perpetual.

Apart from civil remedies, criminal sanctions are provided for profit-making infringing activities, with penalties up to seven years imprisonment and substantial fines. Despite the Copyright Law, and China's membership of both Conventions, Berne and the UCC, and despite attempts by the authorities to clamp down, piracy of all sorts of copyright material is extensive. The concept of copyright infringement as a breach of another's property rights, still less as a crime, may be slow to take hold in China. The Chinese professor who could not understand the problem and said to the present author 'If your book is translated and published in China you will become famous and will be invited to give lectures', was betraying honest ignorance.

TWO OTHER DISTINCTIVE SYSTEMS

SOUTH AFRICA

After the turgid verbiage and convoluted arrangement of the former UK Copyright Act of 1956 which had been closely followed in the South African Copyright Act 1965, the new Copyright Act, No. 98 of 1978 was a model of clarity. It did not, however, please everybody. A reviewer in the *South Africa Law Journal* ((1979) 96 SALJ, 521) of a book on the new copyright law expressed himself in strong terms:

> it is such a lousy piece of legislation. Were our draftsmen wise in following so closely the compromise and sometimes unintelligible wording that emerged from the Paris modification of the Berne Convention in 1975 [*sic*, it should read 1971]? How long will the public have to endure all of the inanities?

One particular point noticed by the reviewer, that the Act was silent about an employer's rights in employees' work, was subsequently rectified by an amending Act of 1980, and there have been other amendments.

South Africa has a distinguished tradition of legal scholarship. The legal system is a composite one resulting from the modification of Roman-Dutch law, brought by the original settlers at a time when Leiden, in the Netherlands, was probably the most important centre of legal learning in the Civil Law, by the Common Law of England. (A somewhat similar hybrid system emerged in Ceylon (Sri Lanka) where the earlier Dutch regime gave way to British rule in 1798.) The Copyright Act shows this dual nature. The word copyright is used throughout the English version of the Act; in the Afrikaans text the word is *outersreg* (cf. Dutch, *auteursrecht*), suggesting the 'author's right' of the Civil Law tradition. An author's moral rights are protected by s. 20. Even after transfer of the copyright the author has the right 'to object to any distortion, mutilation or other modification of the work where such action is or would be prejudicial to the honour or reputation of the author'. This reproduces almost word for word the relevant part of Art. 6 *bis* of the Paris text of the Berne Convention. A leaning towards the Civil Law's insistence on an author's intellectual creativity rather than the mere 'sweat of the brow' may be seen in *Waylite Diaries* v. *First National Bank*, 1993, where considerable input and effort in producing diary pages was not sufficient if the work did not have 'meritorious distinctiveness'.

However, the influence of UK copyright law is seen in the provisions relating to cinematograph films which are the subject of copyright as in the UK, vested in the author who, in the case of a film, is the person by whom the arrangements for the making of the film were made. This effectively bypasses the difficulties of protecting the rights of all others concerned with making the film, which have given such trouble in Civil Law countries.

Remedies for infringement are both civil and criminal. The civil remedies are, as in the UK, damages, interdict (injunction), account and delivery up. Additional damages may be awarded for flagrant or particularly profitable infringement. Criminal penalties, which mainly cover commercial dealings in infringing material, are severe with up to 10 years imprisonment and a heavy fine at the maximum. There was acute controversy within the judiciary over the introduction of a search order on the lines of the UK Anton Piller order but its value was eventually recognized and accepted. The Act provides for the establishment of an advisory committee on copyright, an idea which has much to recommend it compared with the *ad hoc* committees of inquiry used in the UK. South Africa acceded to the Berne Convention as long ago as 1928 but has not joined the Universal Copyright Convention.

UNITED STATES OF AMERICA

After nearly 12 years gestation, a complete revision of US copyright law was enacted in 1976 and came into force on 1 January 1978. This marked the first major revision for nearly 70 years and swept away most of the provisions of the Copyright Act of 1909, leaving only a few issues, mostly concerned with rights in pre-1978 works. It introduced for the first time a single federal, that is nationwide, system of copyright protecting intellectual works from the time they are created. One of the difficulties which the USA faces is that there is not one, but some 50, legal systems, in the individual states. Under the old law, copyright in published works was provided for under federal law, whilst state laws governed unpublished works. There are still some grey areas where the states are able to exercise jurisdiction in ways that can vary considerably from state to state. The situation is, strictly speaking, that federal legislation pre-empts state laws except in certain areas not covered by the Act, but in practice it does not work out so clearly and neatly, and the limits of this provision have been the subject of many court actions.

The USA, like most former British possessions, has a Common Law system (though the state law of Louisiana still shows its French Civil Law ancestry) and the approach to copyright law is similar to that of England and the other Common Law countries. The attitude is materialistic, moral rights are protected under federal law by the Visual Artists Rights Act 1990 but are limited to artistic works only and only for the artist's lifetime. Otherwise, some states protect some moral rights, and federal law in other areas can give incidental protection. The introduction of *droit de suite* was considered quite recently but was rejected; it appears only in the state law of California. As in other countries, copyright is primarily a civil matter but criminal prosecutions can be brought in cases of infringement for commercial advantage or private financial gain: the authorities do not usually prosecute except where large-scale piracy is involved. Maximum penalties are draconian: up to five years imprisonment and a fine of $250 000 (approximately £170 000 at the exchange rate current in February 2001).

The USA was from 1955 a member of the Universal Copyright Convention (UCC) but not of Berne. The UCC, instituted in 1952, owed its existence to a desire to bring into an international convention those countries whose domestic laws on copyright gave a reasonable degree of protection but did not meet the more stringent requirements of Berne. In the nineteenth century the USA had a bad reputation for piracy even though copyright legislation dated back to 1790. (It is said that Robert Louis Stevenson was particularly annoyed because not only were his works pirated but the pirate also mis-spelled his name as 'Stephenson'.) The 1909 Act fell far short of the minimum conditions of the Berne Convention, but the 1976 Act narrowed the gap between US law and Berne requirements. It established a uniform nationwide system of protection which would certainly simplify the protection of foreign works if the USA joined Berne. It brought the duration of copyright (formerly 28 years from publication, renewable for a second 28-year period) up to the Berne level of 50 years *post mortem auctoris*, extended in 1998 to 70 years *pma* in parallel with the European Union. Anonymous and pseudonymous works, and 'works made for hire' (copyright in which belongs to the employer) were protected for 75 years from publication or 100 years from creation (now 95 and 120 years), whichever expires first.

The Act gives protection to 'works of authorship fixed in any tangible medium of expression'. The definition is all-embracing and the (non-exhaustive) list of kinds of works included is apt to cover nearly anything which one might expect to be copyrightable. Computer programs have long been regarded as subject to copyright, and loading a work into a computer's memory comes within the definition of fixation. One provision in the Act which attracted a lot of adverse criticism was the continuance of the notorious 'manufacturing clause' (first introduced in 1891) which insisted that 'non-dramatic literary material' by a US author could not be imported or distributed unless manufactured in the USA. The aim was to protect the printing industry and copyright protection was in effect denied to copies manufactured in violation. The clause, after undeserved extensions of its life, died an unlamented death in 1986.

The biggest stumbling block to the USA's joining Berne lay in the formalities which the 1976 Act required for acquisition or enforcement of copyright. These were much watered down from former provisions but still clashed with the Berne requirement of automatic protection without formalities. They were tidied up in 1989 as a preliminary to joining Berne and it is no longer compulsory to place the copyright line, © (or Copyright, or Copr. with the year of first publication and the copyright owner's name) on every publicly distributed copy. Nonetheless, it is advisable as it precludes a defence of innocent infringement. Under the 1909 Act omission of the notice would prove fatal to an infringement suit: the 1976 Act made it possible to cure an omission under certain circumstances. Copyright registration is optional but the owner of copyright in an unpublished or published work may register it by depositing copies, with the application and fee, with the Copyright Office, and provided that the Register of Copyrights (the Register is a person, not a record) is satisfied with the formalities, the work is registered. (Legal deposit of published works with the Library of Congress is compulsory; it is distinct from registration.) The advantage of registration is that no infringement action regarding a US work may be commenced until the work is registered. This does not generally apply to foreign works. Also compensation for infringement which took place before registration is strictly limited. Thus registration may be seen as some insurance in case the author subsequently has to assert his or her copyright in the courts. All was not plain sailing – the registration system had its adherents – but the USA was able to join Berne in 1989.

The USA has been a pioneer in the legal protection of semiconductor chips. The Semiconductor Chip Protection Act 1984 added a whole new chapter at the end of the 1976 Act. These provisions protect what are known as 'mask works' for a period of 10 years. An exception is made for what is known as 'reverse engineering'. This is the process of reproducing the mask work for the purposes of teaching, analysis and the like, and the results of this process may be incorporated in a new original mask work. The word original would seem to be significant here. Most recently, the

Digital Millennium Copyright Act 1998 has addressed some of the problems relating to the Internet, including reducing or ending the liability of online service providers when innocently handling infringing material. The Act also implements the two WIPO treaties of 1996, on Copyright and on Performances and Phonograms. It should be noted that the USA, as a major exporter of copyright works, including films, recordings and software, has been vigorous in promoting adherence to copyright in foreign countries, not infrequently by exercise of its considerable economic muscle.

This chapter has done no more than use a selection of national copyright regimes to illustrate different approaches to similar problems in different countries. It is not easy to keep up to date, but there are specialized journals and looseleaf works which are helpful, and some are mentioned in the Bibliography.

8 Transnational protection of intellectual property

The value of intellectual property is not confined neatly within national frontiers and the activities of the infringer can spread across many countries. The earliest attempts to protect within one country the intellectual property of another took the form of bilateral agreements between two states. Some states built up extensive networks of bilateral agreements, often as part of wider commercial treaties. The Paris Convention on industrial property (that is, mainly patents) of 1883 marked the beginning of a new phase, this time of multilateral agreements. It was followed three years later by the Berne Convention, concerned with the rights of authors. Since that time a considerable number of multilateral conventions, treaties or agreements have extended the transnational protection of most kinds of intellectual property on a worldwide, or more strictly limited, basis. The word transnational rather than international has been used in the title of this chapter for only in a few cases do we see any genuinely international protection. Rather there is national protection guaranteed by international agreement: each separate state applies its own law but undertakes to provide the protection of its laws for the intellectual property of other states. The various international agreements in the field of copyright and in other fields of intellectual property will be described in this chapter. Many, but not all, of these are administered by the World Intellectual Property Organization (WIPO), and a mention of that organization's activities will be included. The work of the European Union in this field fits most easily into this chapter rather than elsewhere and will also be dealt with.

COPYRIGHT: TRANSNATIONAL PROTECTION

Most countries (though not all) have their own copyright laws but the protection accorded by the copyright law of any particular country applies, of course, only within its own frontiers and may be restricted to its own nationals or to works published within that country. There is no international copyright law. However, a very large number of states have signed the Berne Convention or the Universal Copyright Convention (UCC), or both, though in many cases accession is recent, including two giants, China (Berne 1989, UCC 1992) and Indonesia (Berne 1997). These are the two major international copyright agreements: they protect the rights of authors of literary, scientific, dramatic, musical and artistic works, widely defined. Cinematographic films are also within the protection of these two conventions. They are not concerned with the rights of the makers of sound recordings, nor of performers, nor of broadcasting organizations. (Other agreements which cover these will be mentioned later.) Under these conventions each country agrees that it will give the protection of its own copyright law to the nationals of other signatory states and to works first published in those states. Thus, for example, a British author can bring an action in the French courts if his work (although published in the UK) is infringed in France. It is important to remember that each state applies its own national law, but the conventions do require each signatory state to provide by its law certain minimum standards of protection.

BERNE CONVENTION

Origins

The Berne Convention for the Protection of Literary and Artistic Works celebrated its centenary in 1986. With the rapid expansion of publishing in the eighteenth century, and then the advances in printing technology in the nineteenth century, the question of transnational protection became urgent. Many countries had adopted some form of protection of the rights of authors but such protection was confined within the borders of each state and gave no protection to works published elsewhere. Piracy was rife. In the many small German states the problem was especially severe: Goethe was one author who suffered. France and the UK, using two of the main international languages, were also affected. As a result some countries began to draw up and sign bilateral treaties providing for mutual protection of authors' rights. The German states, spurred on by the German book trade federation, the *Börsenverein des Deutschen Buchhandels* founded in 1825, built up a network of bilateral treaties early in the nineteenth century. In France the initiative came more from the authors: a considerable number of bilateral treaties had been signed by 1870.

In England it was made quite clear in a case reported in 1831, *Guichard* v. *Mori*, that there was no protection for a work written by a foreigner and published abroad. Some 30 years later Miss Maria Cummins, an American lady domiciled in New York, wrote a book called *Haunted Hearts* which was published by Sampson Low in two volumes, priced 16 shillings. Another publisher, Routledge, promptly brought out a one-volume edition for two shillings. Routledge resisted right up to the House of Lords, *Routledge* v. *Low*, 1868. Their Lordships disagreed whether the work of a foreigner resident abroad, which was first published in the UK, was entitled to copyright. However, Miss Cummins had taken the precaution of moving for a few days to Montreal, within the Queen's dominions, at the time when the book was published, so Sampson Low and Miss Cummins won their case and an injunction against Routledge. Already, following the International Copyright Act 1844, a number of treaties had been entered into by the UK with other countries, providing for mutual copyright protection. However, the USA was to retain a bad name for piracy of English language books for a very long time as no treaty was negotiated.

The *Société des Gens de Lettres* in France and other organizations of writers and artists continued to press for international action. The German Börsenverein and the newly-formed *Association littéraire internationale* (of which Victor Hugo was honorary president) got together and approached the Swiss government. Eventually at a conference at Berne in 1886 a multilateral Convention was signed by 10 states, France, Germany, the UK, Belgium, Italy, Spain, Switzerland, Haiti, Liberia and Tunisia. The Convention came into force in the following year. Although intended from the beginning to be open to all states, the Berne Union was slow to attract members from outside Europe. In fact a number of Latin American countries formed their own Montevideo Convention in 1889 and there were several attempts to establish a Pan-American copyright union. The Berne Convention has been revised and updated seven times, though the members are often slow to ratify the revised version: the UK needed to amend her law before it was possible to accept the most recent version, the Paris Act of 1971. The CDPA 1988 made ratification possible and it took place in 1990. A number of states (including the UK) accepted only part of the Stockholm revision of 1967.

The Convention today

From quite modest beginnings the Berne Union has grown and had at the beginning of 1990 a total of 84 member states. The 1990s saw a rapid expansion bringing the number up to 140 by mid-1999. (Updated lists of members of Berne and the other conventions are published annually in the World Intellectual Property Organization monthly *Intellectual Property Laws and Treaties*, and recent accessions as they occur.) The original 10 members are still members today (though there was a hiatus in the membership of Haiti and Liberia and they have only recently rejoined). The copyright law of the USA did not meet the criteria for membership, specifically on the duration of copyright (until the new US Act of 1976) and on non-compliance with Berne's requirement of automatic copyright without registration or other formalities. The Soviet Union also stayed outside: both these states became members of the Universal Copyright Convention. The Russian Federation and other successor states have joined Berne.

The full Assembly of members meets every three years and elects an Executive Committee. The Convention is administered by WIPO. Each member state agrees to pay a contribution to WIPO for the running costs of WIPO and six Conventions including Berne, on one of 14 scales. Only five countries (France, Germany, Japan, the UK and USA) pay the highest, Class I, contributions, the contributors at the lowest levels are developing countries.

Protection

The Berne Convention protects works first published in any of the member states (or first published simultaneously in a member and a non-member state), even if the author is not a citizen or resident in a member state. It also protects any published or unpublished works of a citizen or resident. The scope of the Convention is tersely summarized in Art. 1: 'The countries to which this Convention applies constitute a Union for the protection of the rights of authors in their literary and artistic works.' Art. 2(1) defines literary and artistic works as including 'every production in the literary and artistic domain, whatever may be the mode or form of its expression', and continues with a lengthy list of examples. Any form of written material is included, as are lectures, addresses, sermons and the like, dramatic works, choreography and mime, musical compositions, all kinds of two or three-dimensional works of art (including maps, prints, models and works of applied art) and architectural works. Photographs and cimematographic films (and works expressed by analogous processes) are included. Translations and adaptations as well as collections such as anthologies or encyclopaedias are protected, without prejudice to copyright in the original work. However, news of the day and mere items of press information are excluded.

Individual member states are allowed some latitude in certain fields. Works of applied art and industrial designs and models are one area where the extent of protection is left to the particular state (Art. 2(7)), and so are official legislative, administrative and legal texts (Art. 2(4)). Such things as industrial designs are in some countries (as in the UK) the subject of separate treatment. The texts of legislative enactments and official material of a similar nature are made freely available in some countries. (In the UK Crown copyright applies but is often waived.) Some latitude is allowed to individual states as regards political addresses and judicial proceedings, as well as the dissemination of public speeches and the like in the media for information purposes. Article 2(2) leaves it to individual states to decide whether or not protection shall apply if a work has not been fixed in some material form.

Acquisition and duration of rights

It is an important feature of the Berne Convention that copyright is automatic, with no formalities of registration or deposit of copies necessary for the author to acquire the rights which the Convention provides. These rights (which are reflected in UK copyright legislation) are primarily the exclusive rights to authorize reproduction, translation or adaptation, public performance or recitation, broadcasting and cinematographic production. The banning of formalities for the acquisition of copyright was one of the stumbling blocks to membership for certain countries (including, until 1989, the USA) which required registration or deposit as a condition of granting copyright. The other major stumbling block was the duration of protection required, a minimum of 50 years from the author's death. In fact more and more countries have adopted this term (or even a longer one). The minimum period of protection is 50 years from publication for anonymous or pseudonymous works and generally the same for films. In the case of photographs or works of applied art the minimum term fixed by a member state's law must be at least 25 years.

Moral rights and *droit de suite*

The Berne Convention attempts to harmonize the Civil Law view of author's right accepted by nearly all the original members, with the Common Law approach to copyright developed in the UK. Two issues where the approaches are at odds relate to moral rights and the so-called *droit de suite*. Article 6 *bis* (articles inserted by the later revisions are distinguished by the Latin numbers *bis*, *ter*) provides for recognition of an author's moral rights; the right, even after transfer of the economic rights, to claim authorship and to object to any distortion, mutilation, or other derogatory action in respect of the work which would be prejudicial to the author's honour and reputation. These rights survive the author's death (exercised, of course by the author's heirs or other persons or institutions having the legal right to do so) at least as long as copyright survives. There is, however, an exception for countries whose laws did not provide for such protection *post mortem* at the time when they accepted the revisions to the Convention. Even so, the UK's copyright law under the 1956 Act did not fully comply: the Copyright, Designs and Patents Act 1988 introduced at least minimal moral rights. *Droit de suite* is the right of an artist to claim a royalty every time his or her work is resold after the artist has disposed of it. (The right can also apply to an author's or composer's original manuscript.) In fact Art. 14 *ter* envisages this only when the laws of both the artist's own country and the country of sale (if different) provide for it. In fact *droit de suite* is not widespread among the countries of the Berne Union, it was expressly rejected in the UK 1986 White Paper on intellectual property.

One other area where the Civil Law and Common Law approaches differ is in the ownership of rights in a cinematographic film. Whilst in the UK the film company or producer will normally own all the rights in a film, the Civil Law approach allows rights to be claimed by a large number of people who made a creative input. Article 14 *bis* evades the issue, leaving the ownership of copyright in a cinematographic work to the legislation of each country, but providing that the owner (whoever or whatever he, she or it may be) shall enjoy the same rights as the author of an original work.

UNIVERSAL COPYRIGHT CONVENTION

A new convention

Although the Berne Convention was able to attract many states into membership, a number of countries, the most important being the USA and the Soviet Union, were unable to accept some of the conditions. In particular, the lengthy period of protection for 50 years *post mortem auctoris* excluded those countries with a shorter period, or one which might be related to the date of publication rather than the date of the author's death. Insistence on registration or other formalities as a prerequisite for protection excluded others. As a result, on the initiative of the United Nations Educational, Scientific and Cultural Organization (UNESCO) a second international agreement, the Universal Copyright Convention (UCC), came into being in 1952. The Convention had 83 members by 1990, a number which had risen to 97 by 2000.

Unlike the Berne Convention which is one of the many agreements administered by the World Intellectual Property Organization the UCC is administered by UNESCO but retains links with WIPO. It is governed by an intergovernmental committee of representatives of 18 member states selected to give a fair balance of national interests on the basis of geographical location, population, languages and stage of development. There is a considerable overlap of membership with Berne: the UK, a founder member of Berne, signed the UCC in 1957.

Rights and their duration

In many ways the UCC reflects the compromise necessary to bring in the countries which could not meet the more demanding requirements of Berne. It provides for 'adequate and effective protection' of the rights of authors and other copyright owners in their literary, scientific, musical, artistic and cinematographic works, though those rights are defined less extensively than in the Berne Convention: a state may legislate for exceptions which do not conflict with the provisions and spirit of the Convention. The rights include 'the basic rights ensuring the author's economic interests', including the right to authorize reproduction, performance or broadcasting. Protection extends to the original work or to 'any form recognizably derived from the original'. Whilst the author enjoys the exclusive right to authorize translation, a member state may restrict this by legislation to provide for the grant of a compulsory licence to somebody who wants to translate and publish a written work which has not been published in a language in general use in that state. This is subject to stringent conditions and the rights owner must receive satisfactory compensation. The UCC, like Berne, adopts the principle of national treatment, that is, each signatory state applies its own national laws to protect works first published in other member countries, or the published or unpublished works of nationals of the other states.

The difficulty over the minimum period of protection was met by providing for a minimum period of 25 years after the author's death, whilst (simplifying rather complicated provisions in Art. IV) allowing states which did not compute protection by reference to the author's death to use a minimum period of 25 years from publication or pre-publication registration. This met the situation of the USA which at that time allowed only 28 years protection, renewable once. (This was extended to 50 years *pma* by the 1976 Copyright Act, and subsequently to 70 years *pma*.) The question of registration or other formalities as a prerequisite for protection was met by permitting signatory states to retain this. However, the work of an author from another UCC country, or a work published in another UCC country, is protected if it bears the copyright line, usually shown as © with the copyright owner's name and the year of first publication.

One problem which had to be met was that members of the Berne Union would desert it and join the less demanding UCC. In order to avoid conflict between the two conventions it is expressly provided in the Universal Copyright Convention that if a country has withdrawn from Berne its works cannot be protected by the UCC (except in the case of a developing country for as long as it retains developing status, an exception which was added in 1971). Moreover, in the case of countries belonging both to Berne and the UCC, protection of works originating in a Berne country shall be governed by Berne, that is by the more demanding conditions of the former convention rather than by the easier conditions of the UCC.

Success of the Universal Copyright Convention

On the whole the UCC proved to be a satisfactory second-tier agreement, bringing around 25 countries, notably the USA, which could not accept the more rigorous conditions of Berne, into the international copyright community. However, many of these subsequently amended their laws and became members also of the senior convention, leaving only eight members of the UCC by January 2000 which are not also members of Berne. For a Berne Convention state there is no great advantage in adding UCC membership and around 50 Berne members, or over one-third of the membership, have not joined the UCC.

With the large majority now accepting the more rigorous Berne requirements the minimal formalities now required for a foreign work to obtain copyright protection are now unimportant. The 'adequate and effective' protection under the UCC contrasts with the more specific requirements of Berne but the effect of the difference has probably been more important in theory than in practice. What is most important is not the commitments which the state has undertaken but the level of enforcement, and there are some signatory states even of the Berne Convention in which the level of protection for foreign works is in practice appallingly low. (This applies not only to copyright but also to other forms of intellectual property: the fake Rolex watch is as much a symbol of the counterfeiter as fake software or compact discs.) The rights of authors and publishers often take a low priority with the law enforcement agencies, court processes can be dilatory and judges unsympathetic. Public opinion often does not condemn piracy and sees no moral issue involved in the exploitation of the work and investment of foreign authors and publishers. Even where the government is sympathetic, as for example in Egypt where there was a separate police unit concerned with intellectual property and the copyright law, modelled on that of France, is clear and well-drafted, the pirates can be slippery and can evade without much difficulty the relatively modest operations which the police can mount against them.

DEVELOPING COUNTRIES AND THE STOCKHOLM PROTOCOL

The Berne Convention has been revised several times and in 1967 a conference was held in Stockholm to update it in the light of recent developments. At this conference a number of developing countries, led by India and Tunisia, brought strong pressure for extensive concessions to developing countries. They sought relaxation of the restrictions on translation and reproduction of foreign works, more particularly in the scientific and educational fields, with a view to aiding economic development. The high prices of foreign textbooks had serious effects on higher education. It hardly needed to be stressed that publishing costs in the European countries whose textbooks were in demand in the Third World were very high and the cost of textbooks was often far beyond the means of students in developing countries. The widespread use of the English language, a legacy of British colonialism, had meant that works of British and US publishers and authors were particularly in demand. There was also a considerable demand for books in French, particularly in the former French territories of Africa. There was (and indeed still is) some feeling in developing countries that in some way the more developed countries owe them a debt arising from colonial 'exploitation' in the past, and that in seeking copyright concessions they were asking no more than they were morally entitled to. Although the colonial powers probably gave far more to their colonies than they took out of them, the argument appealed to new-found nationalist aspirations, and it was sympathetically received by many other nations represented at the Stockholm conference. As a result a Protocol Regarding Developing Countries was added to the Berne Convention.

The Stockholm Protocol allowed a developing country, recognized as such by the United Nations, to make a declaration that it proposed to take advantage of the special concessions. The main concessions provided that any national of a developing country could obtain from that country's government a non-exclusive compulsory licence to translate or reproduce (and export to other developing countries) any work which had been published not less than three years previously and had not been translated or published, as the case may be, in that developing country, provided that the permission of the owner of the rights in that work had been sought and refused. (A 'compulsory licence' means that the rights owner is compelled to grant it, it is 'non-exclusive' so other applicants could also apply for one.) The concession was limited to works to be used for teaching, study or research and the original rights owner must receive adequate compensation. An original author would, in any case, lose the translation right if it were not exercised within 10 years of publication. Furthermore, a developing country could reduce the lengthy Berne period of protection to 10 years in the case of photographs and 25 years for other works.

THE PARIS ACT

In fact the Stockholm Protocol was largely a dead letter. Publishers and authors in the developed countries not surprisingly complained that their rights had been taken away over their heads. It took four years before a satisfactory compromise was worked out but in 1971 new provisions, the Paris Act, were added as an Appendix to the Berne Convention, and in almost the same terms as Articles V *bis*, V *ter* and V *quater*, to the Universal Copyright Convention.

The provisions are complicated, reflecting the hard bargaining which took place before they were enacted. Simplifying rather drastically, they provide that compulsory licences to publish translations for the purpose of teaching, scholarship or research may be obtained if the work has not been translated and published in a language in general use in the developing country within three years of original publication. Similarly, a compulsory licence may be obtained to publish an edition 'for use in connection with systematic instructional activities' if the work has not been published in the devloping country at a price reasonably related to local prices for comparable works within a certain period from publication. The period is three years for scientific and technical works, seven years for fiction, poetry, drama and music, and for art books, and five years for other works. The original rights owner must receive compensation equivalent to normal royalties and works produced under the concessions may not be exported. Audio-visual works are included (but not sound recordings).

The general effect, then of the concessions to developing countries added by the Paris Act to Berne and the UCC is that the copyright owner cannot object to the publication of a local edition or translation of a work if authorized by the competent authority, but will get reasonable compensation from the publisher. The Stockholm concessions on duration of copyright were met by an escape clause allowing developing countries to leave Berne and join the UCC.

PAN-AMERICAN COPYRIGHT CONVENTIONS

Various conventions have been concluded between countries of North and South America, the most important being that of Buenos Aires (1910) with around 20 members, including the USA: a work protected by copyright in one Convention country will automatically be protected without formalities in another. The earliest American copyright convention was that of Montevideo of 1889. By what are in effect bilateral arrangements some Latin American countries have mutual relationships with others in Europe.

THE ROME CONVENTION

Neighbouring rights

The Berne Convention and the Universal Copyright Convention cover the same subject matter, broadly speaking the rights of authors or creators of literary, dramatic, musical and artistic works. In addition these conventions protect rights in cinematographic films. Their subject matter is, in effect, works of creativity, and they leave certain other important areas without transnational protection. These areas might well be protected in individual states, under copyright legislation or analogous laws. Thus in the UK sound recordings and broadcasts are protected under copyright law and the rights of performers under the performers' protection legislation.

Sound recordings became important around the first decade of the twentieth century; sound broadcasting developed in the 1920s and 1930s; television took off in the 1950s. Not only did these new media for entertainment and information pose problems relating to their own protection but they also made possible the reproduction of an actor's, singer's or musician's actual live performance. Thus there was a number of attempts to give to performers, to producers of sound recordings and to broadcasting organizations, rights which transcended the limits of national frontiers. Such rights fitted rather uneasily (in the view of many experts) into copyright law, or particularly into the *droit d'auteur* or *Urheberrecht* of the Civil Law countries. Hence they tended to be placed in a special category as 'neighbouring rights' or 'related rights'. Owing to the different approaches of different countries it was necessary to leave the ownership of copyright (or whatever right was given in an individual country) in a cinematographic work to the legislation of individual countries. Neighbouring rights were eventually provided for in a separate convention: it is not easy to see any logic in that, except in the fact that many Berne and UCC countries were not ready to extend protection that far.

The Rome Convention, which finally emerged after a very long gestation in 1961, is sometimes described as the convention on neighbouring rights but its full title is the International Convention for the Protection of Performers, Producers of Phonograms and Broadcasting Organizations. The word 'phonogram' has not passed into current use: it means a sound recording, 'an exclusively aural fixation of sound' as the Convention defines it, thus excluding videos (which count as cinematographic works, though they are not expressly mentioned in the conventions). Membership was rather slow to take off, reaching only 35 by 1990 and 61 10 years later. The UK signed in 1964 but the USA stayed out and Asia is almost unrepresented.

Protection

The Rome Convention, like Berne and the UCC, applies the principle of national treatment. Each signatory state applies its own law to protect the rights against infringement. Owing to the three diverse subjects, performers, phonograms and broadcasts, the provisions are rather complicated. Simplifying somewhat, a phonogram is protected if the producer is a national of a signatory state or if it was first made or published in a signatory state. For a broadcast the qualification is transmission or headquarters in such a state. A performer has rights if the performance appears in a phonogram or broadcast as above, or if it took place in a signatory state. A performer can object to the broadcast, recording or reproduction of a recording of the performance. Broadcasting organizations can object to re-broadcast, recording or reproduction of recordings. Producers of phonograms have the right to authorize or prohibit reproduction. Protection must be for at least 20 years.

A state may grant exceptions for private use or teaching or scientific research and may apply other exceptions which appear in its literary and artistic copyright law. If a country imposes registration or other formalities for the grant of protection to phonograms it must be satisfied with the symbol P in a circle with the year of first publication and the names of rights owners.

THE PHONOGRAMS CONVENTION

The Phonograms Convention, instituted at Geneva in 1971, is aimed at piracy of sound recordings. It is short, terse and straightforward: Article 2 is the important one:

> Each Contracting State shall protect producers of phonograms who are nationals of other Contracting States against the making of duplicates without the consent of the producer and against the importation of such duplicates, provided that any such making or importation is for the purpose of distribution to the public, and against the distribution of such duplicates to the public.

Each country is left free to decide how best to do this, whether by copyright or another specific right, by criminal sanctions or by unfair competition law. In the UK it might be said that all three methods are in use. The Copyright, Designs and Patents Act provides both civil remedies and criminal sanctions in respect of infringement, and although we have no law of unfair competition as such, a passing-off action is available to the producer whose goods are passed off by another manufacturer as those of the genuine producer. The UK became a party to the Convention, with other founding members, in 1973 and hence has an obligation to make similar remedies available to nationals of other signatory states. A minimum duration of protection of 25 years is prescribed and any formalities may be satisfied by use of the symbol ® with the year of first publication and identification of the rights owner. Fifty-seven states had signed by mid-1999: although China, India and Japan had signed, Fiji and Korea were the only other Asian members.

OTHER INTERNATIONAL AGREEMENTS IN THE FIELD OF COPYRIGHT

The Satellite Convention (Brussels 1974) binds its members to take measures to prevent distribution of satellite broadcasting programmes to the public on or from its territory by any distributor for whom the satellite signals were not intended. Twenty-three states only had signed by mid-1999, the UK not being among them.

The Nairobi Treaty of 1981 on the Protection of the Olympic Symbol protects the familiar interlaced rings symbol from any commercial use not licensed by the Olympic authorities. The Vienna Agreement for the Protection of Typefaces (1973) has attracted little support so far.

The Council of Europe (not to be confused with the Council of the European Union) has sponsored three agreements relating to broadcasting. The European Agreement Concerning Programme Exchange by means of Television Films (1958) met the difficulty of licensing broadcast programmes which results from the complex *droit d'auteur* rights, by agreement on a simpler right analogous to copyright for this purpose. Of the 15 signatories so far only Tunisia is from outside Europe though the agreement is open to all. Signatories of the European

Agreement on the Protection of Television Broadcasts (1960) agree to protect television broadcasts against unlicensed use other than for private viewing: there are six signatories. The European Agreement for the Prevention of Broadcasts Transmitted from Stations Outside National Territories (1965) binds its 18 members to apply their criminal law to control pirate broadcasting stations. The UK has signed all three of these.

INDUSTRIAL PROPERTY: THE PARIS CONVENTION

ORIGINS

Although the grant of monopolies to inventors has a long history it was really with the rapid development of industry in the nineteenth century that many countries were moved to adopt modern patent laws to protect and encourage inventors. Such laws, of course, gave protection only in one country, indeed national protectionist sentiments were strong and states were frequently unwilling to give protection to foreigners' inventions except under conditions of strict reciprocity. Thus (as in the copyright field) various bilateral agreements emerged between particular countries, often half-hidden within more general commercial treaties. In the 1870s moves began towards an international agreement concerning the protection of patents. Eventually, on the initiative of the French government, a conference of states was held in 1880, and in 1883, at Paris, an International Convention for the Protection of Industrial Property was signed by representatives of 11 states and came into force in the following year.

To start with, as may be expected, the Paris Union was mainly a European organization. The UK was a member from the beginning, the Scandinavian countries soon joined, and by 1895 all the major states of Western Europe were members except Germany (who joined in 1903). Outside Europe progress was slower. Tunisia was a founder member, the USA joined in 1887 and Japan in 1899. A hundred years later, following a spurt in membership in the 1990s, the number of members stood at 155. (Annual membership lists of all the conventions are conveniently found in the WIPO monthly *Intellectual Property Laws and Treaties*.)

PATENT APPLICATIONS

Unlike the two copyright conventions, the Paris Convention does not provide for automatic rights in other states. Whilst copyright in one Berne or UCC country automatically establishes corresponding rights in any other, the applicant for a patent must make application separately in every country where protection is sought. However, the Convention does mean that a person from one country may apply for, and be granted, a patent under the same conditions as a national of the state where the patent is sought, without any requirement that the applicant must be domiciled or resident, or have an establishment of any kind, in that state. (Whilst some countries grant patents freely to almost any foreigners, many signatory states of the Paris Convention do not grant patents to persons from outside the Paris Union unless they have a domicile or establishment in a Union country.) In patent applications it is always important to get the application in before anyone else and before any information about the invention is made public. This establishes the filing date, or priority date. A priority date established in one Convention country gives priority in any other provided that the application is filed in this other country within 12 months. So any use or publication of the invention in that 12-month period which might have made the second application invalid will not, in fact, affect it. The rights of foreigners to apply for patents under the Convention are specifically included in the UK Patents Act 1977, ss. 5 and 90. These are the two most important provisions of the Convention, equal treatment for nationals and foreigners, and priority backdated to the first application in any Convention country. It will be appreciated that this is a much less comprehensive kind of transnational protection than that given by the copyright conventions.

OTHER PROVISIONS

In addition, the Paris Convention (which is quite a lengthy document) does include a number of other important provisions which have the effect of removing many hindrances to the establishment and exercise of patent rights in a country other than the inventor's own. Thus, for example, whilst some countries will revoke a patent if the patentee is found to be abusing the monopoly rights, the Convention provides that this may be done only if the remedy of compulsorily requiring the patentee to grant licences to other persons to use the patent is not effective to stop the abuse. Temporary protection is granted for goods exhibited at official international trade fairs. It is not infringement to use an invention in a ship, aircraft or vehicle temporarily in a country where it is protected by a patent. Many articles of the Convention are of a detailed administrative nature, restricting to some extent the freedom of individual countries to develop idiosyncratic patent systems of their own. However, the Paris Convention does leave a great deal of liberty to the signatory states: it is very far from imposing a uniform patent system, or an integrated transnational method of application.

International patent law is fiendishly complicated and even the most skilled practitioner cannot hope to attain any degree of expertise in the law of more than a few countries. It is usual to employ the services of a local patent attorney or agent when applying for a patent, or engaging in other patent matters, in a foreign country. Nevertheless, the Paris Convention is probably the most important international agreement in the whole field of intellectual property (indeed it is sometimes called simply The International Convention), benefiting the inventor by allowing him or her to obtain protection in any Convention country, but also benefiting the consumer or user in giving access to products which otherwise might be subject to defensive restrictions by the owner of the original rights, or else to exposure to pirated goods of uncertain quality. The Paris Convention, like Berne (but not the UCC) is administered by the World Intellectual Property Organization. The Convention specifically allows regional or other special agreements between groups of member countries.

OTHER PATENT AGREEMENTS

Patent agreements which, as it were, bring the Paris Convention down to the practical level were discussed in Chapter 6. The European Community Patent Convention, if ever it gets started, will provide a genuinely international single patent, albeit restricted to the member states of the European Union. The European Patent Convention provides a bundle of national patents, chosen from the signatory states, for a single application. On a much wider scale the Patent Cooperation Treaty has a two-stage process which simplifies application for patents in any number of over 100 signatories, and which attracted more than 90 000 applications in the year 2000.

OTHER REGIONAL CONVENTIONS: AFRICA, AMERICA, FORMER USSR

There are several other conventions on industrial property which operate on a regional basis and provide some measure of cooperation in the field of patents or other areas of industrial property. In Africa 14 states which use English as a means of scientific and other communication belong to the African Regional Industrial Property Organization (ARIPO), originally the Industrial Property Organization for English-Speaking Africa, which stems from an agreement signed at Lusaka (Zambia) in 1976. Among other activities it has produced model laws for the guidance of its members. OAPI (in English the African Intellectual Property Organization) brings together 15 states in a Francophone body originating in an agreement at Libreville (Gabon) in 1962. All the parties to OAPI and, with the exception of Somalia, ARIPO are members of the Paris Union. Another regional agreement is a Pan-American convention on trade marks (of limited effect). The Eurasian Patent Organization (formed in Moscow in 1994) brings together the Russian Federation and eight constituent republics of the former USSR, now independent. A Eurasian patent, valid for all the signatories, is obtained by a single application (in Russian) in Moscow, or through the Patent Cooperation Treaty.

TRADE MARKS: PARIS CONVENTION

Although the Paris Convention for the Protection of Industrial Property is generally thought of in the context of patents, its scope is in fact much wider and includes industrial designs and trade marks. There are two advantages in the Convention for the person seeking registration of a trade mark. First, application in a Convention country gives a priority right in any other Convention country provided the later application is not more than six months after the former. Secondly, a trade mark duly registered in the applicant's country of origin is eligible for registration and protection in any other country of the Paris Union, subject to limited general exceptions and the law of that country.

MADRID AGREEMENT

The Paris Convention provides national treatment for trade marks as it does for patents, in other words it does not create an international trade mark, it only promises registration in other countries without hindrance. The Madrid Agreement of 1891 allows the owner of a trade mark in the owner's own country to apply through that country's authorities for registration of the mark with the World Intellectual Property Organization. The applicant designates the member states in which it seeks registration and the mark will, if generally acceptable in each country, be duly registered. The applicant thus gets a bundle of national registrations, not a single international one. For largely procedural reasons the UK stayed outside until a supplementary Madrid Protocol was signed in 1989 which answered the objections. Sixty-one states have now signed the Madrid Agreement and 37 the Protocol. There is a considerable overlap but a few, including the UK, are bound only by the Protocol, and some which have signed the original Agreement have not signed the Protocol. The Trademark Law Treaty, also administered by WIPO, was adopted at Geneva (WIPO's headquarters) in 1994. It provides for a measure of harmonization of trade mark procedures, and so far has attracted rather more than 20 adherents.

WORLD INTELLECTUAL PROPERTY ORGANIZATION

The World Intellectual Property Organization (WIPO) or to use its French abbreviation, OMPI (Organisation Mondiale de Propriété Intellectuelle) was born in an international convention at Stockholm in 1967. It took over from BIRPI, the International Bureaux for the Protection of Intellectual Property, which provided the administration and secretariat for the international conventions. After a short transition period the WIPO Convention came into force and WIPO was recognized as a United Nations specialized agency in 1974. Membership is open to member states of the international conventions, of the United Nations and its agencies, and to other states by invitation. With 175 members at the end of the year 2000, increased from 126 in 1990, there are not many states outside the organization. Most, but by no means all, are members of Berne and the Paris Union. The UK was a founder member.

The Organization's objectives are to promote the protection of intellectual property throughout the world through cooperation among states and, further, to ensure administrative cooperation under the international intellectual property conventions. The definition of intellectual property leaves nothing out. It includes rights relating to literary, artistic and scientific works, performances, phonograms, broadcasts, inventions, scientific discoveries, industrial designs, trade marks and service marks, trade names, unfair competition, and all other rights arising from intellectual activity in the industrial, scientific, literary or artistic fields.

The functions of the Organization are to administer the various intellectual property conventions and other international agreements and to take appropriate measures to facilitate protection of intellectual property throughout the world. It will help to harmonize national laws, encourage international agreements, offer cooperation to states asking for legal or technical help, collect and disseminate information and promote and publish research.

WIPO produces a number of useful publications, including the monthly *Intellectual Property Laws and Treaties* (successor to *Industrial Property and Copyright*) which provides an invaluable updating service. It promotes seminars on special topics for particular audiences. Nearly a score of international conventions, treaties and agreements (the more important of which have been mentioned above) are administered by the secretariat, the International Bureau, headed by the Director General. The headquarters are in Geneva where there is a large staff recruited internationally. The Organization is financed by contributions on various scales from the member states.

THE WIPO TREATIES

A WIPO initiative has been two intellectual property treaties signed in Geneva in 1996. The Copyright Treaty had, by mid-1999, 51 signatories, and the Performances and Phonograms Treaty, 50. The UK has signed both, as have the USA and the European Union. With the exception of Indonesia, Asian countries were conspicuously absent at this stage. The Copyright Treaty clarifies a number of rules and concepts which are already embodied in the international conventions and in the law or practice of many states, for example that copyright protects expression, not ideas, and that computer programs are to be protected as literary works. It adds provisions on rental right, distribution rights of authors, and the duration of protection of photographs (50 years *pma*, instead of Berne's 25 years).

The Performances and Phonograms Treaty, like the Copyright Treaty, clarifies and defines much in existing law and practice, and adds rights which are mostly already to be found in UK law. The function of these two treaties is to reinforce, and perhaps update, the best practice in protection of the rights which they cover.

TRIPS

The TRIPS Agreement, in full the Agreement on Trade-related Aspects of Intellectual Property Rights, including Trade in Counterfeit Goods, stems from the Uruguay Round of the General Agreement on Tariffs and Trade (GATT) which completed its often fraught deliberations in 1994 and created the World Trade Organization (WTO) as the successor to GATT. Included in the Final Act signed by the 128 participating states (plus the European Union) was the TRIPS Agreement. Not everybody was happy with this. Developing countries had often lined up against the economically advanced states, and particularly against the USA whose commercial muscle, rather than genuine consensus, was widely felt to have produced the final agreement. Moreover, TRIPS introduced a new intellectual property regime backed by the threat of trade sanctions which was felt in some quarters to be sidelining the long established organizations in this field, in spite of due respect being paid to cooperation with the World Intellectual Property Organization. The level of protection required is that of the Berne Convention in the copyright field and the Paris Convention for industrial property. Provisions on rights and their acquisition, procedures, infringement and remedies, criminal sanctions and enforcement, accord with good practice already accepted in the UK and other advanced countries. What is novel is that the TRIPS Agreement has teeth, for states (not individuals, but states can back their own individuals or companies) can call on the WTO dispute resolution procedures with the ultimate weapon of trade sanctions against an offending state. With regard to one important point, whether the TRIPS provisions have a direct effect on the law of signatory states, the USA has taken a robust line and said that they do not. In the UK the same view prevailed in *Ex parte Lenzing*, 1997, but the question may not be finally settled.

EUROPEAN UNION

There are currently (Spring 2001) 15 members of the European Union (EU). They are Austria, Belgium, Denmark, Finland, France, Germany, Greece, Ireland, Italy, Luxembourg, Netherlands, Portugal, Spain, Sweden (but not Norway), and the UK. Several applicants for membership are in the pipeline and this list may soon be out of date. All, except Ireland and the UK, adhere to the Civil Law tradition which has not made harmonization easier with the two Common Law countries.

In pursuit of its aim of completing the internal market the EU has carried out a vigorous programme of harmonization and new legislation in the field of intellectual property, to prevent distortion of the market by different laws in individual states. EU legislation most commonly takes the form of Regulations or Directives. A Regulation is directly applicable in every state of the Union. A Directive, on the other hand, must be incorporated in the law of each state by legislation or regulation in that state and a time limit for compliance is usually set.

EU legislation may be found in the massive volumes of the Official Journal (OJ). These are in two series, L for legislation, and C for other matters, and run to 40 or more volumes each year. (References are given as, for example, [1993] OJ L290/9, which, reading from the end, means page 9 of section 290 of the Legislation series of the Official Journal for 1993. A Directive will also have its own number, for example, 98/44, which means item 44 in 1998.)

The Official Journal makes pretty turgid reading, only slightly relieved by the Directives on intellectual property. A Directive will start with a lengthy and wordy preamble of explanatory clauses beginning 'Whereas …' setting out the reasons for the particular piece of legislation, before coming to the (usually terser) substantive part. A Directive is usually incorporated into UK law by a Statutory Instrument (SI) made under the powers conferred on the appropriate Minister by ss. 2(2) and 2(4) of the European Communities Act 1972. The SI will take the form of regulations (distinguish from the EU Regulation), for example, the Duration of Copyright and Rights in Performances Regulations 1995 (SI 1995/3297). (Note the way of referring to Statutory Instruments, alternatively SI 1995 No. 3297: thousands of them on every subject under the sun are produced every year.) These Regulations amend a statute, the Copyright, Designs and Patents Act 1988, to implement the extension of the duration of copyright from, in most cases, 50 years *pma* to 70 years, as required by the EU Directive No 93/98 Harmonizing the Term of Protection of Copyright and certain Related Rights.

A full table of EU measures on intellectual property in force and pending is published at intervals in the *European Intellectual Property Review*. Those which are in force will have been implemented in UK law, which has been discussed in earlier chapters so it is not necessary to give details at this point and we shall confine ourselves to listing some of the more important.

Regulation 40/94 on the Community Trade Marks is very detailed, and sets out the structure and working of the Community trade mark office and all particulars relating to this important innovation.

Directive 89/104 on Trade Marks is different: it requires states to bring their law on trade marks in line with the provisions in the Directive. It is reflected in many provisions of the Trade Marks Act 1994.

Directive 92/100 on Rental Rights provides for authors, performers and others to permit or forbid rental or lending of their works. It was implemented by the Copyright and Related Rights Regulations 1996 (SI 1996/2967) amending the CDPA.

Directive 96/9 on the Legal Protection of Databases was very controversial and the UK fought a rearguard battle to save copyright for databases. The battle was lost and the author's rights were limited to a limited *sui generis* right for 15 years only unless the database exhibited the author's own intellectual creativity. It was implemented by the Copyright and Rights in Databases Regulations 1997 (SI 1998/3032). Here Part II of the Regulations introduce some amendments to the CDPA, but the substance of the Regulations is in Part III which, at some length, actually enacts, without reference to statute, the new provisions.

The volume of paper churned out by the European Union must seriously deplete the forests of Europe and it would not be appropriate to attempt to distill it all here. There are many useful books on European law and enough on intellectual property.

9 Legal cautions for the information provider

This chapter deals with some of the legal curbs on the freedom to supply or disseminate information. Some restraints have already been touched on earlier, for example questions of contract and negligence which were mentioned in Chapter 1.

The topics discussed in this chapter concern the free dissemination of information, taken in its widest sense, and the restrictions which can be of importance to the librarian or information scientist as well as anybody else in the information and media industries. The first, defamation, is an intricate but very interesting subject. It is a matter for the civil courts (if we treat the rare offence of criminal libel logically as a separate matter). Three topics which follow are criminal offences, namely criminal libel, blasphemous libel and obscene libel. Incitement to racial hatred is another criminal matter (it is not the same as racial discrimination). The chapter ends with consideration of breach of confidence in both the private and commercial spheres, and a brief consideration of the impact of human rights legislation.

DEFAMATION

Defamation is the communication or 'publication' to a third person of a statement which tends to lower another person in the eyes of right-thinking members of society, or which tends to make them shun that other person, as Lord Atkin defined it in *Sim* v. *Stretch*, 1936. (The word 'publication' is often used but it does not mean that the statement is published in the usual sense, only that it is communicated to someone else.) There have been various other definitions of defamation which add little or nothing to this. The Faulks Committee on defamation, which examined the law thoroughly and reported in 1975, proposed a statutory definition which read:

> Defamation shall consist of the publication to a third party of matter which in all the circumstances would be likely to affect a person adversely in the eyes of reasonable people generally.

It might be suggested that the substitution of 'reasonable people' for 'right-thinking members of society' is not an improvement: even though 'right-thinking' may be open to various interpretations, it is not so vague as 'reasonable'. We shall deal shortly with the difference between libel and slander: put simply, libel is written (or put in some other permanent form) and slander is spoken.

The first point to note is that there must be some sort of publication to a third party. If you accuse a person in private of being a swindler, or if you post a letter in a sealed envelope to that person making the same accusation, then the person accused cannot bring an action against you for defamation. This rule goes back as far as the seventeenth century when one medical practitioner wrote 'an infamous, malicious, scandalous, obscene letter' to another, sealed it up and addressed it (with some sarcasm, it appears) 'To his loving friend Mr Edward'. The recipient had no case against the writer, *Edwards* v. *Wooton*, 1607. Even when an unsealed letter was opened and read by the recipient's butler the court held that there was no publication of the libel to the butler. He was not supposed to open letters and the sender would hardly expect that this would happen, *Huth* v. *Huth*, 1915. It would probably be otherwise if a letter were sent to somebody's office where it was likely to be opened by a secretary, particularly if the sender knew of the practice in the office. Similarly it would be risky to write on a postcard anything defamatory of the person to whom it was addressed: the postman might read it.

Needless to say, if the recipient communicates the defamatory matter to others there would be no action against the writer: it would be the recipient's own fault that the libel was published to them. It is not possible to defame the dead and the claimant's death puts an abrupt stop to a libel action: the heirs cannot carry it on. A company can sue for defamation in respect of its business reputation but an unincorporated association (like a trade union or a club) cannot sue (though individual officers can, and will frequently have their actions backed and financed by their parent body in cases where it concerns the latter). It was decided in *Derbyshire County Council* v. *Times Newspapers*, 1993, that a public authority could not defend its reputation by a libel action. The accountability of democratic institutions outweighs other factors in such cases.

RIGHT-THINKING PERSONS

The standard as to whether a statement is defamatory does depend on the rather nebulous concept of the right-thinking member of society. In those segments of society which are not right-thinking an accusation of being a police informer might be regarded as the worst form of vilification but it would not be sufficient to found a defamation action. A couple of cases illustrate this.

Edmund Byrne was a member of a golf club. Somebody gave information to the police about illegal gambling machines on the club premises and an anonymous doggerel verse implying that Byrne was the informer was posted on the wall where the machines had stood. The club proprietors allowed the verse to stay there and Byrne sued them for libel. The judges agreed that one of the defendants, if not both, must take the responsibility for publishing the libel by allowing it to stay on the wall instead of removing it. But was it libel? There was a difference of opinion in the Court of Appeal. All three members of the court agreed that it could not be libel to state that somebody had informed the police about criminal activities, but Lord Justice Greer read into the doggerel an additional implication that Byrne was disloyal to his fellow club members and he would have allowed the plaintiff's claim, *Byrne* v. *Deane*, 1937.

In an old Irish case, *Mawe* v. *Pigott*, 1869, the parish priest of Tralee lost his case against a newspaper proprietor. The alleged libel falsely reported the plaintiff as saying that he would watch those men who were rebels (this was the period of Fenian disturbances) and would denounce them to the authorities. The court held that the report, though false, was not libellous. 'The very circumstances,' said the court, 'which will make a person be regarded with disfavour by the criminal classes will raise his character in the estimation of right-thinking men.'

DEFAMATION AND FREE SPEECH

The law of defamation is, of course, closely connected with the right to free speech. It was formerly not unusual for somebody to issue what came to be known as a 'gagging writ', starting a libel action in order to stifle discussion: it can be contempt of court to publish anything that would prejudice a free trial, as long as the case is *sub judice*. Politicians sometimes did this when something discreditable about them was aired before an election: the action would be quietly dropped after the election. In another sphere Dr Wallersteiner issued a libel writ against a shareholder in a company which he controlled and met criticisms of some apparently dubious transactions by the assertion that the matters were *sub judice*. He kept the libel proceedings dragging on for seven years before the Court of Appeal put a stop to them. The lengthy report of the case, *Wallersteiner* v. *Moir*, 1974, with all these transactions detailed, makes fascinating reading.

The Contempt of Court Act 1981 removed the worst abuses, providing that the *sub judice* rule does not apply as soon as the claim is issued but only when the case has been set down for trial or a trial date fixed, which would be much later. Moreover, discussion in good faith of public affairs or matters of general public interest will not be contempt of court if the risk of prejudice is merely incidental to the discussion.

It sometimes happens that the claimant tries to get an interim injunction to stop an alleged libel until the case goes to trial. The courts will not grant this if the defendant intends to plead 'justification' (that is, the truth of the statement), fair comment or privilege (see below), unless the defendant knows that it is untrue and intends dishonestly and maliciously to carry on. (The word 'malice' has a special meaning in the law: it refers to no more than a bad motive rather than the viciousness implied in the usual use of the word.) In other words, it is difficult to get an interim injunction to curb further dissemination of an alleged libel until trial. In *Harakas* v. *Baltic Exchange*, 1982, the Court of Appeal said that this rule is a matter of principle which must be observed. The plaintiff (claimant) shipowner tried to stop the second defendant, a bureau set up to combat maritime fraud, from communicating certain suspicions to persons contemplating business with the plaintiff's company.

PROCEDURE

Defamation is normally heard as a civil matter, in the Queen's Bench Division of the High Court. (Criminal libel is dealt with separately below.) Much of it derives from old case law, supplemented by the Defamation Act 1952, and recently by reforms in the Defamation Act 1996. Although the number of cases which reach the courts in any year is quite small, they often concern prominent public figures and tend to hit the headlines. Unlike nearly all civil cases, defamation trials are heard before a judge and jury unless the parties consent to dispense with a jury, or unless the trial will involve prolonged examination of documents or accounts. The judge decides whether the words complained of are capable of bearing the meaning alleged by the claimant and of being defamatory, whilst the jury has to decide whether they actually did bear that meaning and were indeed defamatory. This will, of course, involve the jury in deciding on any defence of justification, that is that the allegations were true. The jury must also decide, where it is relevant, whether the defendant made the statement with 'malice' (in the legal sense).

An unprecedented decision of the Court of Appeal concerns Mr Bruce Grobbelaar, a professional footballer, who brought a libel action against *The Sun* newspaper for allegations that he had taken bribes to influence the results of football matches. The jury at first instance found in his favour and awarded him substantial damages. The Court of Appeal examined the evidence in the trial, held that the jury's decision was totally unreasonable and overturned the jury's verdict (*The Times*, news item 20 January 2001, and other newspapers). Normally a jury's decision is sacrosanct: the only, and rare, recourse on appeal is an order for a new trial.

DAMAGES AND COSTS

If the jury finds in favour of the claimant then it is the jury which assesses the damages. Formerly they had no guidance from the court and were often influenced, it seems, by spectacular cases with very high awards of damages which had got into the popular press. As a result damages were frequently set at unreasonably high levels. When the defendant has acted especially viciously, or has profited considerably from his act, the jury may award additional or exemplary damages. The leading case is *Broome* v. *Cassell*, 1972, in which the House of Lords refused to upset a large punitive award against the defendant publishers for serious allegations about the plaintiff as a naval officer escorting a wartime convoy which was destroyed by the enemy. The late Mr Robert Maxwell, publisher of the *Daily Mirror*, was awarded £5000 for insinuations in *Private Eye* that he was financing the travels of the then Labour Party leader in order to get a peerage. In addition the jury awarded £50 000 exemplary damages, *Maxwell* v. *Pressdram*, 1987. On the other hand, the jury may take the view that the claimant's case has little merit, even though technically successful, and may award only derisory damages, perhaps a farthing when that coin was still current. Mr Pamplin ended up with ¹/₂p (and a substantial bill for costs) after a retrial ordered by the Court of Appeal, instead of the original award of £12 000 for being described as an unscrupulous spiv, *Pamplin* v. *Express Newspapers*, 1985. Under section 8 of the Courts and Legal Services Act 1990 the Court of Appeal may now substitute its own assessment of damages, but before that it could upset a jury award only by ordering a retrial. The Act helped to curb excessive damages. Perhaps the beginning of a new attitude may be seen in *Rantzen* v. *Mirror Group*, 1994. Esther Rantzen, a well-known broadcaster as well as founder of Childline, a support service for distressed children, was accused in an article in *The People* of protecting a child abuser in order to get information from him. Her award of £250 000 was reduced by the Court of Appeal to £110 000. However, it was the Court of Appeal's decision in *John* v. *MGN Ltd*, 1996, which now enables the judge to guide the jury by drawing their attention, by way of comparison, to the level of awards in personal injury cases. Mr Elton John, a popular musician and entertainer, had been accused in the *Sunday Mirror* of bizarre and rather disgusting eating habits but found his total damages, including an exemplary award, reduced by the court from £350 000 to £75 000. Counsel for either party may also suggest an appropriate award to the jury. This means that the bad old days of pop stars' collecting huge sums from newspapers, and a victim's receiving less for being rendered paraplegic than for an injury to reputation, are happily gone.

Inflation makes it difficult to compare the damages recovered by successful plaintiffs but when Princess Irina Youssoupoff recovered £25 000 in 1934, *Youssoupoff* v. *Metro-Goldwyn-Mayer*, a skilled workman's weekly wage would have been around £5. In other words, her damages amounted to 100 years of wages for the workman. Lord Keyes recovered £40 000 in 1959 against the author and printer of a letter circulated to shareholders of a company he was associated with, *Keyes* v. *Nutt*. That would be at least 10 times as much today, probably more: a young schoolteacher's salary was then around £900 per year. Jeffrey Archer's much publicized action against the *Star* newspaper for allegations of association with a prostitute produced £500 000 in damages. In spite of public agitation for libel damages to be taken out of the hands of the jury, a jury awarded no less than £1.5 million to Lord Aldington in 1989 for allegations, admittedly very serious, that he had sent prisoners of war back to their death in the Soviet Union over 40 years earlier. This case was taken to the European Court of Human Rights by the author, *Tolstoy Miloslavsky* v. *UK*, 1995: the Court concluded that this award was excessive and could not be regarded as proportionate to the legitimate aim in a democratic society of protecting Lord Aldington's reputation, and hence led to a breach of the author's right of freedom of speech under Art. 10 of the Human Rights convention.

Defamation actions are often hard-fought, long drawn-out and very expensive. The small handful of top libel barristers are among the best-paid in the profession. It is by no means unusual for the legal costs to run into hundreds of thousands of pounds. Although it is the normal rule for the loser to pay the costs of both sides, the judge has some discretion to refuse the winner costs if the winner's conduct has been such as to justify this.

LIBEL AND SLANDER

Defamation in English law is rather oddly divided into 'libel' and 'slander'. (This is not the case in Scotland, where the law of defamation is significantly different – see p. 25.) If the statement is in writing, or some other permanent form, it is libel. If it is spoken (or implied in gestures) it is slander. Modern technology has blurred this distinction between written and spoken defamation and it has been suggested frequently that the distinction should be abolished. In the famous case *Youssoupoff* v. *Metro-Goldwyn Mayer*, 1934, the Court of Appeal agreed that defamation in a film is libel, not slander. The plaintiff, a Russian princess, won enormous damages for an imputation that she had been seduced (or perhaps raped) by the mad monk Rasputin.

A statement in a broadcast is libel, not slander (Defamation Act 1952) and the same applies to a cable programme (Cable and Broadcasting Act 1984). The Theatres Act 1968 lays down that defamation in a theatrical production also constitutes libel. A video recording would count as a film and a sound recording is obviously a permanent record of the statement. It is still early to disentangle these legal matters with regard to the Internet: defamation on the net is a very real danger and would presumably be libel in English law, not slander.

The distinction between libel and slander is important for one reason. If someone slanders you then you will have to prove that you have suffered actual damage, not just injury to your feelings or reputation, before the courts will give you redress. In the case of libel, the mere fact that the libellous statement has been made is enough to give you good cause for an action for damages. The importance of the Youssoupoff case lay in the fact that Princess Youssoupoff had not suffered any damage beyond the injury to her reputation: this would not have been actionable if the imputation in the film had been held to be slander.

However, there are a few instances in which proof of actual damage is not necessary even in a case for slander. If somebody slanders you by saying that you have committed a crime then you do not have to prove actual damage, nor if the imputation is that you have an infectious disease. This certainly includes a sexually transmitted disease, and probably leprosy (the relevant reported cases are rather old), and Aids would be an obvious modern example: it is unlikely that the courts would look kindly on an action in respect of an allegation of, say, influenza. Slander which may 'disparage' the claimant in respect of his or her trade, profession or office is actionable. The slander need not refer directly to the claimant's job if it is likely to reflect the claimant's fitness for it, a change introduced in the Defamation Act 1952.

In a case before the 1952 Act an unfortunate headmaster in Pwllheli was falsely accused of adultery with the wife of the school cleaner, and could have lost his job if the accusation had been true. The defendants tacitly admitted its falsity but the House of Lords denied him compensation for his injured reputation or feelings because the slander did not relate directly to his profession or office as headmaster (*Jones* v. *Jones*, 1916). (Incidentally, among the galaxy of legal talent, including three King's Counsel, who appeared in the case, one of the barristers for the defendants was T. Artemus Jones, who had been the plaintiff in *Jones* v. *Hulton*, mentioned below, a few years earlier.)

Lastly, the Slander of Women Act 1891 gives a woman a right of action without proof of special damage for a slanderous imputation of unchastity. The Act restricts the amount of damages which may be awarded and in the more permissive society of our present day it would probably require a strong accusation before it would be worthwhile bringing an action. However, the Act is not quite dormant. In 1990 a Pakistani woman won £20 000 damages against her former husband and his parents for allegations that she was not a virgin when she married him. The High Court judge, Mr Justice Michael Davies, commented:

> In some spheres in 1985, 1981 or 1990, an accusation of sex before marriage would not be regarded as a very serious matter. But I am satisfied that in the community of which Miss Seemi was part it is regarded as a very grave insult. (*The Times*, news item, 3 May 1990.)

In *Kerr* v. *Kennedy*, 1942, Lady John Kennedy had said to a mutual acquaintance that

Mrs Kerr was a lesbian. The court held that this came within the Act and awarded Mrs Kerr £300 damages, a not inconsiderable sum when an employer could get a well-qualified 16-year-old school-leaver for £1 a week.

The distinction between libel and slander is rather artificial and introduces added, and probably unnecessary, complications in what is already an intricate branch of the law. Indeed there have been a good many proposals that it be abolished, starting with the report of a Select Committee of the House of Lords in 1843. Well over a century later the Faulks Committee on Defamation (1975) reiterated the recommendation that the distinction be abolished. There is no sign yet that the recommendation will be put into law.

UNINTENTIONAL DEFAMATION

The law of defamation has many pitfalls for the unwary and perhaps the most dangerous concerns unintentional or innocent defamation. What happens if a writer picks a fairly unusual name for a character and there really is somebody with that name? In 1908 the *Sunday Chronicle* published a lighthearted article about the social scene in Dieppe, including a reference to an imaginary 'Artemus Jones with a woman who is not his wife, who must be, you know, – the other thing!' Unfortunately there was a real-life Artemus Jones, still more unfortunately he was a barrister whose field included libel law. He was able to call a number of witnesses who had thought that the article referred to him. The jury found that he had been libelled and awarded him £1750 against the newspaper proprietors. Although the defendants appealed, the House of Lords upheld the original decision; *Hulton* v. *Jones*, 1910. (The interesting detail is to be found in the report of the Court of Appeal hearing, *Jones* v. *Hulton*, 1910.) It was unfortunate that the writer chose a very unusual Christian name: as Lord Justice MacKinnon remarked in a later case, *Newstead* v. *London Express Newspaper*, 1940, if the name had been John Jones it would not have been possible for the very many people with that combination of names to have sued. In the latter case the *Daily Express* published a perfectly true account of the conviction of a 30-year-old man for bigamy. The bigamist, Harold Newstead, was a barman, but it so happened that a Camberwell hairdresser, also aged about 30, was also called Harold Newstead. He sued the newspaper proprietors and recovered one farthing damages (and a perpetual place in the law textbooks). This case illustrates why cautious journalists often give enough detail of occupation and so on to identify an individual positively.

It is by no means necessary for the subject of the libel to be named if he or she can be otherwise identified. A kennel girl, potential witness against a dog doping gang, was described in the *Sun* as having been kidnapped by members of the gang. In fact she had spent some time in the flat of one Johnny Morgan. He was not named in the newspaper but witnesses who had seen him with the girl thought that he might have been involved in kidnapping and dog doping. He won his case in the High Court; the Court of Appeal reversed the decision; finally the House of Lords, by a 3–2 majority, decided that Morgan had been libelled (but regarded the original damages, £4750, as excessive in the circumstances) (*Morgan* v. *Odhams Press*, 1971).

There was some relief, under s. 4 of the Defamation Act 1952, for the person who unintentionally defamed someone, allowing that person to make an offer of amends and a published apology. The procedure was complicated and s. 4 has been repealed by the Defamation Act 1996. Sections 2 and 4 of the 1996 Act provide a new procedure. Before serving a defence the defendant may offer amends, that is a correction, apology, compensation (if any) and costs. If the claimant accepts the offer, or if the parties do not agree the details, there is a quick court procedure to conclude the matter. Section 8 provides for summary disposal without a jury instead of a full trial where either party, in the court's opinion, has no realistic prospect of success, on the application of either party or on the court's own initiative. These reforms should do much to reduce the length and cost of defamation litigation. One further procedural reform is a 'pre-action protocol' which will encourage the parties to define the dispute more closely, with the claimant identifying the meanings attributed to the statement complained of, and to show that they have given serious consideration to arbitration or mediation in place of a trial. This encouragement of alternative forms of dispute resolution is a key notion of the Woolf reforms of the civil justice system in general.

The Defamation Act 1996 also reduces drastically the risk that a printer or even a retailer might face in distributing a publication which contained a libel when that person might not know, nor have reason to know, about the libellous matter. In the past a plaintiff would often join the printer and commercial distributor in the action if they would be more likely to have the assets to meet a judgment than the author or publisher. Now, under section 1 of the new Act, a defendant who is not the originator of the statement (unless it was not intended to be published), or the editor or the commercial publisher, has a good defence of not knowing (or having reason to believe) that he or she was causing or contributing to publication.

As a matter of interest, there is one old reported case concerning a library, *Vizetelly* v. *Mudie*, 1900. The plaintiff had been sent by a New York newspaper on an expedition to Africa. A book published by a reputable English publisher contained some defamatory remarks about his sobriety and the way he obtained the reports which he sent back. The publishers settled and advertised in appropriate journals to recall copies of the book. Mudie's (the well-known commercial circulating library) took the journals but did not see the notices and continued to circulate the book. There was evidence of lack of due care by the defendants and the plaintiff recovered £100 damages. Recent legislation means that this case would not be followed today.

DEFENCES TO A DEFAMATION ACTION

Justification

There are certain defences to an action for defamation: truth, absolute privilege, qualified privilege, fair comment. Probably the most important is that the words complained of were true: the defence is technically called 'justification'. It is the defendant's responsibility to prove that the actual allegedly defamatory statement is true. Sometimes where the allegations can be separated the defendant can prove only some of them: this will probably reduce the damages payable. However, the Defamation Act 1952 takes a common-sense line in laying down that even if every separate allegation is not proved true it will be a sufficient defence if those not proved are of minor importance only. Justification is the strongest defence to a defamation action but it does place a heavy burden on the defendant to produce real proof that the statement was true, to the satisfaction of a court of law.

Absolute privilege

Absolute privilege exists to protect those engaged in the law courts and in parliament from looking over their shoulder for fear of a libel claim. Judges, counsel, solicitors or witnesses cannot be sued for defamation in respect of words written or spoken in judicial proceedings, and the privilege extends to certain quasi-judicial proceedings such as tribunals and inquiries. Sometimes it may happen that somebody who has been severely criticized in court, with no right to bring a defamation action, will apply to a judge for permission to make a statement in open court. It is at the judge's discretion whether or not to allow this, but it will frequently be allowed unless there are good reasons otherwise.

Fair and accurate reports of judicial proceedings heard in open court in the UK, if published contemporaneously in newspapers or broadcasts, are also privileged, so the newspaper need not fear a libel action for repeating what somebody said in court. The privilege extends also to the European Court of Justice and the European Court of Human Rights, and certain other international tribunals.

Statements made in parliamentary proceedings also have absolute privilege (though a Member of Parliament or of the House of Lords may waive it, section 13 of the 1996 Act), and so do the official Hansard reports, but not other reports which enjoy only qualified privilege (see below). In a House of Lords debate the Bishop of Southwark criticized in strong terms a schoolmaster whose complaints about excessive punishments in the school led to an official inquiry. The proceedings in the Lords were fully reported in the *Daily Telegraph* but in addition the newspaper published a shorter account emphasizing the bishop's attack. The schoolmaster sued the paper for libel in respect of the latter, *Cook* v. *Alexander*, 1974. The Court of Appeal held that the account was a fair and honest account of parliamentary proceedings, made without malice, and so had qualified privilege, and the plaintiff lost his case. The bishop himself would, of course, have had absolute privilege. Communications in the course of duty between officers of state (ministers, senior civil servants, senior armed forces officers) have absolute privilege, and there are a few other official bodies similarly enjoying absolute privilege. These are fairly obvious: most people would agree that in judicial or governmental matters those concerned should be free to speak their minds without fear.

Lastly, there is absolute privilege for anything which passes between a lawyer and client; as Lord Justice Scrutton said in *More* v. *Weaver*, 1928:

> there are certain relations in life which it is so important that people engaged in them should be able to speak freely that the law takes the risk of their abusing the occasion.

In this case a serious dispute had arisen between a lady who had borrowed money to start a hotel, and the lender. The latter made, in letters to her own solicitor, severely critical statements about the other. The Court of Appeal upheld absolute privilege in these circumstances.

Qualified privilege

The essential difference between absolute and qualified privilege is that for the latter to be claimed the allegedly libellous statement must have been made without malice in the legal sense. Qualified privilege is much broader and its scope less well-defined. It falls into two categories. The first allows newspapers, periodicals and broadcasts to give fair and accurate reports of meetings and proceedings of legislatures or courts anywhere in the world, local authority meetings and various other bodies listed in Schedule 1 to the 1952 Act. The second category is rather tricky. A person cannot be sued for defamation for a statement made when that person has a legal or moral duty to make it to a particular person. The obvious example is a reference to a prospective employer. The same is true where there is some common interest or duty between the person making the statement and the recipient, which the statement will protect or further. This will cover, for example, communications between members of a society or company on matters of common interest, as well as, to take another example, complaints through official channels. Thus, a Member of Parliament who took up a constituent's complaint about a firm of solicitors and wrote to the Law Society and the Lord Chancellor was protected by qualified privilege, *Beach* v. *Freeson*, 1972. (There was, of course, no question of parliamentary privilege: the matters were outside Parliament.) It is important to remember, however, that qualified privilege applies only when the statement is made honestly. The person making it must not be actuated by 'malice', which means, to the libel lawyer, that he must not be dishonest, reckless, spiteful, or affected by any other improper motive. An agent for an insurance company for whom the company provided, apparently negligently not maliciously, a damning reference which would make him virtually unemployable in his field faced a defence of qualified privilege, *Spring* v. *Guardian Assurance plc*, 1995. (A claim in negligence, rather than libel, might well have succeeded.)

Anybody is entitled to make fair comment on a matter of public interest, even if the expression of opinion is exaggerated or even prejudicial, provided it is not dishonest, reckless or actuated by an improper motive. This will make a good defence to an action for defamation and is available to private individuals, as well as broadcasters, publishers, corporations, and indeed anybody else. The word 'fair' does not add much to 'comment', in fact the Faulks Committee recommended that the word comment alone is enough. It is important, however, that the matter is of public interest. Examples are the insanitary state of miners' houses owned by a colliery, *South Hetton Coal Co.* v. *North-Eastern News Association*, 1894; the findings of an official bribery enquiry, *Perera* v. *Peiris*, 1949 (a Privy Council appeal from Ceylon); or even the private life of a public figure if it is relevant to his or her public duties, *Lyle-Samuel* v. *Odhams Ltd*, 1920. The person making the statement must get the facts right. The defence of fair comment protects the comment; it is not an excuse to publish untrue factual allegations (though it is not necessary to prove every single minor allegation of fact). Lastly, the comment must be made honestly, without malice. The author cannot disguise a vituperative attack on another as fair comment. The court in *Reynolds* v. *Times Newspapers Ltd*, 1998, laid down three criteria: (1) the defendant must have a legal, moral or social duty, (2) the public must have an interest to know, (3) the material must have been acquired in a way which justified publication.

CRIMINAL LIBEL

The reader who has a Latin dictionary to hand can look up the word *libellus* and will see that it means a little book, or something written, from which stem various other meanings, including an accusation or indictment. It has passed into modern English with the familiar connotation of a defamatory writing. But the term has long been used in English law for other kinds of writing, namely an obscene libel or a blasphemous libel, to give them their traditional names. Thus we have a trio of related criminal matters which are linked by the fact that they are (usually) written and that they are deleterious to the good of the general public, as opposed to that of a specific individual. They are criminal libel, obscenity and blasphemy. Only in the first of these is the word libel retained in ordinary speech. There is a fourth offence, seditious libel or sedition, which involves words aiming to incite disaffection against the sovereign and government. It is a lesser offence than treason. In the secure society of the present day government, attitudes to political protest have softened and reputable speakers and authors use words which once would have attracted severe punishment. On the rare occasions when the abuse of freedom of speech goes beyond that which is acceptable in the UK today it is likely to be controlled by the ordinary law, so we shall not consider seditious libel further. Incitement to racial hatred has been made a specific offence and we shall discuss this later.

Although criminal libel is often treated in the textbooks as an offshoot of (non-criminal) defamation, it does seem more logical to treat it here. It dates back to the days when the courts were concerned as much with the potential for breach of the peace as for the private reputation of the individual. That is why justification, proving the truth of the libellous statement, is not always a good defence to a prosecution for criminal libel; it is also necessary to prove that publication was for the public benefit (to provide some curb on unjustified and vicious muckraking). Further, it is not necessary for the libel to have been published to someone other than the person libelled: this again relates to the old fear of a breach of the peace, which might well be anticipated following the receipt of a potentially libellous statement by the person defamed alone.

Under the Law of Libel Amendment Act 1888 permission must be sought from a judge in chambers (in the judge's private room) to bring a criminal libel prosecution over something published in a newspaper. Criminal libel prosecutions are rare and usually relate to a serious or sustained campaign of vilification. Two cases which were heard in chambers, but in which the judge's decision was given in open court and reported, were both private prosecutions, *Goldsmith* v. *Pressdram*, 1977, and *Desmond* v. *Thorne*, 1982. Sir James Goldsmith (he was Mr Goldsmith at the time), a prominent businessman, had been the object of a persistent campaign of a defamatory nature in the pages of the satirical magazine *Private Eye*. Eventually, following an article which imputed that he was a party to an attempt to obstruct a murder inquiry, he sought permission to commence criminal libel proceedings against the magazine, its editor and its principal distributors. The judge decided that the libel was a serious one and that the public interest required the institution of criminal proceedings. What happened in the end was that a compromise was worked out, when the case came up at the Central Criminal Court the prosecution quietly dropped it so the defendants were formally found not guilty. At the same time most of a large number of civil actions against the magazine and its wholesale and retail distributors, which had beeen started at the same time, were also dropped. Presumably the desired effect had been achieved and the magazine became rather more circumspect in its dealings with Sir James.

Desmond v. *Thorne* was a case in which the judge refused permission for a private prosecution against the authors of an article in the *Sunday People*, together with the editor and proprietors of the newspaper. The applicant, an Irish poet, was the subject of an article in the newspaper alleging continued violence by him against a wealthy society girl with whom he lived for a time. If untrue the article was obviously a very serious libel. However Mr Desmond did admit one single assault on the girl and had apparently attempted to sell to the paper his own story which bore out some parts of the article. Looking at both sides of the matter the judge decided that there was nothing to justify, let alone require, the bringing of criminal proceedings.

Gleaves v. *Deakin*, 1980, was an extraordinary case. Mr (or Bishop) Gleaves was a bishop in a tiny unorthodox church and for a time ran a hostel for homeless boys. In this case the alleged libel was in a book *Johnny Go Home*, not a newspaper, so no consent was required to institute a private prosecution. There had been the normal committal proceedings before the magistrate, to make sure that there was a prima facie case before the defendants were sent for trial. At the magistrate's hearing the defendants (who were the authors and publishers of the book) tried to bring up Mr Gleaves' general bad character as a reason for stopping the prosecution, on the grounds of a formidable record of convictions for homosexual offences and violence. The book made very serious allegations of sexual offences, fraud, theft, Fascist sympathies, and other matters. The stipendiary magistrate (a paid, legally-qualified magistrate) refused to hear evidence of general bad character, she decided that there was a prima facie case and committed the defendants for trial. The defendants appealed against the orders to commit them for trial and the matter went right up to the House of Lords on this preliminary point. Their Lordships said that the magistrate was right. The prosecutor's bad reputation was a matter which must be left to the trial of the case, when it would be relevant to the question whether publication of the book had been in the public interest. In the event, after a lengthy trial at the Central Criminal Court (the Old Bailey) the defendants were acquitted on all the charges.

Following this, the Attorney-General (the senior government legal officer) stepped in and put a stop to other prosecutions for criminal libel which Mr Gleaves had brought against other individuals. The subject matter of the book (Deakin and Willis (1976)) formed the basis of a notable TV production.

In the Gleaves case their Lordships drew attention to the unsatisfactory state of the law relating to criminal libel. Their views were echoed by the Law Commission (an official panel of distinguished lawyers which examines and makes recommendations on selected aspects of the law) in its Working Paper on Criminal Libel in which the Commission recommended, provisionally, the replacement of the existing provisions by a much narrower statutory offence to deal with really serious cases of 'character assassination', with prosecutions being in the hands of the Director of Public Prosecutions only.

Under Scottish law there is no offence of criminal libel though libel as a civil matter bears some resemblance to the English criminal law: a statement may yet be libel even though not communicated to anyone except the person defamed. (Other points to notice about libel in Scotland are that a suit is not affected by the death of either party, there is no distinction between libel and slander, and the courts do not award exemplary damages.)

OBSCENE PUBLICATIONS

The point at which the principle that cultural works shall be freely disseminated, comes up against the concern for public order and morality, is the subject of strongly held (and expressed) views. Nearly everybody is prepared to argue that some measure of restraint should be applied to the dissemination of some kinds of material, but there is little agreement as to exactly what should be restrained. For reasons which are difficult to understand, the most ardent advocates of censorship lump together sex and violence: to the impartial mind the two seem to have no connection. Others will wish to censor anything to do with the former but remain unmoved by television's nightly offerings of guns and crime. Yet others worry about the portrayal of minority ethnic groups, or homosexuals, or women, and so on.

Obscenity originated as an offence against the law of the church and indeed was still held to be such in a case as late as 1708, but soon after that the criminal courts began to take cognisance of it. Before that censorship was much more concerned with religious and political dissent. However, it was really in the nineteenth century that the anti-pornography campaigners began to gain the ascendancy: the trade in pornography continued but at constant risk of prosecution. Obscene publications are now dealt with in the Obscene Publications Act 1959, with some additions in the Obscene Publications Act 1964. The Acts penalize a person who has an obscene article (which could be virtually anything intended to be read, listened to or looked at) for gain, even if that person is not the one who would gain from it. It is also an offence actually to publish an obscene article, whether for gain or not. The word 'publish' means distribute, sell, let on hire, give or lend, offer for sale or for letting on hire. The definition does not leave much out, but in addition it includes showing, playing or projecting the article if it is a recording or contains matter to be looked at. It is most unlikely (though theoretically possible) that a prosecution would follow if you were to lend an obscene book to a friend, but a librarian who lent an obscene book could be committing an offence. The Acts have been specifically extended to cinemas (though the consent of the Director of Public Prosecutions is required before a prosecution may be commenced in respect of feature films). Broadcasting is covered under separate legislation. It is an offence under the Post Office Act 1953 to send an indecent article through the post.

ORDER FOR FORFEITURE

The Acts make provision for another method of clamping down on pornography, which is quite frequently used. A Justice of the Peace can issue a warrant enabling the police to enter (if necessary by force) premises (or a stall or a vehicle), search for and seize any articles which the police have reason to believe are obscene and are being kept for publication for gain. The magistrate will have to be satisfied before the warrant is issued, on the basis of a sworn statement by the police (or by, or on behalf of, the Director of Public Prosecutions), that there are reasonable grounds for suspicion. A Justice of the Peace may summon the occupier to show cause before the magistrates why the articles which have been seized should not be forfeited. Anybody else concerned (for example the owner, author, wholesaler) is entitled to add their arguments as well. If the magistrates are satisfied that these were obscene articles kept for publication for gain (and a defence that publication is for the public good is not made out) then they may order them to be forfeited.

What frequently happens in actual fact is that the trader does not think it worthwhile to argue about it and in effect acquiesces to the forfeiture order, treating it as a risk of the trade. The procedure has its critics. Different magistrates may have very different views as to what is obscene, though it is possible to appeal to the Crown Court against a forfeiture order. However, in *Burke* v. *Copper*, 1962, magistrates made an order for forfeiture of some of a number of articles forfeited, but not others. The selection was apparently quite arbitrary, copies of one photograph appearing in one bundle to be forfeited and in another that was not. Here the informant appealed to a Queen's Bench Divisional Court (a court of High Court judges to which certain matters can be referred) which ordered nearly all the other articles to be forfeited.

One good defence to a forfeiture order, or to a prosecution, is to prove that publication is justified as being for the public good in the interests of science, literature, art or learning, or other object of general concern. If the public good defence is raised the jury (or magistrates) must first decide if the work is obscene. If so, they then decide whether publication is justified, duly weighing up the tendency to deprave and corrupt (for example, numbers of people likely to be affected, and to what extent) against the merits claimed for the work. Both the prosecution and the defence may call expert witnesses to testify as to its scientific, literary or other merits (or otherwise).

Whilst publishers and booksellers can attempt to justify profitable material as having properties conducive to the public good, their motives are not always, by any means, impure. Long before the 1959 Act Mr Benjamin Hicklin, 'a metal broker, residing in the town of Wolverhampton, and a person of respectable position and character', sold over 2000 copies of *The Confessional Unmasked*, a pamphlet containing extracts from Latin authors (with translations) relating to the practice of confession in the Roman Catholic church. About half of the pamphlet was castigated as obscene, part of it relating to questions put to females in confession. Mr Hicklin made no profit from it, he acted from the purest motives (however misguided some may think them) as a member of the Protestant Electoral Union who published the work, to expose what he deemed to be the errors of the Church of Rome. Nevertheless, the Court of Queen's Bench (precursor of the Queen's Bench Division of the High Court), with some hesitation on the part of one of the judges, upheld an order by the justices for seizure and destruction, *R. v. Hicklin*, 1868. (A later version of the pamphlet, contained, or disguised, within an account of Hicklin's trial, met the same fate, *Steele* v. *Brannan*, 1872). Hicklin's case is remembered particularly because it enshrined the 'deprave and corrupt' test for obscenity which has remained in the law to the present day.

The defence of literary merit under the 1959 Act was successfully raised, with a formidable array of expert witnesses, in the Lady Chatterley case, mentioned below. In *Director of Public Prosecutions* v. *Jordan*, 1976, expert evidence to support a defence contention that sexually explicit material could have psychotherapeutic value for certain categories of persons was not allowed. However, a psychiatrist's evidence for the prosecution on the effect on children of 'battle cards' given away with bubble gum, was held admissible in *Director of Public Prosecutions* v. *A and BC Chewing Gum*, 1968, but this was to prove that the cards were obscene, not to raise the public good defence. The law report gives no indication of the nature of the cards but it seems likely that the matter complained of was brutality rather than sex.

The other important defence is if the person handling an obscene article, or having it for gain, can prove that he or she had not examined the article in question and had no reasonable cause to suspect it. This can protect an innocent bookseller or newsagent. A librarian might find it more difficult to prove since a book is presumably examined for the purpose of cataloguing and so forth. It might be easier to raise this defence in the case of a video or sound recording, or a computer disk, which would not reveal its nature on casual inspection.

WHAT IS AN OBSCENE ARTICLE?

The main difficulty with the law on obscene publications is that there is very little agreement as to exactly what is obscene, except that practically always it relates to sex or homosexuality. The test for over a hundred years has been the tendency to deprave and corrupt. The 1959 Act circumscribed this to some extent, applying the test to those who are likely, having regard to all the circumstances, to see, read or hear it. Moreover, the work must be considered as a whole: it is not enough to pick out a few corrupting passages if the general tone is not unsuitable. The old test envisaged those whose minds were open to immoral influences and into whose hands the work was likely to fall.

Obscenity is very much a subjective matter, and as the case reports do not generally repeat the substance of the work in question there is not all that much guidance in them. Social attitudes do alter: sexual and homosexual mores have changed unbelievably in the past two or three decades. As society's attitudes have become less inhibited matters which were touched on only coyly and obliquely in the 1970s and 1980s are now discussed openly and without restraint. Books are now set as school texts which not so long ago would have been bought furtively in seedy backstreet bookshops. The court is not an arbiter of good taste and sheer vulgarity is not necessarily obscene. The target for prosecution now is mainly what is vaguely categorized as 'hard-core' pornography, featuring probably sadistic excesses, bestiality or, particularly, paedophilia, whether disseminated in print, by the Internet or otherwise. With regard to paedophilia, this is the one area where social attitudes have become much more restrictive in the past few years.

The effect of pornography on children has always been a major concern of the law. Misgivings over imports of American horror comics led to the Children and Young Persons (Harmful Publications) Act 1955 banning the publication, sale or hire of picture books portraying crime, violence, cruelty or repulsive incidents which might be likely to fall into the hands of children or young persons and corrupt them. A rather emotive campaign led to the Protection of Children Act 1978 prohibiting the taking of indecent photographs of children under 16, as well as distributing or showing them (or possessing for such purposes). What was meant by an indecent photograph was not clear but the Act was aimed at so-called 'kiddy-porn' publications and films which could not be touched by other legislation. The Criminal Justice and Public Order Act 1994, s. 84, extends the meaning of 'photograph' to include a photograph stored by electronic means, and adds a 'pseudo-photograph', meaning an image which appears to be a photograph, whether computer-generated or not. It seems that pictures of adults which have been doctored to look like children would be covered by this last provision.

One couple narrowly escaped prosecution when perfectly innocent nude photographs of their children were passed on to the police by the processing firm, no doubt covering their own back. There have been many prosecutions of people who have downloaded pornographic pictures of children from the Internet. Indeed, as is well-known, pornographic Internet sites of all kinds attract very large numbers of surfers and attempts to control them or restrict access have so far met very limited success in spite of severe sentences.

The magazine *Oz* published in 1970 a 'School Kids Issue', partly compiled by children, which contained a good deal of overt sexual matter. A lengthy and well-publicized trial resulted in convictions. On appeal, however, the convictions (except on one count) were quashed, the principal reason being that the judge's direction to the jury might have led them to believe that the word 'obscene' implied repulsive, filthy, loathsome or lewd, *R. v. Anderson*, 1971. The *Oz* case rather overshadowed the successful prosecution before London magistrates in the same year of *The Little Red Schoolbook*, the name and format of which evoked the little red book of Mao

Tse-tung's quotations, then in vogue. The book combined some sexual matter with the advocacy of anti-authority views. There was suspicion that the anti-establishment tone, rather than the sexual content, influenced the prosecution, *R. v. Handyside*, 1971.

Although obscenity nearly always refers to sex (or homosexual behaviour), in *Calder Publications* v. *Powell*, 1965, drug-taking was the subject. The book in question, *Cain's Book* by Alexander Trocci, had been seized by the police with a number of other publications from a newsagent's shop in Sheffield. The shopkeeper did not defend the proceedings but the publishers were entitled to appear before the magistrates and they called expert witnesses to testify that the book had literary and sociological merit. The magistrates ordered forfeiture. On appeal two questions arose, first whether a book condoning, indeed positively advocating, drug-taking came within the Obscene Publications Act: the court held that it did. On the second question, whether the magistrates were justified in deciding that publication could not be defended as for the public good, the court held that the magistrates were entitled to reach this decision. Although the law on drugs today is no less restrictive than in 1965 it is unlikely that publication of such a book would lead to a prosecution now. The public good defence was attempted again in *R. v. Calder and Boyars Ltd*, 1969. Again the defendants were a highly reputable publishing business: the book was *Last Exit to Brooklyn*, by Hubert Selby Jnr. The defence was that far from depraving and corrupting, the book would tend to produce in most readers reactions of horror and pity at the descriptions of homosexuality, drug-taking and senseless brutality. The result was ambivalent: on appeal the defendants were not guilty, but largely because of shortcomings in the original trial.

The famous case of *Lady Chatterley's Lover* by D H Lawrence, *R. v. Penguin Books*, 1961, is generally regarded as marking a turning point in the law's attitude to obscenity. The book already had a considerable reputation: an expurgated edition was in circulation but the full unexpurgated version was available only in copies smuggled in from abroad. The trial was by way of being a test case. The defendants produced no fewer than 35 expert witnesses to testify to the book's literary merits. The verdict was not guilty (and subsequent sales were phenomenal). It must be noted, however, that this was a book with high literary merit by a distinguished author: the case did not indicate that every other book using Lawrence's words and imagery would be similarly treated. A few years earlier the highly reputable publisher Secker and Warburg had been found not guilty in respect of publication of *The Philanderer* by Stanley Kauffman, *R. v. Secker and Warburg*, 1954. In his summing up Mr Justice Stable asked 'Are we to take our literary standards as being the level of something that is suitable for a fourteen-year-old girl?' (For some reason teenage girls are always assumed to be more open to corruption than boys!) The 1960s have been regarded in retrospect as the time when society became liberated from puritanism, but in fact that decade saw only the beginnings of the decay of censorship.

Before leaving that era it is worth briefly mentioning two interesting cases regarding the effect of obscene articles on those to whom they are sold. Can experienced police officers from Scotland Yard's obscene publications department be depraved and corrupted by such material? Two plain-clothes detectives bought photographs in a bookshop. Under cross-examination they admitted that they had seen so many similar photographs that these aroused no feelings whatever in them. The shopkeeper and assistant appealed successfully against charges in respect of the sale (though losing the appeal on other grounds), *R.* v *Clayton and Halsey*, 1963. A somewhat similar defence was tried in *Director of Public Prosecutions* v. *Whyte*, 1972. The defendants' bookshop customers were mainly middle-aged addicts of this kind of material, whose morals were already in a state of depravity and corruption. The House of Lords decided by a 3–2 majority that pornography addicts were not exempt from being further depraved and corrupted, and the defendants lost their appeal.

BLASPHEMY

'Blasphemous libel', as it is called in full if it is written, is a criminal offence. It applies only to vilification of the Christian religion. In earlier times this was regarded as a serious matter: to seduce ignorant people away from those beliefs which alone led to ultimate salvation was rightly, in the eyes of most people, deserving of criminal sanctions. Attitudes have changed and in *Bowman* v. *Secular Society*, 1917, it was held that serious and restrained argument that Christian doctrine is mistaken does not fall under the law against blasphemy. Nevertheless, in 1922 John William Gott was prosecuted for selling in Stratford Broadway two twopenny pamphlets, *Rib Ticklers, or Questions for Parsons* and *God and Gott*. He had three previous convictions for similar offences and on this occasion was sentenced to nine months imprisonment with hard labour. (Hard labour in a prison sentence was abolished in 1948.) It could well have been assumed that the offence of blasphemy had fallen into abeyance after that, for there was no further prosecution for over half a century. However, a private prosecution by Mrs Mary Whitehouse, a well-known anti-pornography campaigner, against the homosexuals' magazine *Gay News*, revived the offence, *Whitehouse* v. *Gay News and Lemon*, 1979. The magazine had published a poem about Jesus Christ with a strong homosexual tone: undoubtedly it was deeply offensive to many Christians. The House of Lords rejected the argument that the offence of blasphemy no longer existed and that there was, in any case, no intention to blaspheme. It was enough that the matter was blasphemous and that there was an intention to publish it. The editor, Denis Lemon, received a nine-month suspended prison sentence and was fined £500; the publishers were fined £1000. Given the change in attitudes to homosexuality since

1979, such a prosecution would be unlikely to succeed today but blasphemy remains an offence and a prosecution for other matter remains feasible.

SALMAN RUSHDIE

In 1990 the *cause célèbre* of Salman Rushdie's book *The Satanic Verses* led to an attempt by a Muslim body to invoke the law of blasphemy as applicable to the Islamic religion. The Chief Metropolitan Magistrate had refused to grant summonses against Mr Rushdie and Viking Penguin, publishers of the book, for the common-law offences of blasphemy and seditious libel. The convener of the British Muslim Action Front, Mr Abdul Choudhury, challenged the magistrate's decision. Three distinguished judges in a Divisional Court of the Queen's Bench unanimously upheld the original decision, *R.* v. *Bow Street Magistrates Court, Ex parte Choudhury*, 1990. (*Ex parte* in this context means 'on behalf of'.) Lord Justice Watkins accepted that the book had deeply offended many law-abiding Muslims in the UK. However, a review of previous cases made it clear that the law of blasphemy protected the Christian religion only and this case, apparently the first in which it had been sought to extend the blasphemy law to other religions, failed. (The side issue of sedition also failed on the ground that it required the intention to incite violence against the government or constituted authority, not just to provoke hostility between different classes of subjects. This is a fairly restrictive interpretation of sedition, but not unreasonable.)

The Salman Rushdie affair provoked some considerable debate on the law of blasphemy. On the one hand some argue that it is anomalous in a multicultural society to uphold the faith of one segment of the population only, even though over 90 per cent of the population are at least nominal adherents of that faith. The law, it is argued, should be extended to other religions. Others feel that there could be considerable difficulty in defining the limits of religion and meeting the sensibilities of all groups. Moreover, atheists and agnostics might feel that their views should also be protected from vilification. So, it is argued, the law should be abolished. In Italy, that most Catholic country, the Constitutional Court recently removed blasphemy against the Christian religion from the penal code, as incompatible with equality for all religions (*The Times*, news item, 22 November 2000). Indeed, a law of blasphemy can be criticized as an unwarranted curb on free religious debate. The one view which seems to command little support is that the law should stay as it is, but so far no legislation is in prospect. A curious twist to the Salman Rushdie saga came when the British Board of Film Classification refused a certificate for a video from Pakistan, *International Guerrillas*, on the ground that it would expose Mr Rushdie to hatred and be cause for a prosecution for criminal libel. However, the ban was lifted on appeal to the Video Appeals Committee, Mr Rushdie himself supporting the appeal.

INCITEMENT TO RACIAL HATRED

Part III of the Public Order Act 1986 brings together and strengthens measures concerning acts intended or likely to stir up racial hatred, as well as possession of racially inflammatory material. Racial hatred means 'hatred against a group of persons in the UK defined by reference to colour, race, nationality (including citizenship) or ethnic or national origins'. Religion was not included until the government proposed anti-terrorist measures in December 2001. However, the House of Lords accepted Sikhs as a racial group in a race discrimination case (schoolboy's right to wear his *pagri* (turban)), *Mandla* v. *Dowell Lee*, 1983. The same would be true of Jews. The situation of a group of converts to Sikhism or Judaism might be doubtful.

What we are concerned with here is a criminal offence relating to stirring up racial hatred: although acceptable to most right-thinking people, it has to be recognized that this law can be a severe curb on the freedom to disseminate opinions or information. (Discrimination on grounds of race in employment, education and other fields is something quite different: it is against the law but it is in general a civil matter. There is parallel legislation on sex discrimination. However, there is no criminal offence of stirring up hatred against people by reference to their sex, not entirely a fanciful notion.) The Act concerns words, behaviour, written material, films, videos and sound recordings, public performances, broadcasts and cable transmissions, if they involve threatening, abusive or insulting words, behaviour, visual images or sounds, and the person (or corporate body) concerned intends to stir up racial hatred, or in the circumstances it is likely that racial hatred will be stirred up. The maximum penalty is two years imprisonment and a fine. With regard to written material the offence includes displaying it (except privately in a dwelling) as well as publishing or distributing it to the public or a section of the public. Innocent contravention is a defence, where the person did not intend to stir up racial hatred and did not suspect it, or have reason to suspect. Fair and accurate reports of judicial proceedings published contemporaneously are permissible, as are fair and accurate reports of Parliament.

It is also an offence to possess material of an offending nature with a view to its being used as above by the person in possession or by anybody else. This could prove tricky for a library or archive which had a collection on race relations containing inflammatory material. A prosecution on flimsy grounds would be unlikely: a prosecution under this part of the Act may be commenced only by, or with the consent of, the Attorney-General. However, the cautious information provider might be well advised to handle such material circumspectly.

Two recent statutes give some protection to a person who is the target of serious abuse. The first is the Malicious Communications Act 1988 which makes it an offence to send a communication which is false or believed by the sender to be false and is intended to cause distress or anxiety to the direct or indirect intended recipient. The second is the Protection from Harassment Act 1997. Like other forms of harassment, harassment by the use of words which cause alarm or distress constitutes an offence.

FREE SPEECH AND FREEDOM OF INFORMATION

Librarians, as principal guardians of the nation's corpus of knowledge, are frequently seen as advocates of freedom of information. There are really two facets to this. First, there is the right of the individual to express and disseminate views, even if they are unpopular, and to hear what others have to say. Secondly, there is the duty of the government to make information which affects the citizens of the country as freely available as possible.

UNOFFICIAL CENSORSHIP

Popular opinion, whether of the majority or of a forceful minority, is one factor restricting the free dissemination of information: some libraries apply, willingly or otherwise, a measure of censorship to their holdings. Enid Blyton's 'Noddy' books for children suffered a ban in at least one county council's area on grounds of 'political correctness'. During the labour disputes in the newspaper industry which followed the move of *The Times* to Wapping, certain left-wing local councils banned *The Times* and related titles in their public libraries until the publishers secured a court order to stop this. It is noteworthy that the court was prepared to support the principle of freedom against a public authority, but it may be questioned whether there would have been any possibility of action against a private body. Student unions, particularly in the 1970s and 1980s, denied a platform, often with threats of violent disturbance, to speakers on the campus if they did not subscribe to the current student ideology. Most recently 'Holocaust denial' has become a target of unofficial censorship with certain groups advocating that the expression of revisionist views on the mass murder of Jews, gypsies and others under the Nazi regime in the 1940s should be a criminal offence. In Germany and France this is indeed the case, but it seems unlikely that we shall follow suit in the UK. Nonetheless, unofficial censorship by orchestrated protest on this issue has been exercised on occasion and has succeeded. Censorship by orchestrated protest may be seen as a very real threat to freedom of speech and information even in this country.

OFFICIAL SECRETS

It is in the nature of governments and agents exercising government authority to be secretive. Not infrequently it is necessary for a litigant to seek a court order for disclosure of documents by a government department, and the department, in the name of the minister, may on occasion withhold documents in the public interest.

Official secrets, particularly if they relate to national security, are jealously guarded and are protected by the Official Secrets Acts 1911, 1920 and 1989. The first two Acts are wordy and complicated, attempting to catch every possible misuse of confidential government information from major espionage to carelessness with government documents. The most serious offence involves the collection, recording, publication or communication to another person, for a purpose prejudicial to the interests of the state, of any document or information (or virtually anything else) which might be useful to an enemy (including a potential enemy). This offence can carry up to 14 years imprisonment.

Less serious offences, punishable by up to two years imprisonment came originally in s. 2 of the 1911 Act. This catch-all section penalized the communication of documents or information (or other things) to an unauthorized person, or the use of the information for a purpose prejudicial to the safety or interests of the state, or even unauthorized retention of these things or failure to take reasonable care of them. Other provisions related to receiving documents and the like in contravention of the Act, as well as attempts and persuading others to commit an offence.

The catch-all provisions of s. 2 (slightly amended in 1920) came under a lot of criticism. Two major wars doubtless slowed down the process of reform but eventually the 1989 Act replaced this section by new provisions even more wordy and complicated but of narrower scope. To simplify, a person who is or has been a crown servant or government contractor is guilty of an offence if he or she makes any damaging disclosure relating to security or intelligence, defence or international relations, or a disclosure which results in crime or impedes the apprehension of criminals. Another person into whose hands such information has come as a result of unlawful disclosure is guilty of an offence if he or she reveals it, knowing, or having cause to believe, that this will be damaging. A present or former member of the security services who has had any information in an official capacity and reveals it, also commits an offence. The maximum sentence remains at two years imprisonment and a fine. (It is a pity that the opportunity was not taken to consolidate the law, as it is now spread across the three Acts, of 1911, 1920 and 1989.)

The 1989 Act drastically limited the scope of the previous legislation and it is no longer true to say, as the head of the security service, MI5, told the Franks Committee, 'It is an official secret if it is on an official file.' Governments tend, usually (though not always) with good reason, to be very secretive about their affairs. 'Open government' is now a popular catchphrase and it does seem probable that a Minister of the Crown would prefer, where possible, to deal with lesser lapses of security by internal disciplinary procedures, rather than in the full glare of a public criminal prosecution.

THE *SPYCATCHER* CASE

The *cause célèbre* of the *Spycatcher* book placed the Attorney-General, as the government's principal legal officer, in a very difficult position. Mr Peter Wright was a member of the security service from 1955 to 1976 and was engaged on counter-espionage work. On engagement, and again on retirement, he signed declarations that he was bound by the Official Secrets Acts, as was the normal procedure. After his retirement he wrote the book *Spycatcher*, an autobiography containing a good deal of material about the work which he did in the security service, as well as some serious allegations about MI5 and MI6. The saga, which lasted from 1986 to 1988, may be conveniently, if exhaustively, studied in the collection of *The Spycatcher Cases*, edited by Michael Fysh and published as a special volume of the *Fleet Street Reports*, [1989] 2 FSR. It seems highly probable that a prosecution under the Official Secrets Acts 1911 and 1920 would have been successful. However, Mr Wright was now living in Tasmania and the book was published in Australia. This effectively put him beyond the reach of the Official Secrets Acts. There is no doubt that the Attorney-General was in a serious quandary. On the one hand, he could hardly stand by and allow the law to be flouted. On the other hand, there was no effective way of stopping publication. The only alternative course, which the Attorney-General adopted, was to pursue a series of civil actions based on breach of Mr Wright's fiduciary duty, and breach of confidence, not only against Mr Wright and his Australian publishers, but also seeking injunctions against various English newspapers which published, or proposed to publish, extracts from the book. The Australian actions met with no success, nor did an action against a New Zealand newspaper. In the UK the actions succeeded only to a very limited extent. By the time the matter had dragged through a series of courts, the contents of the book were very largely public knowledge and an injunction to prevent breach of confidence was pointless.

Derbyshire County Council public libraries came into the saga at one point, intervening in the Attorney-General's actions against the *Guardian* and the *Observer* in which he had been granted interlocutory (interim) injunctions to prevent the newspapers' publishing extracts from Mr Wright's book, *Attorney-General* v. *Guardian Newspapers and anor*, 1987. The libraries had received requests from the public for the book, and the Council sought the court's determination whether they could lawfully import copies and make them available.

The court held that they could not. However, on a second issue, there was no obligation on the libraries to act as unofficial censors and examine newspapers and periodicals which they made available, to determine whether they contained material from *Spycatcher*.

SARAH TISDALL

A new appointee to the Civil Service is required to sign a declaration that his or her attention has been drawn to the provisions of the Official Secrets Act as set out on the declaration form, and acknowledging that he or she must not divulge any information gained as a result of the appointment, nor publish on pain of prosecution any such information unless it has already been made public. One case which made the headlines was that of Sarah Tisdall. As a Foreign Office clerk she photocopied two secret documents relating to the arrival of Cruise missiles in the UK and sent them anonymously to the *Guardian* which published one document in full and some details of the other. The deployment of these American weapons in this country was at that time a matter of intense public interest and considerable public concern, not only in pacifist circles. Sarah Tisdall was a well-educated young woman of excellent character, with no previous convictions, and she acted on strongly-held moral grounds. But, as the Lord Chief Justice said, 'She knew she was breaking the law, she knew she was committing a gross breach of trust', and the Court of Appeal upheld a six-month prison sentence (*R. v. Tisdall*, 1984).

CONFIDENTIAL INFORMATION

In one case in the *Spycatcher* saga, *Attorney General* v. *Guardian Newspapers (No 2)*, Sir John Donaldson MR said

> There is an inherent public interest in individual citizens and the state having an enforceable right to the maintenance of confidence. Life would be intolerable in personal and commercial terms, if information could not be given or received in confidence and the right to have that confidence respected supported by the force of law.

The law will give a civil remedy affording protection against the unauthorized disclosure or use of information which is of a confidential nature, and which has been entrusted to a person in circumstances which impose or imply an obligation to respect its confidentiality. This can apply to commercial or to private confidences.

Some of the older cases are interesting and illustrate the evolution of the remedy. One of the earliest was *Morison* v. *Moat*, 1851. (Note the spelling of

Morison with one 'r' – like the name of the author of this book, Marett.) Morison (Senior) invented Morison's Universal Medicine (unfortunately the recipe does not seem to have survived) and went into partnership with Moat who 'in breach of faith and contract' communicated the secret formula to his son. After the deaths of both partners Moat's son started making the medicine. The court granted Morison's sons and heirs an injunction to stop him. A couple of years earlier we have the case of the Queen's husband, Prince Albert, the Prince Consort, suing somebody who had come into possession (not completely innocently) of some private etchings made by Queen Victoria and the Prince Consort. The prince obtained an injunction to stop an exhibition of the etchings and publication of an annotated catalogue, *Prince Albert* v. *Strange*, 1849. In both these cases the breach of confidence was committed by a third party, by Moat Senior and, in Prince Albert's case, probably by a printer, but the court was prepared to restrain the end-recipient of the information. Nobody seems entirely sure even nowadays what is the theoretical legal basis of the law in this area, whether it is a question of contract, of intangible property or of equity (that branch which developed to give flexibility to the rigid rules of the law but which in time became almost as inflexible). Sopinka J in a case before the Supreme Court of Canada saw it as a *sui generis* action relying on all three to enforce the policy that confidences be respected; *LAC Minerals* v. *International Corona Resources*, 1990. The Vice-chancellor (second judge in the Court of Chancery in those days) seemed in *Morison* a little uncertain whether breach of contract came into the matter or not, and indeed later cases commonly treat breach of confidence as a breach of an implied term in a contract (for instance between employer and employee), though this is not helpful when there is no contract.

Very often, of course, there is an express term in a contract that one party will not disclose the confidential information of the other. For example, a supplier of a computer system may well have to make a thorough examination of a client's business, involving access to much confidential information, and the contract will probably include an express condition of non-disclosure. Even if there is no express term that matters will be kept confidential the court will often be prepared to find an implied term. In *Weld-Blundell* v. *Stephens*, 1920, Mr Weld-Blundell had employed a chartered accountant to advise him concerning the financial affairs of a company and wrote him a letter which contained some libellous remarks about two officials of the company. The accountant passed the letter on to his partner who went to see the company's office manager and carelessly dropped the letter out of his pocket. The contents of the letter thus became known to the two people defamed who brought successful libel actions, and Weld-Blundell had to pay out nearly £1700. He thereupon sued his accountant in an attempt to recover this money. The Court of Appeal decided that there was indeed an implied term in the contract between Weld-Blundell and his accountant that the letter would be kept confidential. However, the court was not prepared to give him recompense for his own fault in writing the defamatory letter and restricted the damages to £1 and no costs.

INVENTORS

Companies which receive proposals from inventors and others regarding suggested new products have to be cautious that, having rejected an idea, they do not subsequently develop a product that is based, even subconsciously, on that idea. A company may well establish 'Chinese walls' between relevant departments to ensure that confidentiality is not breached. A certain Mr Seager had an inventive turn of mind and was determined to interest the representatives of Copydex Ltd in his invention of a toothed metal carpet-retaining strip (with the name 'Invisigrip'). In fact, in spite of Mr Seager's loquaciousness (commented on by one of the judges), negotiations came to nothing and no contract was made. However, the idea was developed by Copydex which was soon marketing an 'Invisigrip' carpet strip very similar to Mr Seager's. However innocently, this did seem to be based on the information given in confidence by Mr Seager and when the matter came before the Court of Appeal he won damages for the use of his confidential information, *Seager* v. *Copydex*, 1967.

Mr Marco Paolo Coco designed a moped engine and then held discussions with Messrs Clark, an engineering company. However, they could not reach agreement as the company was not happy with Coco's friction transmission onto the tyre. Shortly afterwards the company developed and marketed their own machine. Although Mr Coco lost his case against the company for misuse of information given in confidence (*Coco* v. *Clark*, 1969) the case is important for Mr Justice Megarry's analysis of the three elements essential to a cause of action for breach of confidence. It must be shown that (a) the information was of a confidential nature, (b) it was communicated in circumstances importing an obligation of confidence, and (c) there was an unauthorized use of the information. In fact, the plaintiff was not able to show that the information which he gave to the defendant was really confidential, nor that the similarities between the two engines arose from misuse of the information.

INNOCENT THIRD PARTY

It is difficult to imagine circumstances in which damages would be awarded against a defendant who revealed, or otherwise made use of, material which he or she had no idea was confidential. However, the plaintiff may well seek an injunction to stop the third party from making use of or divulging the confidential matter, but by this time, of course, the third party will have been told that it is confidential. This is what happened in *Stevenson Jordan and Harrison Ltd* v. *Macdonald and Evans*, 1952. A certain Mr Hemming had a senior position with the plaintiff firm of management consultants. After he left the firm he put into shape a lot of notes and other material detailing the methods used in the plaintiff's business and the defendant publishers agreed to publish it as a book, *Flexible Budgetary Control and Standard Costs*. The defendants maintained that they were unaware at the time that Mr Hemming was breaching confidence in releasing the material in the book; indeed, when Mr Hemming died before publication they asked a director of the plaintiff firm to read the proofs, which was how the matter came to light. Nevertheless, the judge granted an injunction to stop publication (with the prospect of loss to the defendants who had gone to considerable expense by that stage). The judge emphasized the cardinal principle that the court will grant an injunction to stop anyone taking advantage of a supposed right arising from a breach of confidence. It seems necessary to act swiftly: the plaintiff firm might have had no remedy if it had not made Macdonald and Evans aware of the breach of confidence before the book was actually published. In other words, total innocence seems to protect a third party, but that party is no longer innocent as soon as he or she knows that the material is confidential. (Of course, had he been alive, the plaintiffs would have had a good cause of action against Mr Hemming, whilst the defendant publishers could have recovered against him for the money they had wasted.) Macdonald and Evans subsequently appealed and were able to persuade the Court of Appeal that the material in the book was not really confidential after all. However, the Court of Appeal studiously avoided giving any different opinion on the principles which the judge at first instance had set out.

A case where the third parties were perhaps not completely innocent was *London and Provincial Sporting News Agency* v. *Levy*, 1928. The plaintiff agency provided information on racecourse betting prices to its subscribers, a term in the contract requiring that it be used only on the subscribers' own premises. A subscriber, Mr Joe Levy, a bookmaker, passed the information on to Solomon Pell and another agency which disseminated it to its own clients. Pell and the second agency should have suspected, at the very least, where the information came from. The plaintiffs obtained nominal damages from them, an injunction against all three and larger damages against Levy.

A case in which an innocent third party got involved in different circumstances was *Booker McConnell and anor* v. *Plascow and ors*, 1985. Mr Plascow was employed in a senior position with the second plaintiffs and his employment contract included a comprehensive clause preventing him from revealing his employers' secrets even after leaving them. He accepted a job with a rival company and before he left he obtained computer printouts of a lot of highly confidential information, leaving with a bulging briefcase. The plaintiffs' suspicions were aroused and they went to court *ex parte* (without notifying the other party) to obtain a whole battery of orders restraining use of the confidential material, as well as an Anton Piller (search) order for a search of Plascow's house and his new employers' premises. Here the plaintiffs over-reached themselves: the new employers were highly reputable and were not a party to Plascow's actions, and the news of the search damaged their standing in the business community. They went to court and won the unusual remedy of having the Anton Piller order cancelled, even though it had been executed, thus restoring their reputation for business probity.

COMMERCIAL INFORMATION

Confidential information cases which come to court are, of course, likely to involve information of commercial value, the protection of which makes the expense of legal action worthwhile. Not surprisingly, these often involve employees or ex-employees who are trying to profit from knowledge gained in their employment. It is common practice to put a clause in the employee's contract restraining the employee from direct competition with his or her former employers after leaving.

Mr Robb (*Robb* v. *Green*, 1895) had a large business supplying live pheasants and pheasant eggs to country gentlemen and their gamekeepers from his two game farms in the south of England. In 1890 he engaged Mr Green as a manager (at a salary of £100 p.a. plus a cottage). At the end of 1893 Mr Green left and soon afterwards his former employer saw an advertisement in the country magazine, *The Field* (still, of course, flourishing today), from which it transpired that Mr Green was now running a game farm elsewhere. Eventually he admitted that before leaving he had secretly copied lists of Robb's customers and their gamekeepers and was now sending circulars to them (offering, incidentally, a $7^{1}/_{2}$ per cent bonus to head keepers who placed orders). The misuse of this information was held to be a breach of an implied term of the employment contract and the plaintiff was awarded £150 damages and an injunction to stop further misuse.

Faccenda Chicken

Ninety years after *Robb* v. *Green* the Court of Appeal gave judgment in a somewhat similar situation, providing an up-to-date analysis. Faccenda Chicken Ltd was a company with a prosperous business selling fresh chickens to supermarkets, restaurants and the like. Mr Fowler, the sales manager, built up this side of the business. Subsequently he left and set up on his own, joined by a number of Faccenda's employees. Using sales information which he had acquired while with his former employers, Fowler's business soon prospered at the expense of Faccenda's. The lawsuit which Faccenda brought against Fowler was complicated by other matters. However, the relevant issue here is the claim by the plaintiffs for breach of an implied term in the employment contract that Fowler (and the others) would not use knowledge of confidential information or trade secrets gained while in Faccenda's employment, to that company's detriment, whilst still employed or after leaving (*Faccenda Chicken* v. *Fowler*, 1986).

In the case at first instance, heard in 1983, Mr Justice Goulding, in an analysis which was approved (with some amplification) by the Court of Appeal, divided into three categories the information which an employee might acquire in the course of his employment. First, there is trivial or generally available information which is not confidential at all. Secondly, there is information which must be treated as confidential because the employee has been told so or because it is obviously confidential, but which, once learned, becomes part of his own skill and knowledge. While still in employment he must not reveal or misuse it, but if the employer wants to protect this information after the employee leaves, he must do so by express stipulation in the employment contract. Thirdly, there are trade secrets so confidential that they cannot lawfully be used by the employee after he has left. The knowledge of customers, prices and so on which Mr Fowler and his fellow ex-employees had acquired fell into the second category. (The situation is different from that in *Robb* v. *Green* in that Mr Green had deliberately copied the lists of customers while still with his employer: there is no reason why he should not have made use of the names which he remembered.)

PRIVACY

English law has long been hesitant about acknowledging a right of privacy as such. Cases where the law is invoked to restrain the disclosure of confidential information which is not of a commercial nature are much less frequent. The marriage of the 11th Duke of Argyll and his third wife ended in divorce. Shortly afterwards the *People* started to publish a series of articles by the Duke: it appeared that they would reveal confidences exchanged between the Duke and Duchess during the time of their marriage. The Duchess was successful in getting an injunction in the Queen's Bench division against His Grace and the newspaper to stop publication of the offending articles, *Argyll* v. *Argyll*, 1967. Much further down the social scale, but almost as newsworthy for the popular press, were details of the married life of John Lennon, a former member of the Beatles pop group. He tried to stop the *News of the World* from publishing an article by his ex-wife, but was unsuccessful (*Lennon* v. *News Group Newspapers and Twist*, 1978). The Master of the Rolls (senior judge of the Court of Appeal), Lord Denning, said 'It seems to me as plain as can be that the relationship of these parties has ceased to be their own private affair. They themselves have put it into the public domain', a useful reminder that information is not confidential when it is already available to the public.

PUBLIC INTEREST

One important question is how far confidentiality may be overridden for reasons of public interest. There are two facets to this. The public interest may justify the court's requiring a witness to reveal material given in confidence. Alternatively, the public interest may serve as a defence to an action for breach of confidence. An employee who reveals illegality or other shortcomings on the part of his or her employer can be in a difficult situation and the Public Interest Disclosure Act 1998 protects the 'whistle blower' from victimization. It is commonly believed that the secrecy of the confessional is absolute. Certainly, it would be a brave court which would compel a priest to breach it but, in spite of a few old cases to the contrary, it seems that a priest can, and may be compelled to, reveal confidences given under the seal of confession. The same is true of confidential medical information. The only area where confidentiality is absolute is legal professional privilege, involving communications between a lawyer and client. Journalists have fought hard to keep the identity of their informants secret and the Contempt of Court Act 1981, s. 10, gives statutory authority to this. However it may, though in practice rarely, be overridden by a court on grounds of public interest. The public interest defence was successful when the Church of Scientology was refused interlocutory (interim) injunctions to prevent publication of confidential material by ex-students of Scientology training courses; *Hubbard* v. *Vosper*, 1972, *Church of Scientology* v. *Kaufman*, 1973. (Mr Hubbard was the founder of Scientology.) The secretive Church of Scientology's methods had been much criticized in the press around that time as verging on 'brainwashing' and there was government support for regarding the organization as undesirable: the defendants maintained that revelation to the public was in the public interest. In a very different situation it was held to be in the public interest that deficiencies in breathalysers could be be revealed by a former employee of the plaintiffs, *Lion Laboratories* v. *Evans*, 1985. In this case Griffiths LJ pointed out that there is also a public interest in preserving confidentiality within an organization. When the court is asked for an interim injunction to stop publication of confidential information before the trial on the grounds of public interest, this will be granted only exceptionally.

HUMAN RIGHTS

Since the Human Rights Act 1998 came into force on 2 October 2000 it has received a great deal of publicity and few people can be unaware of it. Human rights law has emerged as an important – and doubtless lucrative – specialism: a specialist set of chambers with some notable barristers was an immediate response in the legal profession and more are following. The European Court of Human Rights in

Strasbourg has made decisions on the European Convention on Human Rights for a number of years: cases may be brought by an individual who feels that his or her human rights have not been protected, against the government, but only after all legal processes have been exhausted in his or her own country. The effect of the Act is that now the principles of the Convention must be taken into account in the UK courts. The worst fears, for example that an employer will not be able to tell an employee to get his hair cut as it offends against the latter's right to free expression, will probably not be realized, but having ultimate decisions made by a court of seven judges drawn from the 40 nations of the Council of Europe (the Human Rights Convention has nothing to do with the European Union) with very different traditions from this country, cannot fail to have an effect. The reports of the Court of Human Rights make turgid reading but it cannot be denied that some of its decisions can be startling, if not worrying. The two Articles which may well be felt in the context of our present discussion are loose enough to allow varied interpretation. These are Article 8, the right to respect for private life, and Article 10, the right to freedom of expression. However, as Sir John Donaldson MR pointed out in one of the *Spycatcher* cases, every citizen has the right to do what he likes provided that it is within the law: the right to freedom of expression contained in Article 10 is already assumed in this universal basic freedom of action, *Attorney-General* v. *Guardian Newspapers (No 2)*, 1989. We might add, with regard to Article 8, the familiar principle 'an Englishman's home is his castle', long accepted in the courts as well as in everyday life.

10 The future

FORCES AT WORK

The law is a fast-moving subject, and few areas are moving faster than those dealt with in this book. Whilst the most obvious reason for this is the revolution in the technical handling of information, brought about by the still continuing developments in electronic storage and communication, there are other forces at work. Realization of the commercial value of information, and indeed of all forms of intellectual property, continues to grow, but just as illicit exploitation becomes technologically easier, protection becomes more difficult.

We have long been accustomed to exploitation of copyright in academic circles, but the commercial exploitation by universities, on a wide scale, of patented discoveries and business know-how is relatively new. Even the name and coat of arms of a university can produce an income in this commercialized world. There is an explosive growth in the desire for knowledge, for information, for education. At the same time, social forces are at work to denigrate and oppose traditional rights of property in the fruits of intellectual endeavour and research, and of talent and entrepreneurship in the creative industries. Freedom of information challenges long-held restrictive attitudes. Freedom of speech is sweeping away old taboos, but orchestrated protest is showing its power as it sets up new ones.

INFORMATION LAW IN THE NEWS

A trawl through the author's files of news cuttings give some pointers to the future. Here are a few interesting items.

INTERNET SECURITY

Internet security seems likely to remain a problem for some time in the future. A teenage hacker living in a small Welsh village entered American corporate databases, took details of 23 000 credit cards and caused damage estimated at £2 million (*The Times*, 21 April 2001).

MUSIC FROM THE NET

The Napster case in the USA was discussed in Chapter 5. Whilst a court case brought Napster to heel, the fall of 1.3 per cent by value in record sales in the year 2000 and a dramatic fall in sales of singles recordings, particularly in the USA, was blamed on Napster and other free online music services. Illegal copying of music onto blank CDs rose sharply in France, Italy and Germany (*Financial Times*, 20 April 2001). Victory over Napster is still (April 2001) not complete and in any case is only a start: it is likely to be a long struggle before this menace to the rights of composers, performers and record companies is eliminated, if ever.

PORNOGRAPHY

The boundaries between acceptable eroticism and unacceptable pornography are as uncertain as ever. In France *La Vie Sexuelle de Catherine M*[illet]was fourth in a bestseller list (*The Times*, 21 April 2001). The British Board of Film Classification recently revised its guidelines for the R18 certificate (for videos to be sold only in licensed sex shops) and the sort of images which are permissible now would have attracted prosecution only a few years ago (*Financial Times* weekend magazine, 31 March 2001). Meanwhile heavy sentences are visited in the UK on Net surfers who download erotic pictures of children.

DRUG PATENTS IN DANGER

Activists across the world hailed a victory for their campaign when leading pharmaceutical companies withdrew their action in the High Court in Pretoria claiming that the 1997 South African Medicines Act infringed their patent rights. The emotive issue of drugs to combat HIV clouded the arguments, but the South African government took its stand on the World Trade Organization TRIPs agreement (the *Guardian*, 19 April 2001). Articles 8, 27(2) and 30 of TRIPs would appear to support the government's claiming the right to override patents in the interests of public health and allow manufacture and import of cheap drugs. Where this much-publicized matter will end remains to be seen. Pharmaceutical companies do not get a good press. Theirs is a risky business, with the failure of a drug common after huge research costs have been expended. Financial incentives, protected by patent law, are essential to the development of new medicines. South Africa is a powerful state: many people will be watching with apprehension to see whether the patent system will face more attacks in less powerful developing countries, and elsewhere.

PROGRAMS AND MAPS

Patentability of computer programs seems likely to come before long: in the USA, software patents are frequently granted and applications to the European Patent Office are common (*Financial Times*, 'Connectis' supplement, March 2001).

An out-of-court settlement resulted in the Automobile Association (AA) paying no less than £20 million to the Ordnance Survey for infringement of copyright in maps, and the AA's becoming a licensee for future publications (*Daily Telegraph*, 7 March 2001).

These files are bulky: the amount of news and articles relevant to the issues discussed in this book which appear in the newspapers is considerable, and after only a few months the files of cuttings constitute an invaluable information resource. This concluding chapter is meant to be short, but briefly covered below are some more fields where interesting developments are likely.

CONTROL OF THE INTERNET

Control of the Internet is obviously going to loom large. The Yahoo! case in France (see Chapter 5) has shown that it is possible for a government, at least, to exercise some sort of control through the courts when the defendant can be brought to submit to the jurisdiction. In an area admittedly marginal to our concerns in this book, 'cybersquatting', monopolizing Internet domain names for profit, the British courts have been able to control the miscreants. Cybercrime is worrying, money laundering, fraud, hacking for the purpose of electronic theft, copyright piracy, are all relatively easy on the Net. Government, and international, initiatives are still in their infancy, but it would be wrong to be too optimistic of more than limited success in the near future.

DOT-COM MILLIONAIRES

A couple of years ago wise money was going into dot-com companies, where millionaires were made almost overnight. Then the bubble burst and the believers in miracles realized that the cyber world was in evolution, not revolution, and a new caution is likely in the future.

THE END OF PAPER?

Turning to happier themes, the demise of paper continues to recede over the horizon. The technology is already in existence to operate a complete switch from paper to the computer, but the paperless office has not materialized yet. In fact, as we mentioned earlier in this book, the computer has facilitated a vast increase in communication on paper. Newspapers flourish which were in dire straits a decade or two ago. The word processor has advanced productivity in everything from junk mail to legal textbooks. On-demand publishing on paper may well be the future for books rather than publishing in electronic form. Will CD-ROM, or technology's next invention, take-off as a format in its own right, or will it remain as an adjunct to hard copy? However, e-mail and e-commerce are advancing rapidly. The 'written' word can now have a transience and mutability which are quite new: how shall we cope in an electronic world in which nothing is certain?

HUMAN RIGHTS

Privacy will undoubtedly be a major issue. The Human Rights Act, coupled with the new Data Protection Act, are likely to give us in the UK something like the French *droit de personnalité*. It is to be hoped that the Human Rights Act will not lead to the absurdities which were forecast when it came into being. Indeed, it seems that a new sanity is appearing in some fields, most notably in race relations, where it has appeared in the past few days (as this is written in late April 2001) that racism is not the monopoly of one only of the many communities in the UK. The treatment of incitement to racial hatred, discussed in Chapter 9, may well be modified. Freedom of speech and assembly is still under threat from orchestrated, and sometimes violent, protest.

OTHER POINTS

Some other points may be worth making. The blasphemy law (Chapter 9) must disappear soon: although Christians are in a huge majority in the UK, there is strong feeling that a law which protects only one faith is inequitable, and any other solution is unworkable. Defamation law has been reformed, both in the new statute and in the practice of the courts, and the indications are that the excesses of the unreformed law will not return. Criminal libel may well disappear, and the long-discussed end of the curious distinction between libel and slander must surely come to be. However, defamation on the Internet may prove rather intractable. It is probable that alternative dispute resolution and arbitration will be increasingly used for settling intellectual property disputes: they should make it easier and cheaper to protect one's rights. It is to be hoped that understanding of intellectual property rights will grow. It is not so long since drink-driving was regarded as a bit of a joke: nobody passes it off like that nowadays. Similarly, we hope, the person sporting a fake Rolex, illicitly copying music or buying counterfeit software will come to be shunned by right-thinking persons.

We have probably reached a point now when we can reasonably forecast, at least in broad outline, the technological shape of the future information structure. In the future information world the technologist and the information or media manager will play complementary roles, but they will need the work of the lawyer to prevent their efforts from ending in chaos.

Appendix I Overview of the Copyright, Designs and Patents Act 1988 (CDPA)

The CDPA started life with 306 sections. A number of interpolated sections has increased the total: these are designated by the addition of the capital letter A, B, and so on, and are placed immediately after the section bearing the original number. Thus, sections 50A, 50B, 50C and 50D follow section 50. (The UK does not follow the common international practice of designating interpolated articles by the Latin numerals *bis*, *ter*, *quater* and so on.) Most of the interpolated sections, as well as other amendments, have been added to implement European Union Directives. The mechanism by which these sections are added, or amendments carried out, involves the Minister's making regulations under powers conferred by the European Communities Act 1972, s. 2(2) and (4). The regulations, incorporated in a Statutory Instrument (SI), carry out the necessary additions or amendments, and the CDPA thenceforth stands amended accordingly. This procedure bypasses the need to take an amending bill through Parliament on each occasion that an EU Directive requires changes. It does mean that to be up to date one must have access to an amended copy of the CDPA, or the Act and regulations. The Act may be found conveniently in Michael Henry's *Current Copyright Law* (Butterworths, 1998) incorporating amendments and additions resulting from a spate of EU legislation in the 1990s.

This overview is intended to provide a quick guide to the CDPA, as discussed in preceding chapters, not a complete summary.

The Act is divided into seven Parts, as follows:

Part I Copyright
Part II Rights in Performances
Part III Design Right
Part IV Registered Designs
Part V Patent Agents and Trade Mark Agents
Part VI Patents

Part VII Miscellaneous and General

(Parts I and III are subdivided into Chapters.)

There are eight Schedules at the end of the Act.

Regulations amending the Act are referred to below by the year of issue. These are:

1989 Design right (semiconductor topographies) Regulations

1992 Copyright (computer programs) Regulations

1995 Duration of copyright and rights in performances Regulations

1996 Copyright and related rights Regulations

1997 Copyright and rights in databases Regulations

PART I COPYRIGHT

Chapter 1, Sections 1 to 15A: Subsistence, Ownership and Duration of Copyright

Section 1 defines copyright and lists the material affected

Section 3 defines literary, dramatic and musical works: amendments add preparatory design material for a computer program, 1992 Regulations, and databases, 1997 Regulations

Section 3A is added by the 1997 Regulations: it defines a database

Section 4 defines artistic works

Section 5 defining sound recordings and films is replaced by ss. 5A and 5B, 1995 Regulations, expanding the definitions

Section 6 defines broadcasts: it is amended in respect of satellite broadcasts by the 1996 Regulations, which also add

Section 6A relating to the place from which a satellite broadcast is deemed to be made

Section 7 defines cable programmes

Section 8 defines a published edition

Section 9 defines an author; important amendments to the authorship of sound recordings and films are made by the 1996 Regulations

Section 10 concerns joint ownership, with an amendment in respect of films, 1996 Regulations

Section 11 on first ownership of copyright includes the position of employees' works

Sections 12 to 15 deal with the duration of copyright and are amended in accord with the 1995 Regulations, extending copyright in most works to 70 years pma, and also substituting ss. 13A and 13B for the original s. 13; s. 13A makes important changes to the duration in respect of films

Section 15A, added by the same regulations, defines the country of origin

Chapter II, ss. 16 to 27: Rights of Copyright Owner

Section 16 lists the acts restricted to the copyright owner, and these are detailed
in subsequent sections, copying (s. 17), issuing to the public (s. 18), rental or
lending (s. 18A added by the 1996 Regulations), performance or showing in
public (s. 19), broadcasting (s. 20), and adaptation (s. 21)
Sections 22 to 26 deal with secondary infringement, and
Section 27 defines an infringing copy

Chapter III, ss. 28 to 76: Permitted Acts

This Chapter deals at length with exceptions to the copyright owner's exclusive
rights; research and private study is dealt with in s. 29, with an important
amendment excluding commercial research in a database added by the 1997
Regulations
Sections 32 to 36A are applicable to educational establishments
Section 36A, added by the 1996 Regulations, allows lending by an educational
establishment
Sections 37 to 44 cover the library and archive exemptions
Section 40A was added by the 1996 Regulations and applies to lending of
copyright works by a library or archive
Sections 45 to 50, headed *Public administration*, deals with exemptions for
Parliamentary and judicial proceedings, and related areas, also (s. 50) acts done
under statutory authority
Sections 50A to 50D were added by the 1992 Regulations and provide certain
exemptions relating to computer programs, and (s. 50D) databases
Sections 51 to 56 provide exemptions in respect of designs, typefaces (ordinary
use for printing is not infringement, s. 54) and works in electronic form
Sections 57 to 65 cover acts permitted after the presumed death of an anonymous
author (s. 57), use of records of spoken words (s. 58), public recitation (s. 59),
abstracts (s. 60), folksongs (s. 61), and certain other matters
Section 66 (relating to public lending) was amended and 66A (acts done after
presumed expiry of copyright in films) was added, by the 1996 and 1995
Regulations respectively
Section 67 permits use of a sound recording by a club under certain conditions
Sections 68 to 75 permit certain acts with broadcasts and cable programmes; note
particularly s. 70 allowing recordings of a broadcast or cable programme for
time-shifting
Section 73 was amended, and 73A added, by the Broadcasting Act 1996; they
relate to re-transmission of broadcasts and resulting royalties

Chapter IV, ss. 77 to 89: Moral Rights

This Chapter introduces moral rights, an innovation of the CDPA, although long known on the continent; see also ss. 94 and 95

Chapter V, ss. 90 to 95: Dealings with Rights in Copyright Works

This Chapter deals with the transfer of copyright; ss. 93A to 93C, added by the 1996 Regulations, deal with transfer of rental right in respect of a film and resulting remuneration

Sections 94 and 95 cover assignability of moral rights (not assignable) and their transmission after death

Chapter VI, ss. 96 to 115: Remedies for Infringement

Sections 96 to 106 deal with civil remedies, and
Sections 107 to 110 with offences

Chapter VII, ss. 116 to 144A: Copyright Licensing

Sections 116 to 135 deal with licensing schemes run by licensing bodies and applications to the Copyright Tribunal; these are followed in

Sections 136 to 144A by other provisions relating to licensing; s. 144A was added by the 1996 Regulations

Sections 117 and 124 are explanatory and were substituted for the original sections by the 1996 Regulations

Sections 135A to H were added by the Broadcasting Act 1990 and refer to use as of right of sound recordings in broadcasts and cable services

Section 142 was added by the 1996 Regulations and deals with applications to the Copyright Tribunal to settle certain royalties

Section 143 (certification of licensing schemes) was amended, and s. 144A (compulsory collective administration of certain rights) added, by the 1996 Regulations

Chapter VIII, ss. 145 to 152: The Copyright Tribunal

The Copyright Tribunal replaces the former Performing Right Tribunal with jurisdiction now extended to hear proceedings relating mainly to licensing of copyright: its jurisdiction is listed in s. 149 (as amended by the Broadcasting Act 1990 and the 1996 Regulations)

Chapter IX, ss. 153 to 162: Qualification for and Extent of Copyright Protection

Section 154 Qualification by author

Section 155 Qualification by country of first publication
Section 156 Qualification by place of transmission of a broadcast or cable transmission
Sections 157 to 162 Geographical extent of copyright protection and application to other countries

Chapter X, ss. 163 to 176: Miscellaneous and General

Section 163 and 164 Crown copyright and copyright in Acts, and Measures of Church Synod
Sections 165 to 167 Parliamentary copyright
Section 168 Copyright vesting in certain international organizations
Section 169 Folklore
Sections 172 to 179 Interpretation of Part I of the Act
Sections 178 and 179 Definitions: these sections are valuable for reference: certain changes have been made by the 1992, 1995 and 1996 Regulations and by the Broadcasting Act 1990

PART II, SS. 180 TO 212: RIGHTS IN PERFORMANCES

Before the CDPA came into force remedies for infringement of live performances were limited. This Part remedies that situation.
Section 180 defines performance and states the rights of a performer and person having recording rights in a live performance
Section 182 has been amended, and ss. 182A to 182D added, by the 1996 Regulations; they relate to consent and (s. 182D) right to remuneration for exploitation of a recording
Section 189 Permitted acts: these are listed in Schedule 2 at the end of the CDPA
Section 191 Duration of rights; amended by the 1995 Regulations expanding the original provisions
Sections 191A to 191M Performers' property rights; added by the 1996 Regulations
Sections 192A and 192B Non-property rights; substituted for the original s. 192 by the 1996 Regulations
Section 194 Civil remedy; amended by the 1996 Regulations
Sections 198 to 202 Offences
Section 198 Criminal liability relating to illicit recordings
Section 198A Duty of local weights and measures authorities to enforce s. 198; added by the Criminal Justice and Public Order Act 1994
Section 205A Licensing of performers' property rights added in Schedule 2A by the 1996 Regulations
Sections 211 and 212 Definitions

PART III DESIGN RIGHT

Design Right (unregistered) is an innovation in the CDPA and must be
distinguished from the right in a Registered Design covered in the Registered
Designs Act 1949; this Part must be read alongside the 1989 Regulations
which introduce modifications where semiconductor topographies are
concerned

**Chapter I, ss. 213 to 225, outlines design right, its ownership (s. 215) and duration
(s.216)**

Chapter II, ss. 226 to 235, deals with infringement and remedies

Chapter III, ss. 236 to 245, gives exceptions to the rights owner's rights

**Chapter IV, ss. 246 to 252, explains the jurisdiction of the Comptroller of Patents,
Designs and Trade Marks, and of the court**

Chapter V, ss. 253 to 264, covers miscellaneous issues:

Section 253 gives a remedy for groundless threats of infringement proceedings
analogous to that in the Patents Act 1977
Sections 263 and 264 Definitions

PART IV REGISTERED DESIGNS

This Part introduces some amendments to the Registered Designs Act 1949:
some further amendments are in Schedule 3 and the full amended text of the
Act may be found in Schedule 4

PART V PATENT AGENTS AND TRADE MARK AGENTS

Miscellaneous provisions relating to patent and trade mark professionals

PART VI PATENTS

Sections 287 to 292 deal with the new Patents County Court

PART VII MISCELLANEOUS AND GENERAL

Section 296, amended by the 1989 Regulations, gives a copyright owner rights
    against anyone who provides or offers a device, or publishes information,
    designed to circumvent copy protection

Section 297 makes it an offence fraudulently to receive broadcasts or cable
    programmes

Section 297A Supplying or advertising unauthorized decoders for encrypted
    transmissions is an offence; added by the Broadcasting Act 1990

Section 301 Provides royalties for the Great Ormond Street Hospital for Sick
    Children, from performance or publication of the play *Peter Pan*

SCHEDULE 1
Copyright: transitional provisions

SCHEDULE 2
Rights in performances: permitted acts

SCHEDULE 2A
Licensing of performers' property rights

SCHEDULE 3
Minor amendments of the 1949 Act

SCHEDULE 4
The Registered Designs Act 1949 as amended

SCHEDULE 5
Patents: miscellaneous amendments to the Patents Act 1977

SCHEDULE 6
Provisions for the benefit of the Hospital for Sick Children: Interpretation

SCHEDULE 7
Consequential amendments to other statutes

SCHEDULE 8
Repeals of other statutes in part or in whole

Appendix II   Duration of protection for intellectual property

COPYRIGHT

Note (a) With regard to copyright, time runs from the end of the calendar year in which the relevant event (for example, death of author) took place. (b) The duration of copyright given below follows the Duration of Copyright and Rights in Performances Regulations 1995 which took effect from 1 January 1996. However, reg. 15 provides that copyright will continue to subsist in a pre-existing copyright work until the date on which it would have expired if that date is later than the date on which it would expire under the 1995 Regulations, and reg. 28 makes a similar provision for performances.

Literary, dramatic, musical or artistic works – CDPA s. 12
(a) 70 years from the year in which the author, or last surving joint author, died;
(b) Unknown author(s): 70 years from the year in which it was made, or if made available to the public in that period, 70 years from the date when first made available; (c) but if the identity of one or more authors is known before that period expires then 70 years from year of the death of the last surviving known author;
(d) if the country of origin is not a state of the European Economic Area (EEA) and none of the authors is a national of an EEA state then that duration to which the work is entitled in its country of origin (provided it does not exceed the appropriate period in (a) to (c) above);
(e) Computer-generated work: 50 years from the year when it was made.

Sound recordings – CDPA s. 13A
(a) 50 years from the year in which it is made, or if released in that time, 50 years from the year of release;
(b) if the author is not a national of an EEA state then that duration to which it would be entitled in the state of which the author is a national, but no more than would be appropriate in (a) above.

Films – CDPA s. 13B
As for literary, dramatic, musical or artistic works, but the relevant death is the last
to die (or the last known one to die if any is unknown) of:

the principal director,
the author of the screenplay,
the author of the dialogue, or
the composer of music specially created for and used in the film.

Broadcasts and cable programmes – CDPA s. 14
50 years from the year in which a broadcast is made or a cable programme included
in a cable programme service, but

if the author is not a national of an EEA state then the duration to which it
would be entitled in that state, but not more than that given above.
There is no extension for repeats.

Typographical arrangement of a published edition – CDPA s. 15
25 years from the year in which first published.

Publication right – Copyright and Related Rights Regulations 1996, reg. 16
25 years from the year in which first published.

Crown copyright – CDPA ss. 163 and 164
125 years from the year in which made, or

if published commercially within 75 years from the year when it was made,
then 50 years from that year;
but 50 years from Royal Assent to an Act of Parliament or Measure of the
Church of England General Synod.

Parliamentary copyright – CDPA s. 165
50 years from the year when made;
parliamentary bills: until Royal Assent, rejection or withdrawal – s. 166.

Copyright vesting in certain international organizations – CDPA s. 168
50 years from the year when it is made.

Perpetual copyright under the Copyright Act 1775 – CDPA Schedule 1, para. 13
Rights conferred on certain universities and colleges are extinguished 50 years
after the end of the year (1989) in which the CDPA came into force.

Moral rights – CDPA s. 86

So long as copyright subsists in the work (right to be identified as author, right to object to derogatory treatment, and right to privacy in certain photographs and films), but

> false attribution, 20 years after death.

Performers' rights – CDPA s. 191

50 years from the end of the year of performance, or

> if a recording is released in that period, 50 years from the end of the year of release; but if the performer is not a national of an EEA state, the period which his or her state would grant provided it is not longer.

Databases – Copyright and Rights in Databases Regulations 1997, reg. 17

A database is protected by copyright as a literary work only if it constitutes its author's own intellectual creation – CDPA s. 3A.

Database right: 15 years from the year it is made, or

> if made available to the public before the end of that period, 15 years from the year when it is first made available.

A substantial change, including one resulting from accumulated small changes, in effect creates a new database with a fresh 15 year term of protection.

If a database was a copyright work before commencement (1 January 1998) and was created on or before 27 March 1996, copyright continues to subsist for the remainder of the copyright term – Copyright and Rights in Databases Regulations 1997 reg. 29.

DESIGNS

(a) Design Right – CDPA s. 216

> 15 years from the end of the year in which the design was first recorded in a design document, or an article was made to the design, whichever is first, or

10 years from the end of the year in which articles made to the design are first made available for sale or hire if that occurs within five years of the the end of the first year above.

(b) Registered designs – Registered Designs Act 1949 s. 8

> Five years from registration, which may be extended for a further four five-year periods, making a maximum of 25 years.

(c) Design derived from an artistic work – CDPA s. 52

> 25 years from end of the year in which articles made by an industrial process from the artistic work are first marketed.

SEMICONDUCTOR TOPOGRAPHIES – Design Right (Semiconductor Topographies) Regulations 1989 reg. 6

10 years from the end of the year in which the topography or articles made to it were first made available for sale or hire, or

> if not made available within 15 years from the earlier of the time when first recorded in a design document or articles made to the topography, then the end of the 15 years.

PATENTS – Patents Act 1977 s. 25

20 years from the filing date;

a Supplementary Protection Certificate extending protection for up to five years may be obtained under certain conditions for a patent for a medicinal product – Patents (Supplementary Protection Certificate for Medicinal Products) Regulations 1992 (SI 1992/3091).

TRADE MARKS – Trade Marks Act 1994 s. 42

10 years from the filing date, renewable indefinitely for 10 years at a time.

Select bibliography

Law books get out of date probably more quickly than books in any other discipline: it is necessary to check that you are using the latest edition. They are also rather expensive. Whilst some introductory texts cost under £20, most student textbooks are between £25 and £30. Standard practitioners' texts are commonly around £100, often much dearer, looseleaf works are £150–£250 with updating costing £200 a year. Journals concerned with specialized fields have proliferated in recent years: subscriptions usually cost around £150–£200 and upwards. Publication of books and journals on CD-ROM, with two or more updates a year, is increasing, often with preferential rates for purchasers of the hard-copy version. Law publishing at all levels has expanded and whilst the two old-established publishers, Sweet and Maxwell, and Butterworths, retain their pre-eminence, they have been joined by a number of others. Hammicks Legal Bookshop (192 Fleet Street, London EC4A 2NJ, also in Bristol and Manchester) must have the largest law stock and their annual Legal Catalogue is virtually a complete bibliography of law books published in Britain.

This is not a comprehensive bibliography, rather a quick guide to some standard and useful works. Many of these books are very expensive but an asterisk indicates those which are likely to cost less than £35 (at 2001 prices).

Serial publications

Computers and Law. Society for Computers and Law.
European Intellectual Property Review. Sweet and Maxwell.
Intellectual Property Laws and Treaties. WIPO [Switzerland]
Intellectual Property Quarterly. Sweet and Maxwell.
International Internet Law Review. Euromoney Legal Group.
Managing Intellectual Property. Euromoney Legal Group.
World Intellectual Property Report. BNA International [USA]

Books

For well over a century Intellectual Property has been represented on practitioners' shelves by successive editions of *Copinger and Skone James on Copyright* (14th edn 1998, supplement 2002), *Terrell on the Law of Patents* (15th edn 2000) and *Kerly on the Law of Trade Marks* (13th edn 2000), all published by Sweet and Maxwell. However, they have now been joined by many other good texts.

Allinson, J.R.J. (1999). *Understanding Patent Law*. Ashgate.*

Bainbridge, D. (1999). *Data Protection Act and Privacy in Communications*. CLT Professional.*

Bainbridge, D. (2000). *Introduction to Computer Law*. 4th edn Pitman.*

Brown, H. and Marriott, A. (1999). *ADR Principles and Practice*. 2nd edn Sweet and Maxwell.

Burke, J. (1977). *Jowitt's Dictionary of English Law*. 2nd edn Sweet and Maxwell.

Butterworths E-Commerce and IT Law Handbook. (2000). Butterworths.

Carey, P. (1998). *Guide to the Data Protection Act 1998*. Blackstone.*

Carter-Ruck, P. and Starte, H. (1997). *Carter-Ruck on Libel and Slander*. 5th edn Butterworths.

Chartered Institute of Patent Agents. (2000). *CIPA Guide to the Patents Acts*. 5th edn Sweet and Maxwell.

Cohen, M.A., Bang, E.A. and Mitchell, S.J. (1999). *Chinese Intellectual Property Law and Practice*. Kluwer.

Cornish, W.R. (1999). *Intellectual Property: Patents, Copyright, Trade Marks and Allied Rights*. 4th edn Sweet and Maxwell.*

Cornish, W.R. (1999). *Cases and Materials on Intellectual Property*. 3rd edn Sweet and Maxwell.*

Edenborough, M. (1999). *Intellectual Property Law*. Sweet and Maxwell.*

Fisher, D.I. (1997). *Defamation via Satellite*. Kluwer.

Garner, B.A. (1999). *Black's Law Dictionary*. West.*

Geller, P.A. (2000). *International Copyright Law and Practice*. (Looseleaf.) Matthew Bender. [USA]

Henry, M. (1998). *Current Copyright Law*. Butterworths.*

Holyoak, J. and Torremans, P. (1998). *Intellectual Property Law*. 2nd edn Butterworths.*

'Internet and Author's Rights'. (1999). *Perspectives in Intellectual Property*. Sweet and Maxwell.*

Johnston, D. (1995). *Design Protection*. Gower.*

Kelleher, D. and Murray, K. (1999). *IT Law in the European Union*. Sweet and Maxwell.

Laddie, H., Prescott, P. and Vitoria, M. (2000). *Modern Law of Copyright and Designs*. 3rd edn 3 vols. Butterworths. [£465]

Lindbergh, E. (1992). *International Law Dictionary: English, French, German.* Blackstone Press.*

Marett, P. (1996). *Intellectual Property Law.* Sweet and Maxwell.*

Mehigan, S. (1999). *Confidential Information.* Butterworths.

Merkin, R.M. (1999). *Arbitration Law.* (Looseleaf.) Informa Publishing.

Metaxas-Maranghidis, G. (1995). *Intellectual Property Laws of Europe.* Wiley.

Mutti, A. and Adams, J. *Union Catalogue of Intellectual Property Holdings in London Libraries.* Butterworths.

Prime, T. (2000). *European Intellectual Property Law.* Ashgate.

Reed, C. (2000). *Internet Law: Text and Materials.* Butterworths.*

Reed, C., and Angel, J. (2000). *Computer Law.* Blackstone.*

Robertson, G. and Nicol, A. (1999). *Media Law.* 4th edn Sweet and Maxwell.

Rowe, H. (2000). *Data Protection Act 1998: a Practical Guide.* Tolley.*

Rowland, D. and Macdonald, E. (2000). *Information Technology Law.* 2nd edn Cavendish Publishing.*

Rutherford, L. and Bone, S. (1993). *Osborn's Concise Law Dictionary.* 8th edn Sweet and Maxwell.*

Thomas, P.A. and Cope, C. (1996). *How to Use a Law Library.* 3rd edn Sweet and Maxwell.*

Wall, R.A. (1998). *Copyright Made Easier.* 2nd edn ASLIB.*

Williams, P. and Nicholas, D. (2001). *The Internet and the Changing Information Environment.* ASLIB.*

List of relevant addresses

British Copyright Council	29–33 Berners Street, London W1P 4AA
CEDR (Centre for Dispute Resolution)	Prince's House, 95 Gresham Street, London EC2V 7NA
Chartered Institute of Arbitrators	12 Bloomsbury Square, London WC1A 2LP
Chartered Institute of Patent Agents	Staple Inn Buildings, High Holborn, London WC1V 7PZ
Commission for Racial Equality	Elliot House, 10–12 Allington Street, London SW1E 5EH
Copyright Licensing Agency	90 Tottenham Court Road, London W1P 0LP
Her Majesty's Stationery Office [HMSO] (Licensing Division and Copyright Unit)	St Clement's House, 2–16 Colegate, Norwich NR3 1BQ
Information Commissioner	Wycliffe House, Water Lane, Wilmslow, Cheshire SK9 5AF
Patent Office	Cardiff Road, Newport NP9 1RH
Performing Right Society	29–33 Berners Street, London W1P 4AA
Publishers Association	1 Kingsway, London WC2B 6XF
Registrar of Public Lending Right	Bayheath House, Prince Regent Street, Stockton-on-Tees TS18 1DF

Register of Copyrights	Library of Congress, Copyright Office, 101 Independence Avenue, SE, Washington DC, 20559-6000, USA
Society for Computers and Law	10 Hurle Crescent, Clifton, Bristol BS8 2TA
The Stationery Office Ltd (Publications Centre)	51 Nine Elms Road, London SW8 5DR
World Intellectual Property Organization [WIPO]	34 Chemin des Colombettes, 1211 Geneva 20, Switzerland

Index